PO[LITICS]
AND
ECONOMICS
IN AMERICA

THE WAY WE CAME TO BE

RICHARD E. CARMICHAEL

KRIEGER PUBLISHING COMPANY
MALABAR, FLORIDA
1998

"I saw a startling sight today, a politician with his hands in his own pockets." — Mark Twain

Original Edition 1998

Printed and Published by
KRIEGER PUBLISHING COMPANY
KRIEGER DRIVE
MALABAR, FLORIDA 32950

Library of Congress Cataloging-In-Publication Data

Carmichael, Richard E., 1947-
    Politics and economics in America: the way we came to be/
Richard E. Carmichael
        p.   cm.
    Includes bibliographical references and index.
    ISBN 1-57524-056-4 (alk. paper)
    1. Economics—United States—History.   2. United States—Economic conditions.   I. Title.
HB119.A2C29   1998
338.973'009—DC21   97-20172
                                                                    CIP

10   9   8   7   6   5   4   3   2

ACKNOWLEDGMENT

I would like to thank those authors that I have quoted throughout this book. Without the previous works of these authors, this research would not have been possible.

Also, I would like to especially thank my wife Kay for the numerous hours that she spent proofreading this book. I hope that she enjoyed the story, I most certainly appreciated the help.

INTRODUCTION

The outlook in the twenty-first century for the world's industrial countries can not be forecasted by use of mechanical extrapolation. This is because each of these countries, be it Western Europe, or Japan and the "Asian Tigers," or the United States, has its own separate history, its own culture.

In the twenty-first century, market niche competition will give way to head-to-head competition among the industrial giants of the world. The key to competing in this environment will be the ability to create and sustain a competitive advantage over a company's or country's economic rivals. Each country has a unique culture that determines how it approaches the marketplace. This will require that each of the major countries look to its history to determine its strengths and weaknesses, its opportunities and threats, relative to the competition. Also, many companies look to their national government for different levels of assistance in accomplishing their business goals. Some companies form a partnership with government in order to enhance their competitive positions, while others emphasize a hands-off policy in trade and commerce. Therefore, this book examines the historical and continuing role of government in business.

The purpose of this book is to examine the evolution of economic thought and the historical events that affected the economic growth of the world's industrialized countries, with particular emphasis on the United States. During specific times in its history, the United States was the envy of the entire world. In the nineteenth century, the Europeans recognized that the American approach was different. It was the Europeans, who coined the term the "American System." After World War II, the United States dominated the world in almost every aspect of global business as they were clearly the world leader in manufacturing in both new product and new process development. However, starting in the 1980's the rest of the industrialized world began to catch up.

America's current problem is not winning the new economic game, but forcing itself to notice that the game has changed. America must recognize that it has some problems and to develop specific strategies in order to compete in the twenty-first century. This book develops several strategies that America can implement in order to improve its competitive position as follows:

- Consumption and Investment: American companies should increase their productivity relative to their competitors. The federal government's fiscal policy should emphasize investment over consumption expenditures.
- National Strategies: America must at least develop defensive strategies to match the industrial subsidies that are provided to companies by their governments.
- Education, Training and Accountability: In the knowledge society of the twenty-first century, the school must become accountable for the future performance of its students.

America has one important intangible. This country has a certain dignity, a certain class, based upon individual accomplishment, that no country has ever been able to achieve. If, in addition, the American government would adopt some of the strategies currently used by Japan and Germany and form a partnership with business, it would make the task of winning the twenty-first century, much easier.

CONTENTS

---

x   Contents

LIST OF TABLES AND FIGURES

CHAPTER 1

THE ECONOMIC WAY OF THINKING

"Political Economy or Economics is a study of mankind in the ordinary business of life." —Alfred Marshall

WHAT IS ECONOMIC HISTORY

After World War II, the United States dominated the world in almost every aspect of global business. Mass marketing was effectively an American monopoly. American companies were superior in technology, their workers were better educated and more skilled, and American managers were the best educated and trained in the world. The United States was clearly the world leader in manufacturing in both new product and new process development. In the twentieth century almost everything that plugged into an electrical outlet was invented in America and this country was the clear leader in determining what new products would be manufactured and how they would be made. However, America no longer dominates the world in the field of new process engineering. Japan's consumer electronics three largest chemical companies in the world are located in Germany. One of today's most prevalent management theories "Total Quality Management," was invented by American Scholars, but its application was perfected in Japan.

America has lost its position of world dominance in manufacturing. There is now a three way race between the European Union, Japan, and the United States. The race is to determine who will be the leader of the industrial world in the twenty-first century. When the top contenders for economic supremacy are analyzed, it is discovered that each has definite strengths and weaknesses. America is still the leading contender for economic supremacy. However, America no longer enjoys the economic dominance it had in the past. The question in the twenty-first century will not be who is perfect, but who is doing the best job, and who is creating the most value for its customers. In order to plan for the future, a company or a country must first understand its past. In the nineteenth century, the American forte was not as the original inventor but as the innovators. American businessmen acquired technological processes from abroad and then experimented with them, often greatly improving on the original invention. The Europeans themselves were the first to recognize that the American approach was different. It was the Europeans, who coined the term the "American System." America does not need to "reinvent the wheel" to win the twenty-first century; however, it needs to understand that it has problems and to develop specific strategies for the purpose of solving these problems. America needs to look at the past, and to understand what made it the greatest county in the world. For it is only with an understanding of past events that a country effectively plans for the future.

The purpose of this book is to examine the evolution of economic thought and how historical events have affected the economic growth of the world's industrialized countries. The first step in this analysis is to examine the field of economics itself. First, the basic theory of modern day economics will be explored in order to give the reader some understanding of what economics is and what economic theory attempts to accomplish. The theories of many famous Europeans and American economists are then described and placed in a historical context.

Economics has always been a reflection of historical events and has evolved as a field of study that proposes to explain current events. Economic forecasting is a product of the 1970's and is discussed in later chapters. Therefore, the focus of this book is to trace the evolution of economics, referred to as Political Economics until 1776, and to examine how the evolution of economic belief served to explain the growth of the economies of the leading industrialized countries of the world. Our exploration of economic history will begin with ancient history, which traces political economics all the way back to the writings of Aristotle. However, the emphasis of the book is the United States, and its continuing debate as to the proper role of government in controlling economic activity. Still, this analysis will not arbitrarily end in the 1990's. In addition to attempting to explain the past, this book analyzes the strengths and weaknesses of the Industrial World's leading economies and provides a picture of what these countries might look like in the twenty-first century.

BASIC ECONOMIC TERMS AND THEORY

Economics can be defined as the social science that seeks to examine and understand the choices people make in using scarce resources to meet their demands. Economic history is the subject that deals with the ways in which man has used his limited resources to satisfy his wants and with the institutions he has developed to organize economic activity.

"Political Economy or Economics," according to Alfred Marshall, "is a study of mankind in the ordinary business of life".[1] However, for practical purposes, the scope of this book is limited to the analysis of the questions that are most commonly asked by economists and other interested persons. Central to the study of economics is the question of what determines prices, how proceeds of economic activity are distributed and what determines the share of income that goes to wages, profits, interest and rents.

In every economy, certain basic choices have to be made. Among these choices, the most important are what goods will be produced, how will they be produced, who will do which jobs and for whom the results of economic activity will be made available. Each of these choices is made necessary because of scarcity, and each can be used to introduce key elements of the historical as well as the current economic way of analyzing a situation. To define the economic way of thinking, exploring the key elements of economic analysis, is useful.

Deciding What to Produce

In any economy the number of goods and services that could be provided is immense. The impossibility of producing as much of everything as people want reflects a scarcity of the productive resources that are used to make all goods. Many scarce productive resources must be combined to make even the simplest product or to produce a simple service. These productive resources are referred to by economists as the factors of production and are usually grouped by labor, capital and natural resources. Labor can be defined as the contribution to production made by people working with their minds and muscles. Labor can further be divided into those persons who organize the factors of production, i.e., the business owners, and those who actually perform the physical tasks required to produce a product, the workers.

Capital is the means of production that are created by people, including structures, machines, tools and systems. In economics, capital is defined as goods that are produced and used for the purpose of increasing the quantity of future goods. Natural Resources is anything that can be used as a productive input in its natural state, such as farmland, residential and commercial building sites, forests, fossil fuel and mineral deposits.

Deciding How to Produce

There is more than one way to produce almost any product. As a nation's economy advances, new methods of production are continually being developed. Business owners operate to make a profit. In order to make a profit, they have to find a way to allocate the factors of production efficiently. The owners of a business usually organize their company in an attempt to operate efficiently. Efficiency means producing a product with a minimum expense, effort and waste. However, over time, production potential can only be expanded by accumulating more of the factors of production and finding new technology to make the factors more productive. The act of increasing the economy's supply of production inputs made by people is known as capital investment. Investment is the act of increasing the economy's stock of capital. To accumulate capital, individuals have to save some of their income.[2]

Deciding Who Will Do the Work

The question of who will do the work, who will organize the tasks, who will develop the systems and who will do the physical work is a matter of organizing the social division of labor. Will everyone do everything independently, or will people cooperate? Economists answer these questions by pointing out that it is more efficient to cooperate. Three things make cooperation effective; they are, teamwork, learning by doing and comparative advantage. Teamwork requires that people work together to accomplish a task more efficiently than if they work independently. Learning by doing implies that people get better at some jobs by doing the work repeatedly. Comparative advantage is the ability to produce goods or services at a relatively lower opportunity cost than someone else.[3]

Deciding for Whom Goods and Services Will be Produced

In any economy, a decision has to be made about who will receive the benefits of production. Are goods and services to be distributed equally to everyone? Or are they to be sold to those willing and able to pay. If the goods produced are distributed only to those persons that are willing to pay, people with higher incomes will enjoy more and better products than people with lower incomes.

Distribution of purchasing power is never perfectly equal because some people have the financial resources to enjoy great quantities of goods and services. Other people, even in a nation as wealthy as the United States, live in poverty. No society has yet discovered how to provide equally for the demands of everyone, and at the same time, to provide the incentives that encourage high quality production and continued technological innovation.[4]

The question of distribution of output, among members of society, has implications in terms of both efficiency and fairness. Efficiency is the part of economics that is concerned with facts and the relationships among them. This is referred to as positive economics. However, a great portion of economic analysis is based on the fairness of distribution. This part of the analysis is called normative economics which is the area of economics that is devoted to judgments about which conditions and policies are good or bad.[5]

Additional Questions that Concern Economists

Another question that concerns many economists is what variables depress or stimulate total economic growth and what are the causes of the uneven levels of severity of business cycles. Also, emerging as a ponderable question is why it is so difficult in the modern economy to find useful employment for people that are willing and able to work.

In addition to these questions, the role of institutions such as business enterprises, banks and central banks, and government policies must be considered. All these questions, the solutions past, present, and the courses of action that are taken are the subject of economic history.

SCOPE OF THE BOOK

The study of American economic history is a study of change, from the merchant capitalism that preceded the American revolution, to the industrial revolution and the productivity revolution, through the Great Depression of the 1930's, two world wars, and culminating with the head to head competition of the modern day global economy.

Economics does not consist of one theory; it consists of many theories that have evolved throughout the history of the modern world. While examining every economic theory in the context of one book, is not possible, the objective of this work is to analyze historical events through the use of the most prevalent economic theory and the most noted economist of the time under evaluation.

Modern history has often presented a stage for the debate of the role of government in the economy. In 1576, Jean Bodin defined the role of the leaders of the new "Nation-State," as maintaining the climate for economic growth, keeping taxes low, and defending the realm. In the mid-eighteenth century, a group of French Philosophers called the Physiocrates created the idea of an economic system as an interconnected and interdependent structure. Their system contained a controlling natural law of economic behavior, and a guiding rule of laissez faire, or a hands off policy by government in the affairs of trade. In 1776, Adam Smith wrote "The Wealth of Nations," where he defined the role of government as a source of calculable law, a defender of the nation and a promoter of the freedom of internal and international trade.

In the nineteenth century, economists such as David Ricardo, John Stuart Mill, and Karl Marx, continued the debate which by that time was centered around the fairness of the distribution of profit between the workers and the capitalists. Alfred Marshall took the theories of the classical economists and developed economics as a separate field apart from politics, history and moral issues. Classical economics or Neoclassical economics, as it was now called, supported the basic theory that there was a self-adjusting mechanism that prevented an economy from entering into a long and severe depression. Since, by theory, depression could not be sustained, it was not necessary for government to take an active role in controlling the economy.

During the Great Depression that started in 1929, the leading economists of the day urged their governments to do nothing to improve their economic situation. However, by 1933, the newly elected American president Franklin D. Roosevelt found an economy with 25 percent of its employable workers not able to find jobs. Roosevelt's solution was to put people to work in jobs provided by the federal government and the Federal Emergency Relief Administration was created for this purpose. By 1937, eight million Americans were employed by their government.

In 1936, a new economic theory was created by John Maynard Keynes in his book, "The General Theory of Employment, Interest, and Money." According to Keynes, it is not necessary to wait for the economy to self adjust to a depression. The government should take steps to overcome a shortage of total demand. In a depression, the desire of the federal government to balance their budget must give way to the need to stimulate economic growth. The great depression and the theories of Keynes started the transition of the United States and most of

Europe, from the national state to the fiscal state. The depression gave rise to the belief that the national government should control its country's economic environment.

Joseph Schumpeter pointed out that as long as revenues were considered as a constraint, it was difficult for the government to act as either a social or economic agent. Following World War II, most developed countries adopted the theories of Keynesian economics. Keynes assumed that a wise and efficient government, would apply sound fiscal policy. However, in the hands of modern day politicians, government has become the master of the individual in society.

Schumpeter warned in 1918, that the fiscal state would in the end undermine government's ability to govern. Eighteen years later, Keynes hailed the fiscal state as the great liberator of a depressed economy. Keynes argued that government, no longer limited by restraints on expenditures, could effectively control economic growth by manipulating government spending and taxation. However, in the 1990's many economists and politicians believe that Schumpeter was right. By 1996, most of the governments of the industrialized world had run-up such large federal deficits that fiscal policy became almost useless in fighting either recession or inflation.

The debate has continued into the 1996 American presidential campaign where both the Republican and Democratic parties have attempted to define their positions based on the perceived role of government. The Republicans have defined their position as one of a reduced tax burden on its citizens, along with a smaller, and less intrusive role of the federal government. Their position is similar to the theories of Alfred Marshall and Neoclassical economics. The Democrats have defined their position more along the lines of Keynesian economic theory, calling for a larger role of government in controlling the economy.

The views of the two major American political parties were put to the test of the voters in the November 5, 1996, elections. Americans voted to retain President Clinton to "Build a bridge to the twenty-first century." However, they also voted to keep the Republican majority in both the House and Senate. Americans appeared to have voted for some moderate changes in government programs and some directed tax relief. Still they decided to hedge their bets to be certain that the bridge would not be overburden with government regulations. The debate will probably last long into the twenty-first century. As for the current generation of Americans and Western Europeans, we may never completely settle the question. In life there is only one certainty, for as John Maynard Keynes once wrote: "In the long run we are all dead."

The main purpose of this book can, therefore, be summarized as follows:

- To see economics as a reflection of the world in which specific economic ideas have developed over time.
- To isolate and emphasize the most lasting concepts of the leading economists of their time.
- To go beyond the ideas of the economic scholars to events that shaped the history of economics, its evolving institutions, and its continuing debate over the role of government in controlling the economy.
- To use the lessons from the past so that we can avoid repeating our mistakes in the future.

CHAPTER 2

THE ROOTS OF POLITICAL ECONOMICS

"The lower sort are by nature slaves, and it is better for them as for all inferiors that they should be under the rule of a master. Indeed the use made of slaves and of tame animals is not very different." —Aristotle

THE GREEK INFLUENCE

Central to all economic analysis was the question of what determines the prices that are paid for goods and services and how the proceeds from this economic activity are distributed. Also, there was a continuing debate over what determines the share of income going to wages, interest, profit, rent and other fixed items that are used in production. Over most of the modern life of economics, the following two subjects have been of great concern:

• The Theory of Value and what determines prices.

• The Theory of Distribution and who has benefited.

In earliest times, neither the factors determining prices nor those setting levels of wages and interest, were of much relevance. With production and consumption centered on the household, there was no necessity for a theory of prices; with slaves there was no compelling need for a theory of wages. In nearly all of economic history, most people have been poor and a comparative few have been very rich. Accordingly, there has been a compelling need to explain why this is so.

The basic industry of both Greece and Rome was agriculture; the producing unit was the household, and the labor force was the slave. Discussion of the economic questions of this era is principally to be found in the writings of Aristotle (384 - 322 B.C.). The most important reason that ethical questions were addressed to the exclusion of economic ones in the ancient world was the existence of slavery. According to Aristotle, at all times and in all places, the Greek world relied on some form of dependent labor to meet its needs. Since wages were not paid for labor, it followed that there could be no view of how wages were determined. Because slaves did the work, labor had a derogatory aspect that helped to exclude it from scholarly consideration.

The ethical justification of slavery became the most interesting economic question of the period. In defense of the institution Aristotle wrote, "The lower sort are by nature slaves, and it is better for them as for all inferiors that they should be under the rule of a master. Indeed the use made of slaves and of tame animals is not very different."

In Politics, Book I Aristotle adds, "It is clear then, that some men are by nature free, and others slaves, and that for these latter slavery is both expedient and right." Aristotle was equally certain as regards to women, "The male is by nature superior, and the female inferior; and the one rules, and the other is ruled; this principle, of necessity, extends to all mankind."[1]

Aristotle also strongly condemned the taking of money in the form of interest. Aristotle held that money, was intended to be used in exchange, not as means to obtain a profit. Interest continued to be condemned throughout the middle ages. Without wages and interest in the ancient world, there could not be a theory of prices in any modern sense. Prices derive, in one way or another, from production costs, and production costs were not a visible function in the slave owner household.

Aristotle wrote about another problem that was to be a continuing one for economists. This is the question of value in use and value in exchange. Aristotle wondered why some of the most useful things have a low value, e.g., water, while some of the least useful items command a much higher price, e.g., gold or diamonds. Well into the nineteenth century, economic writers would still be struggling with the difference between value in use and value in exchange.

By Aristotle's time, they had established coinage of metal in Greece. After defining the nature of money and coinage, Aristotle goes on to an analysis of how money is made. According to Aristotle, the making of money, in its pure form, is not permissible. "Some men turn every quality or art into a means of making money; this they conceive to be the end, and to the promotion of the end all things must contribute."[2]

THE CONTRIBUTIONS OF ROME

There was one major contribution to economic thought by the Romans. This was Roman Law that defined the rights of private property. It was Roman Law that gave formal identity to property and to its possessor the dominion or rights, which are now commonly agreed upon. These rights were comprehensive; they included the right not only of enjoyment and use of property, but also to misuse and abuse it. The intrusion on these rights in the future would from that time on require justification by the intruder.

No institution can compare in its importance to private property and no institution has been so productive of social, economic or political discord. If Roman economic comment was slight, it was, nonetheless, the Roman genius to distinguish and give form to the institution that would be central to personal satisfaction, economic development and political conflict in the centuries to come.

THE MIDDLE AGES

Historians have looked, with little success, for any formal expression of economic ideas in the scholarly and priestly thought of the one thousand years that followed the dissolution of the Roman Empire. The basic economic life of the middle ages bore little resemblance to modern economic society. Specifically, the market though growing in importance was still a minor aspect of life in the middle ages. The great rural masses of men and women grew, made or killed what they ate or wore and surrendered a part of it to a hierarchy of Lords or Masters.

However, towns, though small by modern standards, began to appear. Some purchases and sales did take place and they attracted the mind and pen of the greatest of the religious philosophers of his time, the prolific Saint Thomas Aquinas (1225 - 1274). Saint Thomas was the first of the group of religious philosophers and scholars known to history as the Schoolmen.

The craft guilds were strongly characteristic of medieval economic life. They existed for several purposes, for example: assurance as to quality of workmanship, social observances, political influence and regulation of prices and journeymen's wages. This being the case, the question of fairness or justice of the price of a product arose, just as it had with Aristotle. It was to the fairness of prices that Saint Thomas Aquinas addressed his work.

"I answer that it is wholly sinful to practice fraud for the express purpose of selling a thing for more than its just price. To sell dearer or to buy cheaper than a thing is worth is in itself unjust and unlawful." Saint Thomas thus enjoined a fair price as a religious responsibility; default from that obligation made the perpetrator subject not only to the moral condemnation of the community but to appropriate religious sanction.[3]

Saint Thomas also accepted and strongly affirmed the ban on the taking of interest. He also combined this belief with the consideration of the righteousness of trade overall. Trade, according to Saint Thomas, is praiseworthy, because it serves natural needs.

Money, one of the most magically alluring subjects of economics, drew the attention of another articulate religious scholar, Nicole Oresme (1320 - 1382). The term "Merchant Capitalism" is central to Nicole Oresme. The policy of the prince (the leader) should be to encourage trade and arrange the conditions that do so. For Oresme this meant the proper management of money.

Oresme showed how the coinage of such metals as gold, silver and copper, coins of fixed weight and reliable purity, could replace the awkward use of scales, in the weighing of metals. The responsibility for coinage he then placed squarely on the Prince or the government.

According to Oresme, it is the sovereign's function to condemn and punish those who practice any fraud upon money.[4]

Oresme was particularly severe with the Prince of an adjacent province who slipped debased coins (less than claimed amounts of metal) into the monetary circulation of his neighbor, and he was convinced that merchants would avoid doing business in a land where the coinage was unreliable.

The rigid hierarchical structure of feudal society commanded and distributed goods and services not in response to price but in response to law, custom and the fear of punishment. The marketplace was an esoteric exception to the way trade was conducted, and most scholars did not spend time trying to explain it. Oresme, who did, was responding to a new and expanding world in which markets and moneys were strongly emerging as necessary factors of economic life.

MERCHANT CAPITALISM (1450-1776)

Merchant Capitalism extended for three hundred years, from roughly the middle of the fifteenth to the middle of the eighteenth century. The end of merchant capitalism was sealed by the beginning of the industrial revolution, the American Revolution and the publication in 1776 of "The Wealth of Nations" by Adam Smith.

Mercantilism was the product of the minds of statesmen, civil servants, and the financial and business leaders of the day. The merchant emerged from the feudal shadows to become an affluent, distinctive, socially acceptable and a prestigious figure.

By the fifteenth century the merchant towns of Venice, Florence, Antwerp, and London had merchant communities of distinction. In the merchant towns the great merchants were not merely influential in the government; they controlled the power of government. Throughout all of Europe they were influential in the new national states.

The national state arose as a response to transnational drives. The Spanish Empire in the new world produced so much gold and silver that Spain, under Philip II, could finance the first standing army in the sixteenth century, since the Roman legions. Thus equipped, Spain launched the first campaign for the attempt to unify Europe under Spanish rule. Fighting Spain's threat became the motivation and the aim of the inventor of the national state, the French lawyer-politician Jean Bodin, (1530 - 1596). In 1576, Jean Bodin published, "Six Livres de la Republique," that defined the new national state.

What Bodin prescribed was a controlled civil service (answerable only to the sovereign), central control of the military, and a standing army managed by professional soldiers appointed by and accountable to central government. Bodin also recommended central control of coinage, taxes, customs and a centrally appointed professional judiciary, rather than courts staffed by local magnates.

These recommendations were the opposites of what had existed for a thousand years. All of them threatened powerfully entrenched "special interest," for example:

- An autonomous church and exempt bishops and abbeys.

- Local lords of all sizes, each with his own armed mercenaries, and each with his own jurisdiction and his own taxing powers.

- Free cities, self-governing trade guilds and scores of others.

However, the Spanish bid for mastery of Europe left no alternative. The choice was subjection to the national sovereign or conquest by a foreign sovereign. From then on, attempts similar to those of Spain to gain the mastery of Europe, triggered practically every change in the political structure of the national states. Along with the proliferation of markets and the rise of the merchant class, three major developments reflected the economic attitudes and policies of this period.

The first were the voyages to America and the Far East. In 1492, Christopher Columbus, who was trained in Portugal and sponsored by Spain, found America. In 1497 the Portuguese navigator Vasco da Gama sailed to India; and in ensuing decades, others from Spain and Portugal and then from England, France and Holland.

The result of these voyages was a flow of new and exotic products into Europe from the East, and more important, a flood of silver and gold from the mines of the new world. From 1531 to 1570, near the peak of the flood, silver represented an amount between 85 to 97 percent of the total treasury coming into Europe.

The effect of the great inflow of metal was a general rise in prices, an early example of the quantity theory of money. This is the historic theory which argues that if the volume of trade (the velocity of money) is held constant, prices will vary in direct proportion to the supply of money. The relationship between the supply of money and general commodity prices, was a key topic of the economic analysis of the time. Writing in 1576, Jean Bodin said; "I find that the high prices we see today are due to some four or five causes. The principle one is the abundance of gold and silver."[5]

The second development was the continuing effect that the great inflow of silver and gold had on the volume of trade. There was a view in this period that the role of money was essentially neutral. Money is a convenience in the buying and selling of goods, a bridge over the gap in time between the sale and purchases of goods, and a convenient way of holding wealth. It was believed that more fundamental factors govern the state of trade then the changes in the supply of money. Therefore, increases in the supply of money could not be used to stimulate merchant trade.

The third and most important development of the merchant capitalist period, was the appearance and consolidation of the authority of the national state, as previously discussed. The earlier centuries had seen the decline of the feudal and compulsively feuding baronage and the emergence of princely and city authority. The national state was but the final step in a long chain of events. The rise of the national state caused the close association between the state authority and the interest of the merchants.

Mercantilism involved a market break with the ethical attitudes and instructions of Aristotle and of Saint Thomas Aquinas and the middle ages overall. The Merchants were patently in pursuit of wealth, in a society where they were influential. However, society no longer considered the pursuit of wealth by the merchants, to be evil or dubious. Merchants were easy in their conscience. Protestantism and Puritanism may have helped, but the church leaders accommodated religious faith to economic circumstances.

As wealth and the pursuit of wealth, by the merchants, become respectable, the right to charge interest on loans, became acceptable. When the borrower invested and in turn made money from his loan, then, as a matter of simple equity, he should share the gain with the lender who made the investment possible and compensate the lender for their risk of loss of the principle. Both Catholic and Protestant Church doctrine made the necessary concession to economic circumstances. The financing of merchant operations with borrowed money became legitimate. They did not deny merchants access to heaven if they charged interest on their loans. After all, they were among the largest contributors to the Church.[6]

Wages had little or no part in mercantilist discussion and practice.   They accomplished domestic manufacturing   extensively in the household. In their home, husband, wife and children worked the raw material supplied to them by the merchant into finished textile products. Again no wages were paid as such; the merchant simply paid the workers whatever amount was necessary to obtain the finished product.

In summary, the major beliefs of the merchant capitalist were:

- Merchants had a very negative attitude toward competition. Because they didn't relish competition, monopoly or monopolistic control of prices and product offerings were approved.

- The Merchants were extremely influential in the state, and held a strong belief that the government should not interfere in trade or the economy.

- There was agreement that the accumulation of gold and silver should be a primary goal of personal and public policy, and this was the end to which all personal effort and public regulation should always be directed.

Of the total changes that took place during the years of merchant capitalism, none was more important than the arrival of the modern corporation. Initially this was merely a temporary association of individuals joining their efforts and capital for a common task or voyage and to ensure a non-competitive price for the products that they purchased and sold. The roots of such associations extended back to the guilds of the middle ages. In the fifteenth century, merchants selling cloth from England to the continent, often formed a loose federation. The following were the most important of these federations to economic history:

- Muscovy Company of 1555

- The Dutch East India Company of 1601

- The British East India Company (1600-1874)

In the late seventeenth and early eighteenth centuries the chartering of joint-stock companies, as they came to be called, continued. Actually, most trade with the American Colonies was conducted with charted companies. Also, in the early 1700's, there was a further and even more spectacular forerunner of modern corporate business. This was the market for the sale of stocks and bonds that appeared in Paris and London.

Although we can understand mercantilist doctrine primarily through the policies of the time, there were men in all the new states of Europe that articulated its general principles. Thomas Mun, who was one of the most distinguished of these writers, published in 1664, "England's Treasure by Foreign Trade." Thomas Mun offers a dozen rules for maximizing England's wealth and well-being, for example:

- Always sell dear to foreigners what they do not have and sell cheap what they can otherwise obtain.

- Use ones own ships for exports.

- Buy cheaply from far away countries.

- Do not give business to nearby competitors.

DAVID HUME ON THE NEUTRALITY OF MONEY

David Hume, born in 1711, was an early member of the classical school of economics, as well as a noted historian and philosopher. He was a colleague of Adam Smith at Edinburgh University in Scotland. Eighteenth century economists widely agreed that an increase in the money stock, chiefly gold and silver coins at the time, would raise the price level. Price increases had been observed, for example, when the Spanish began bringing gold back to Europe from the New World. A less settled question was whether an increase in the money stock would also cause real economic output to increase. Today economists refer to this issue as whether on not money is "neutral." On the subject of the neutrality of money, Hume said that "although an increase in the price of goods is a necessary consequence of an increase in the stock of gold and silver, it follows not immediately." The change in the money stock does not affect all markets at once. Hume continues by stating that, "At first, no alteration is perceived; by degrees the price rises, first on one commodity, then of another; till the whole at last reaches a just proportion with the new quantity of money." Agreeing with the modern theory, which states that the initial stimulus to real output is only temporary, Hume continues: "In my opinion, it is only in this interval or intermediate situation, between the acquisition of money and the rise of prices, that the increasing quantity of gold and silver is favorable to industry." In Hume's view, there is no long-run effect on real output. In the long run, unlike the short run, money is neutral. A one-time change in the quantity of money has a lasting proportional effect on the price level but on nothing else.[7]

THE FRENCH DESIGN

Merchant capitalism and the craftsmen that it required to produce its products, had also appeared in France. Paris had become a city of merchants along with their suppliers and workers. However, to a larger extent than any other country in Europe, France had retained a powerful agricultural interest and mystique.

In the latter half of the eighteenth century, a highly innovative French contribution to economic thought evolved. This was in the spirit of enlightenment, based on the writings of Voltaire, Diderot, Condorcet and most of all Rousseau. Central to this theory was the role of agriculture as the source of all wealth. The French philosophers combined an assertion of the traditional values of the land and its associated political power, with the advocacy of reform.

Historians of economic thought have given these writers the title of "Physiocrats," those who assert the rules of nature. The physiocrats were a closely knit community and many of their ideas are associated with a common position. An important figure among the physiocrats was Pierre Samuel DuPont de Nemours (1739-1817). In 1800 DuPont immigrated to the United

States, and in 1802 with his two sons, he began construction of a powder mill on Brandywine Creek near Wilmington, Delaware. From these beginnings came one of the largest American industrial corporations. In fact General DuPont became one of the most powerful industrial leaders of the last part of the nineteenth century.

The major contributions of the physiocrats to economic thought were as follows:

- Ledriot Natural (Natural Law): The first and central commitment of the physiocrats was to the idea of natural law, for it was this, they held, which ultimately ruled economic and social behavior. The law of kings and legislators is tolerable only as it is consistent with natural law. The existence and protection of property according to natural law. A society is better off, it was reasoned, if things were worked out in accordance with natural motivations and restraints.

- Laissez Faire: The guiding rule in legislation and in government should be laissez faire. The term laissez faire was the greatest legacy of the physiocrats. However, this phrase has been defined in two different ways. In later times, economists would identify laissez faire with the achievements of the competitive market. The results of a market economy would be preferred to any intervention by the state. However, laissez faire would also be the rallying cry against government intervention in any form for any social purpose. Leave things alone in the widest conceivable area except national defense, and they will work themselves out.

- Product Net: There was another theory that was clearly in opposition to merchant capitalism. This was the idea of product net. It simply held that all wealth originated in agriculture, none in any other industry, trade or occupation. Closely associated with the notion of product net was the physiocratic class structure. In this there were the following categories:

  1. The landlords or proprietors: The people who guided the production of agriculture. To them the product net ultimately accrued and they were accountable for the social and political responsibilities of the community and the state.

  2. The productive class: The people who worked the soil. It was after their reward (wages) was paid that the product net went to the proprietors.

  3. The lower status: The merchants, manufacturers and craftsmen, i.e., the unproductive class.

As with laissez faire this was an idea that did not die. The notion that production somehow creates a surplus of revenue accruing to particular classes was to re-emerge in a different form in the next century. Then it would be the capitalists, not the landowners, whom they would accuse of receiving a surplus value; another and different product net.

There was still another physiocratic contribution, that also has a major resonance in our own time, called the Tableau Economique. The Tableau Economique was developed by Francois Quesnay (1694-1774). This system alleged to show how products flowed out from the worker to the landlords and onto the merchants, manufacturers and other non-productive classes, and how money flowed back to the cultivator. Thus Quesnay showed how each part of the economy served and was compensated by each of the others. He displayed the mechanism of purchase and sale of goods as a complete interlocking system. In 1973, Wassily Leontief was awarded the Nobel Prize for Economic Science. This award was for his work called input-output analysis. This system became the principle building block for the modern popular models for predicting the economic prospect and the effect of changes in prices, wages, interest rates, taxes and demand as these are reflected through individual industries. This was a concept developed by Francois Quesnay.

The French Revolution swept away the world that the physiocrats had sought to defend and save. Left, however, for generations to come were the ideas of an economic system as an interconnected and interdependent structure of concepts; a controlling natural law of economic behavior, the prominence of agriculture, laissez faire, the product net, and the tableau economique.[8]

Adam Smith later wrote: "This system, with all its imperfections, is, perhaps, the nearest approximation to the truth that has yet been published upon the subject of political economy."

CHAPTER 3

AMERICA: THE COLONIAL YEARS

"America was never in higher prosperity, her produce abundant and bearing a good price, her working people all employed and well paid." —Benjamin Franklin

COLONIAL BUSINESS ENTERPRISE

During the colonial period, extremely small business dominated American industry. Most American businessmen were peddlers, blacksmiths, and small shopkeepers. These small business owners did not have the capital or ability necessary to cope with the needs of the widening market. Eventually the petty capitalists' position of dominance in America was taken over by a group of merchants who were better able to take care of the international and domestic economy that the colonies had become as a member of the British Empire.

The merchants came into existence in America, in the middle of the eighteenth century, in the major colonial cities. The original merchants were owners of general stores, shipping companies, brokerage and wholesale operations. The era of the merchant capitalists in the colonies spanned the period from 1750 to about 1850. Thomas Hancock, Stephan Girard and John Jacob Astor were all merchant capitalists. Before the American Revolution there were over 100 merchants in each of the three largest cities, Philadelphia, Boston and New York.

THE INFLUENCE OF BRITISH MERCANTILISM

By the middle of the seventeenth century, Great Britain had not yet achieved her position of world economic domination. Attempts to build an empire were often frustrated by the power and activities of the Dutch and the French. In order to overcome the advantages enjoyed, especially by the Dutch, Britain adopted a set of policies that came to be known as merchant capitalism. Designed principally to build a strong state, mercantilist policies were intended to help the entire empire to compete in the world economy. However, merchant capitalism favored the interests of the "mother country" over those of the rest of the empire.

The American colonies were to be given assistance, but they were also regarded as producers of raw materials for Britain and consumers of British manufactured goods. The intention of the British government was to use force, if necessary, to maintain this arrangement. Beginning in 1649, Britain adopted the first Navigation Acts affecting the colonies, and for the next 200 years these acts were modified for the purpose of preserving the power of the British Empire.

After the French and Indian War in 1763, the regulations imposed by the Navigation Acts began to be applied with an emphasis toward raising revenue to help Britain offset some of the expenses of defending the colonies. In general, mercantilist legislation, as it pertained to international trade, provided for the following:

- All trade to England from the American colonies was to be carried in ships owned and manned by citizens of the British Empire.

- All goods imported into the colonies, except wine and salt from Southern Europe, had to be shipped   via England.

- A major portion of colonial exports, such as tobacco, cotton, indigo, rice and naval stores (pitch, tar,   resin, turpentine, hemp, masts, yards, and bowsprit), could be shipped only to England.

- Extensive tariff regulation was established.

- An elaborate system of rebates, drawbacks, export bounties on designated goods, and export taxes was developed.

    The restrictions on imports and exports were economically disadvantageous to the colonists. An example of British legislation that particularly frustrated American traders was the Molasses Act of 1733, which imposed prohibitive duties on imports of sugar, molasses, and rum from the non-English West Indies. Designed to protect the English West Indies' sugar producers at the expense of the mainland, this Act proved to be a colossal economic and political blunder on the part of the British government.
    However, the British system of mercantilism did present the colonies with some advantages. England protected colonial shipping on the high seas. Also,

generous bounties were paid to the colonists on such goods as tar, pitch, hemp, silk, indigo and lumber. Being members of the British Empire, the colonists also had the advantage of exporting some goods to Britain at lower duties than were required of foreign shippers. In some cases, British restrictions gave the colonists an almost monopolistic position in trade, relative to other countries in Europe. For example, tobacco raising was prohibited in England and a prohibitive duty was imposed on non-colonial tobacco imports.

GREAT BRITAIN'S VIEW OF COLONIAL TRADE

From the British point of view, the colonies never seemed to understand that their function in life was to devote their efforts to the interest of England, the center of the Empire. They were supposed to be producers of raw materials and consumers of English manufactured goods, i.e., the basic goal of English mercantilism.

New England was the worst offender of the system. Because of its geographical disadvantages, New England could not compete in agricultural production with the other colonies. New England did have a large seacoast, and abundant natural resources. This situation resulted in a comparative advantage that gave New England the ability to produce ships at a lower cost than English shipbuilders. Consequently, New England competed with, rather than complemented, England's international trade. This tendency toward competing directly with England with a manufactured product, i.e., sailing ships, was in direct contradiction with England's mercantilist policy.

The middle colonies, New York, New Jersey, Pennsylvania and Delaware, were also not living up to mercantilist expectations. The middle colonies carried on a large trade with Southern Europe and the West Indies.

By 1770, the middle colonies had greatly increased their volume of foreign trade by selling wheat flour and provisions to Southern Europe, the West Indies and England.

The Southern Colonies came the closest to fulfilling the requirements of the mercantilist system. They raised raw materials, mostly tobacco, for export to England and imported manufactured goods from England. In 1700, Virginia and Maryland shipped enough tobacco and imported enough manufactured goods to account for two-thirds of all colonial trade with Britain.

Great Britain was prospering very well during this era, and manufacturing with a built in market for the goods produced, was the key. By far the world's leading manufacturing nation, England was building up an overseas financial empire by exporting more than that country was importing. When a country exports more than they import, they have a balance of payments surplus. However, when one country has a balance of payments surplus, at least one of its trading partners must have a balance of trade deficit. In this case, the colonies had a balance of payments deficit with Britain. In the short run, the colonies were able to cover their balance of payments deficit by borrowing, but eventually the debts became so large that they could not be paid. These debts by the colonies were one of the aggravations that fanned the anti-British feeling that eventually erupted in the revolutionary war.[1]

COLONIAL BANKING

The history of American money and banking has been a story of conflict between different philosophies and disparate beliefs over what money should do and how it should be controlled. The two points of view about the role of money were between those who desired "easy money" versus those who desired "sound money" policies. Those who believed that easy money offered an open door to prosperity argued for a rapidly expanding money supply that was free from strict control by a central authority. For the colonies this meant Great Britain. Their views were opposed by those who believed in sustainable economic growth or a steady progress under a central authority whose primary objectives were safety, solvency, and stability. The debate began before the revolution and has continued ever since.

In early America, capital did not accumulate fast enough to raise the level of living very much. Therefore, many of the colonists, acting on the assumption that money was the same as capital, thought that each addition to the money supply would automatically increase the stock of capital by the same amount. It was commonly believed that a money system should have two functions: it should provide a medium of exchange, and it should augment the supply of capital. However, as David Hume pointed out, there is no direct relationship between the money stock and the amount of capital available for investment. The colonists, in a desperate attempt to expand their business, developed a series of monetary experiments. All of these experiments were resisted and sometimes thwarted by the British, who upheld the conservative view in the monetary debates of that period.

By the middle of the seventeenth century, in order to increase their stock of metallic money, i.e., gold and silver, the colonies resorted to devaluation; that is they cut the amount of metal in their silver coins. However, this attempt to inflate the money supply was also prohibited by British edict. Refusing to accept Britain's distaste for monetary inflation, the colonies, who were desperately in debt to England, began to print paper money. In 1690, Massachusetts issued one-year notes to pay retiring soldiers. The experiment worked out so well that more paper money was quickly printed. Meanwhile, the other colonies, encouraged by Massachusetts' action, also began to issue paper money. Some of these notes were issued by state banks, but there were no banks as we know them today. Colonial banks issued money against mortgages, but they did not accept deposits.

At first, paper money did not depreciate in value. However, in many colonies it was used unproductively and far too much money was printed. As a result of this over expansion of the state's money supply, prices increased on a broad scale. Extreme inflation can disrupt the economy and cause widespread suffering to certain groups of people. However, paper-money depreciation did act to the advantage of colonial debtors and to the disadvantage of British creditors, who eventually prevailed upon the British Crown to prohibit the practice.[2] According to Benjamin Franklin, the British anti-inflation policy was one of the five causes of the America Revolution.

ECONOMIC SEEDS OF REVOLUTION

The major problem that confronted the British in North America after the French and Indian War was that of financing the protection of the colonies and liquidating the debts acquired during the war. The Seven Years War (the French and Indian War was the colonial phase) diverted capital away from British commerce and depleted the royal treasury. The English government believed that it was politically impossible to increase property taxes at home, and argued that the colonists should bear a larger share of the costs of their own defense.

The British response to their money problems created by the North American War was to introduce new revenue measures, tighten up the administration of the colonies, and force the mainland colonies to conform more closely to mercantile expectations. Fiscal reform began in 1762 with the passage of a wartime measure that ordered absentee customs officials to their colonial posts, increased the portion of revenues that they could keep for themselves, and gave the Navy authority to seize cargoes suspected of customs violations. Parliament changed the wartime measures into permanent law in 1763 and in 1764 added the Revenue Act. The Revenue Act included a revision of the Molasses Act of 1733, lowering the duty on molasses from the French West Indies, but also providing the means for strict enforcement of the Act. Also, the British altered the judicial aspects of the Navigation Acts in this 1764 program. The vice-admiralty courts received larger jurisdiction, customs officers were guaranteed freedom from retaliatory suits, and defendants in custom cases were generally denied the due process of law by having to prove their innocence in these cases.

In addition, in 1764 Parliament passed The Currency Act that caused the colonists to be seriously constrained for the first time in the management of their money supply. The Currency Act prohibited the creation of all new land banks throughout the colonies. Also this Act demanded the phased withdrawal of previous land-bank notes, banned additional issues of bills of credit as legal tender, and required a scheduled retirement of all past issues of bills of credit.

The 1764 Currency Act was designed to reduce the exchange rate of the colonial currency in terms of British Pound Sterling. This would increase the cost of colonial products to English buyers and reduce the cost of English products to colonial buyers. The Act resulted in strong protest from the conservative mercantile communities in Philadelphia, New York and Baltimore. In adopting the Currency Act, the English desired the following results:

- To increase the value of colonial currency in which the colonists paid taxes to England.

- To increase the value of debts owed by the colonist to English merchants. This would effectively lower the profit for the colonist on trade with England.

- To increase the colonial demand for English imports, as a result of the increased value of colonial currency, in terms of Sterling.

- To create a decline in English demand for exports as a result of the falling value of Sterling in terms of colonial currency.[3]

Given the negative balance of trade that was already being experienced by the colonial merchants, this Act effectively devalued the British Pound relative to colonial currency. As many American merchants were already in serious debt to their British counterparts, this Act served to worsen an already bad situation.

Further revenue measures followed. The Stamp Act of 1765 placed a levy on commercial papers, newspapers and other printed material. The Chancellor of the Exchequer, Charles Townshend, sponsored a set of duties, which were enacted in the Townshend Acts. These Acts taxed the colonists on their consumption of paper, glass, lead, paints and tea, that was imported from England.

Soon after their introduction, these enactments were repealed: the Stamp Act in 1766 and the Townshend duties (except for the tax on tea) in 1770. However, the capriciousness of all these regulations was an important contributor to the development of a revolutionary atmosphere that was probably more significant than the direct economic burden the regulations themselves imposed. The unpredictability of British regulations, and the potential for substantial damage to colonial interest, fueled a growing lack of respect for British authority. For an example of the potential impact that the Currency Act could have caused, consider the modern monetary policy of the United States being conducted by the Bank of England. Thus, while other irritations and desires fueled the American Revolution, there was probably no single issue more important and more divisive, than the perceived role of government (in this case the British Parliament), in commerce and trade.

AMERICAN COMMERCE AFTER THE REVOLUTION

In 1774 and 1775, the First Continental Congress prohibited trade with Britain. The British followed with the Prohibitory Act of 1775, banning almost all trade with the colonies. Accordingly, the British attempted to blockade the coast of the mainland colonies. This resulted in a decline in trade with Britain. However, American merchants got around the British blockade by developing new trading opportunities. The First Continental Congress opened American ports to all traders, except England, and promoted an expanded trade policy with the friendly European nations. In 1779, the French formed an alliance with America. The result of this alliance was that trade with the French West Indies and Europe expanded. Americans were able to purchase a large amount of European imports through the sale of tobacco and from the procurement of loans from France, Spain and The Netherlands.

When the War ended in 1783, Americans resumed trade with Britain. American consumers had become accustomed to British manufactured goods. Responding to this large market, British merchants again extended credit to American importers, although at levels that were smaller than before the War. However, Americans were able to engage in international trade with the rest of Europe, on a more favorable basis. Part of this improved trading position was a result of freedom from the mercantile system. Relieved of the restrictions of the Molasses and Sugar Acts Americans could trade with greater freedom and at a lower cost with the French West Indies.

American commerce profited in other ways from the demise of mercantilism. Americans gained the ability to export a much greater amount of goods (not just tobacco), directly to the continent, and trade with Northern and Southern Europe increased substantially. Americans were now free to export grain, flour, rice, potash and naval stores directly to France and the Netherlands. Americans also took advantage of their new freedom by developing a direct trade with Asia. As early as 1786, Americans began shipping beef, flour and naval stores to the French Island in the Indian Ocean and at the same time, they opened trade with China.

In summary, the end of British rule in the colonies brought about the end of merchant capitalism and the beginning of the industrial revolution in America. The industrial revolution brought with it a complete change in the way the world conducted its business, and a new economic theory was required to explain this change. To this end Adam Smith published "The Wealth of Nations" in 1776. Several other economists, such as Jean Baptiste

Say, Thomas Malthus and David Ricardo, who by adding and refining Adam Smith's original work, developed the basic theories in a discipline that came to be known as Classical Economics.

CHAPTER 4

THE FOUNDATIONS OF
CLASSICAL ECONOMICS

"It is not its silver or gold that measures a nation's wealth. It is the annual labour of every nation that is the fund which originally supplies it with all the necessaries and conveniences of life." —Adam Smith

ADAM SMITH (1723-1790)

The industrial revolution, which came to England and Southern Europe in the last third of the eighteenth century, brought workers to the factories and the factory towns. These workers previously produced goods in their cottages or food and wool on their farms.

The capital that merchants had invested in raw materials and sent to the villages to be made into cloth was now being invested in factories. However, to operate these new factories a much larger investment was needed in the factors of production, i.e., land, labor, and natural resources.

The dominant figure in this change was the industrialist whose purpose was the increased production of goods. The industrial revolution profoundly shaped the development of economics and from it emerged one of the most celebrated figures in the history of the subject. Adam Smith was the prophet of the industrial revolutions achievements and the original source of its explanation.

Adam Smith is considered to have been the founder of economics as a distinct field of study, although he wrote only one book on the subject "An Inquiry into the Nature and Causes of the Wealth of Nations," published in 1776. Smith was 53 years old at the time. His friend David Hume found the book such hard reading that he doubted that many people would read it. However, Hume's prophecy was wrong. People have been reading The Wealth of Nations, for more than 200 years.

Adam Smith wrote that the wealth of a nation was not a result of accumulating gold and silver, as the mercantilists believed. The wealth of a nation is measured by the outcome of the activities of ordinary people working and trading in free markets. To Smith, the remarkable thing about the wealth produced by a market economy, is that it is not a result of any organized plan but the unintended outcome of the actions of many people, each of whom is independently pursuing the incentives the market offers with his or her own interests in mind. Smith writes that: "It is not from the benevolence of the butcher, the brewer, or the baker that we expect our dinner, but from their regard to their own interest. Every individual is continually exerting himself to find out the most advantageous employment for whatever capital he can command. By directing that industry in such a manner as its produce may be of the greatest value, he intends only his own gain, and he is in this, as in many other cases, led by an invisible hand to promote an end which was no part of his intention."[1]

Much of the discipline of economics as it has developed over the past two centuries consists of elaborations on ideas found in Smith's work. The idea of the "invisible hand" of market incentives that channels people's efforts in directions that are beneficial to their neighbors remains the most durable of Smith's contributions to economics.

In his book, Smith describes the work of a pin factory, but one that was far from characteristic of the industrial plants of later decades. What captured Adam Smith's attention was not the machinery that characterized the industrial revolution but the way the job was divided so that each worker became an expert on his minuscule part of the task. The great efficiencies of contemporary enterprise, combined with man's natural propensity to truck, barter, and exchange one thing for another came from this specialization, this division of labor.

Smith's Lasting Contributions to Economics

Adam Smith's contributions to economics were many. There are, however, four critical areas that provide a starting point. These are his views on economic motivation, the distribution of revenue that was earned from the sale of goods, how prices are determined and the role of government in business and international trade. These issues still survive in today's college textbooks as the study of microeconomics.

Economic Motivation: This for Smith centers on the role of self-interest. The private and competitive pursuit of things that are in ones best interest is the source of the greatest benefit to the public. Smith adds, an invisible hand leads the individual to promote and end which was not part of his original intention. The person concerned with self-enrichment had previously been and object of doubt, suspicion and mistrust, feelings that went back through the middle ages to biblical times. Now, because of his self-interest, he had become the driving force behind the industrial revolution's propensity to produce a whole spectrum of new products.

The Distribution of Revenue: Prices and who gets the proceeds, were the second of the basic issues of economics that Smith addressed. In this regard, Smith analyzed the reasons for the distribution of revenue among the workers, the landlords and the owners. As workers were assembled in the factories, what determined their pay became highly relevant. As the capitalists assumed control of production, the question arose concerning a fair distribution of income to the workers and to the owner of the business.

The wage's that were paid to workers, Smith regarded generally as the price of attracting labor and the cost of sustaining them on the job. Profit, according to Smith is the appropriation of a surplus value that the worker creates over and above what the capitalist pays them. The capitalist, according to Smith, has a seemingly rightful claim. The question here was not if the capitalist deserved a return on the capital that they invested, but how much that return should be. In many circumstances, the amount of return that went to the capitalist was a result of the power that they held over the workers and not their contribution to the value of the goods sold.

The compensation paid to landlords as rent, entered into the composition of the price of commodities, in a different way from wages and profit. High or low wages and profit are the causes of high or low price; high or low rent is the effect of it. "The rent increases in proportion to the goodness of the pasture."[2]

How Prices are Determined: The interesting and disturbing circumstance that many of the best or most nearly essential things in life are virtually free, puzzled Smith. For example, water which was highly useful was very cheap while diamonds which were then, as now, expensive, were not really very useful. From this analysis came the troubling difference between value in use and value in exchange.

Smith resolved the problem in his time by simply setting value in use aside and asserting a value in exchange. This was a version of what came to be known as the "labor theory of value." According to Smith, the value of labor measures the worth of any possession and ultimately the amount for which it can be exchanged.[3]

Government's Role in Business and International Trade: Adam Smith's strongest recommendation as to public policy urges the freedom of internal and international trade. Many of Smith's recommendations come from his observation of the pin factory. According to Smith, only if there is freedom to barter and trade, can some workers specialize on pins. Also, others can devote their efforts to additional tasks, so that all of these efforts will come together for the exchange that satisfies several individual needs. If freedom of trade does not exist, each worker must concentrate incompetently on making his own pins; the economies from specialization are gone. From this analysis, Smith concludes that the wider the trading area, the greater the opportunity for specialization; for the division of labor, and the greater the productivity of labor.

Smith's case for free trade extends to a direct assault on the mercantilist view of gold and silver as the foundation of national wealth and to the belief that trade restrictions can enhance the stock of precious metals. In the opening words of The Wealth of Nations, Smith proclaims that it is not its silver or gold that measures a nation's wealth. It is "the annual labour of every nation that is the fund which originally supplies it with all the necessaries and conveniences of life." Wealth, Smith held, is enhanced by "the skill, dexterity, and judgment with which its labour is generally applied, and, secondly, by the proportion between the number of those who are employed in useful labour, and that of those who are not so employed."[4]

According to Smith the matters of labor and production are the most important ones to address. If they are managed successfully, prices will be low, and supplies of marketable products will be plentiful. Gold and silver will come in from abroad to purchase the products, and the supply of specie will take care of itself. Other countries cannot prevent their people from exchanging their gold and silver for useful products. Smith observes that, "All sanguinary laws of Spain and Portugal are not able to keep their gold and silver at home." Smith adds, "It is not by the importation of gold and silver, that the discovery of America has enriched Europe. By the abundance of the American mines, those metals have become cheaper."[5]

Smith was not totally rigid on the matter of free trade. He would allow tariffs for industries essential for defense and possibly in retaliation for tariff abuse abroad. Also he would be tolerant of protecting new enterprises from competition abroad and recommend a gradual withdrawal of tariffs as these enterprises became capable of competing on an international level. Alexander

Hamilton who recommended tariff protection for new and developing enterprises in America after the revolution, took this argument up later.

Smith's Laws of Accumulation and Population

Smith attempted to answer the question of what pushes a society toward the pursuit of wealth. Smith thought that part of the answer is the workings of the market system itself. The competitive force of the marketplace encourages businessmen to invent, innovate, to take risks, and to expand. Smith identified two basic laws of behavior that propel the market system toward increasing levels of productivity.

The first is the Law of Accumulation. The industrial revolution in its early stages provided many opportunities to obtain wealth for those who were industrious enough and smart enough to take advantage of the situation. The basic objective of most of the early industrialists was to accumulate their savings. Prior to the Civil War in America, bank loans were usually made for purchasing land and investment banking had not yet been developed in this country. Therefore, the money to build manufacturing facilities essentially came from the profit of the enterprise or the accumulated savings of the capitalist.

Smith believed that the accumulation of capital was a great benefit to society. For it was the capital that society invested in new facilities and machinery that provided the division of labor necessary to increase the workers' productivity. However, Smith identified a potential problem as he feared that accumulation could lead to market saturation. This was because accumulation would mean more machinery, and this would increase the demand for workers. The increased demand for workers would lead to higher and higher wages until profits would disappear.[6]

They would surmount this hurdle to economic growth, according to Smith, by the second great behavioral law, "The Law of Population." Smith believed that if wages were high, then the population would increase because families with higher incomes could afford more children and the infant mortality rate would decrease. Therefore, if the first effect of accumulation was to raise the wages of the working class, the second effect would be to encourage the increase in the number of workers. This meant that accumulation might continue for long periods. The increase in population controls the supply of workers and their ability to command higher wages. The growth in population limits the cost of labor which is the major obstacle to increased profits.

Through the laws of accumulation and population, Smith constructed for society an endless chain of increased productivity. The mechanism of the market and the price system first serves to equalize the distribution of income to labor and capital, sees to it that the products demanded are produced in the proper quantities, and further encourages competition that drives prices down to where they are equal to the cost of production. Smith believed that the new industrial society was dynamic, that accumulation of wealth would continue, and that accumulation would result in increased facilities for production and in a greater division of labor.[7]

Smith was the economist of preindustrial capitalism. He saw an evolution for society, but he did not see a revolution. His system presupposes that eighteenth-century England will remain unchanged forever. The system would grow only in quantity, more people, more products and more wealth, but its quality would stay the same. Smith's system is a static one that grows but one that never matures.

Adam Smith emphasized the commitment to competition as a prerequisite to all capitalists' societies. Smith assumed that competition in a capitalist system, would ensure optimal industrial performance. Adam Smith addressed an audience that was ready to receive his message and with his message the remnants of the out-of-date regime of merchant capitalism ended.

For one hundred years after Smith's death, economists would attempt to amend and sharpen his conclusions, and struggle to resolve his ambiguities. In the years following Adam Smith's death, three great figures one French and two British emerged. The main emphasis of their writing was to refine and extend Adam Smith's economic theories. All three witnessed the industrial revolution in full flower, and, improving on Smith, they sought to bring economics abreast of this enormous change. In addition, there was the beginning of economic commentary from America.

JEAN BAPTISTE SAY (1767-1832)

Jean Baptiste Say's business background led him to observe the distinctive role of the entrepreneur; the man who conceives or takes charge of an enterprise; sees and exploits opportunity, and is the motivating force for economic change and improvement. Say later in life was a professor ending his career at the College de France.

However, Say's major, and for a full 130 years, his lasting and most influential contribution to economic theory was his Law of Markets. To this day, economic textbooks continue to refer to Say's law. Say's Law held that out of the production of goods came an effective aggregate of demand sufficient to purchase the total supply of goods.[8]

Put in more modern terms, from the price of every product sold comes a return in wages, interest, profit or rent, sufficient to purchase that product. There can never be a shortage of demand. It is, indeed, possible that some people will save from the proceeds of the sale. However, the amount saved by consumers will be invested by companies in new production facilities. In other words, businesses would spend the saved income of consumers. Even if they hoard the receipts, this does not change the situation; prices adjust themselves downward and adjust to the lesser flow of income. There can still be no general excess of goods, no general shortage of purchasing power.

THOMAS ROBERT MALTHUS (1776-1834)

Thomas Malthus was a British clergyman whom the British East Indian Company employed. Malthus wrote two books on classical economics and the industrial revolution, "An Essay on the Principle of Population" and "Principles of Political Economy." These works cover a wide range of subjects, but to the history of economics he contributed two theories.

Malthus' most noted contribution was the law he saw controlling the growth of population, and on how increased population affected the allocation of wages to the workers. From Thomas Malthus' observations came his basic conclusion:

- The mean of subsistence will limit population growth.

- Population increases when the mean of subsistence allows, and does so geometrically, while the best hope for increase in the food supply is arithmetic.

- This asymmetry will persist, so that the food supply will hold the population in check unless prior checks on its increase are operative. The possible prior checks are moral restraint, vice and misery.[9]

Using data from the United States, supplied by Benjamin Franklin, Malthus asserted that population tends to double every twenty-five years. Franklin also reported that some villages in the new country doubled in only fifteen years. Although Franklin did not provide any information on the food supply, Malthus concluded that output could never keep pace with population. Unchecked population grows at a geometric ratio, Malthus held, whereas food increases at merely an arithmetic ratio.

A geometric ratio means that a number continually multiplies itself by a constant, for example, a perpetual doubling. An arithmetic ratio simply adds a constant. Malthus provided a good example of his theory: where humans would increase by 1,2,4,8,16,32,64,128,256, while food would grow by 1,2,3,4,5,6,7,8,9. In this case if each person had one basket of food at the beginning of a period, two hundred years later, 256 people would have to share just nine baskets of food.

Malthus did not present a pleasant prospect for humanity. He did provide a powerful case against public or private charity and a greatly serviceable support to those who found it convenient to forgo help to the unfortunate.

Malthus' other claim to fame was his doubt about Say's Law. Malthus held that supply would not create its own demand, given the poverty of the workers. The workers have reduced themselves to the lowest levels of sustainable wages by their propensity to reproduce. There would be a tendency for more goods to be produced than could be bought and consumed by these workers. Also, at this time, banks did not make loans to business firms. Therefore, the only way that business owners could obtain capital, was by deferring consumption. This would result in increased savings at the expense of current consumption demand.

DAVID RICARDO (1772-1823)

David Ricardo rescued Say's law from Malthus' attack. According to Ricardo, the flow of income from the production of goods did indeed create its own sufficient demand. Ricardo's writing was not similar to the method used by Adam Smith. Ricardo's work is grim and difficult. Ricardo offered an influential change of method. Ricardo was theoretical and inductive; proceeding from some empirical evidence, he continued by abstract reasoning to the plausible, or perhaps inevitable conclusion.

Ricardo's writing used a method that, in the future, would greatly appeal to economists. His method of writing, reduced the research that is necessary to analyze a theory. It served Ricardo well. His method and his conclusions would lead the later defenders of capitalism, and its most passionate opponents, equally to firm conclusions.

One of Ricardo's most lasting contributions to economic theory was his Law of Comparative Advantage. During Ricardo's time wealthy English landowners attempted to persuade Parliament to impose tariffs on the import of grain. The price of grain had soared during the Napoleonic Wars, partly because of Napoleon's embargo, and the landowners feared that a drop of prices would take place. On the other side of the argument were the new businessmen of the Industrial Revolution who preferred to see lower prices for food. The reason that businessmen preferred low prices is that the price of food affects their major cost, the wages paid to the workers. The landowners won the battle of influence, and in 1815 Parliament passed an act that prohibited imports of grain below a certain price, virtually granting English farmers a monopoly. British dictionaries define "corn" as grain such as oats, rye, wheat and barley. Thus they called the acts "Corn Laws."

Ricardo thought that Britain had two choices as to their position in international trade: as a projectionist island or as an extroverted trader. Ricardo recommended a free trade policy for Britain. Ricardo developed his theory to show that countries should specialize in whatever leads them to give up the least opportunity. This is their "comparative advantage." In addition, the sacrifice they make by not producing a product, is their "opportunity cost." Thus according to Ricardo, specialization is determined by whoever has the lower opportunity cost.

For Ricardo, free trade makes it possible for households to consume more goods regardless of whether trading partners are more or less economically advanced. Ricardo's position on the "Corn Laws" was that if the French farmers are willing to feed us for less than it would cost to feed ourselves, Englishmen would be better off by eating French food and spending their time doing something else. In spite of his constant argument on this topic, Ricardo could not persuade Parliament to repeal these laws and they remained in effect until 1846. Ricardo did, however, provide a powerful argument for subsequent generations of economists. Ricardo's argument is that protection is usually bad for an economy as a whole, though sometimes good for a particular group of people. This debate continues today though in another form, between those who support managed trade and those who still believe that totally free trade is possible.

Ricardo follows Smith in identifying the main concerns of economics. Of the factors determining the value of price (value in exchange) of a product, Ricardo believed that the first must be utility. "If a commodity were in no way useful, in other words, if it could in no way contribute to our gratification, it would be destitute of exchangeable value."[8] Here emerges, in early form, the other side of the modern view of price making, the interaction of supply and demand. After establishing the need for "exchangeable products," Ricardo then saw the value of exchangeable products resulting from scarcity or from the quantity of labor required to obtain them. It is Ricardo's commitment to a firm labor theory of value in exchange that is central to the influence he exercised in the years to come.

Next Ricardo addressed the return to landlords of rent, which he defined as, "That portion of the produce of the earth, which is paid to the landlord for the use of the original and indestructible powers of the soil." From the possession of the better land the landlord would receive a surplus over the cost or rent. The owner of good land was thus the beneficiary not only of his own good fortune but also of the increasing misery or poor fortune of all others. Rent did not force up prices; it was a residual accruing passively from the increase in population and the general progress of the society. The rise of rent is always the effect of the increasing wealth of the country, and of the difficulty of providing for its augmented population.[10]

Returning to wages, Ricardo said, "That wages are the price that is necessary to enable the laborers to subsist and to perpetuate their race, without either increase or reduction." This theory, "The Iron Law of Wages," was to enter history extending far beyond formal economics. The law established that those who worked were meant to be poor and were not to be rescued from their poverty by a compassionate state or employer or through trade unions or by other actions of their own. This, as we shall see was a very fortunate conclusion for the capitalist who received a seemingly excess value for their investment.

The Iron Law was the natural or equilibrium price of labor, the level to which, all else equal, wages tend to settle. However, Ricardo concluded that not only workers' necessities but also conveniences that were essential to them based on previous habit, should be considered. Taken together, these are what economists would now call the workers' accustomed standard of living. Also, the market price of labor in an improving society could be above the market rate in the short run. This could result when the demand for labor was greater than the current supply of labor. However, since higher wages encourage increases in population and as the number of laborers is increased, wages again fall to their natural price and sometimes fall below it. In modern terms, if the demand for labor is greater than the supply of labor, wages will increase. However, when living standards increase, families tend to have more children. This increases the supply of labor and reduces wages to a natural or equilibrium level.

It was for his controlling law of wages that Ricardo was to be remembered. From this controlling law came his commitment to the inevitable misery of those who live under capitalism and to the uselessness of any corrective action by government or by the workers themselves. This action Ricardo specifically condemned as he wrote; "Like all other contracts, wages should be left to the fair and free competition of the marketplace, and should never be controlled by the interference of the legislature." [11]

In the years to come there would be an increasingly angry division between those who spoke for the system and those who spoke for the masses who were perceived as the victims of the industrial revolution. From Malthus and especially from Ricardo came ideas that would serve both sides of the debate.

HENRY CHARLES CAREY (1793-1879)

Until the civil war and even after, what distinguished the American scene was a spacious abundance, a prospect of income and opportunity for farmer and worker, as well as businessman and capitalist, unimaginable in England. The leading American economic scholar of this time was Henry Charles Carey.

In his early work, Carey was a follower of the British classical theory. However, as he sought to apply classical theory to his American surroundings, he came to have his doubts. David Ricardo had seen increasing population and limited land resources pressing labor to an even lower marginal return. Carey saw the same processes leading labor to an ever higher return as it became more productive.

In the new world settlement had begun on the hilltops, where forests were less dense and resistant. Since property on a hilltop usually represented the most prestige to those of noble European heritage, settlers tended to assign the most value to these locations. In America, when the pioneers moved, it was often to more fertile, more productive valleys, thus achieving not a diminishing but an expanding return. The same was true when attention turned to the frontier and the great unexplored resources there.

This tendency rejected the views of Ricardo, and it destroyed those of Malthus. An increasing population was not dividing a stagnant or decreasing food supply, but one that was rapidly increasing. Henry Carey was not averse to the thought that on some distant day there might be too many people. However, he was content to believe that this evil was sufficient unto its own time. God had said "Be fruitful and multiply."[12]

CHAPTER 5

THE FOUNDATIONS OF DEMOCRACY

"We hold these truths to be self-evident, that all men are created equal, that they are endowed by their Creator with unalienable rights that among these are Life, Liberty and the pursuit of Happiness." —Thomas Jefferson

THE CREATION OF THE U.S. CONSTITUTION

To fight the War of Independence, the colonies were loosely tied together by the Articles of Confederation and Perpetual Union that was ratified in 1781. However, after the war, the confederation was too weak to be effective as a framework of national government. In particular, taxing power to pay for the operation of government was left to the individual states. This delegation of responsibility left the new nation in debt and consumed by inflation when the war ended.

In January 1786, Virginia and Maryland appointed commissioners to analyze the potential development of a better form of government. The delegates from these two states met with representatives from the middle states at

Annapolis and issued a call for a constitutional convention. The first meeting was held at Philadelphia on May 14, 1787. Four months later, on September 28, 1787, George Washington, who was president of the convention, sent the completed constitution to the thirteen states for ratification. The constitution required ratification by two-thirds of the states to become law. On June 21, 1788, New Hampshire became the ninth state to ratify the constitution. Congress declared the constitution to be the new law of the land on March 4, 1789. The first ten amendments to the constitution, the Bill of Rights, were passed by the First Congress and became law on December 15, 1791.

The representatives of the individual states were reluctant to give up any power and relinquished to the central authority only those rights they believed were necessary to create a strong central government. To strengthen the reserved rights, the Tenth Amendment was added to the constitution that said:

• The powers not delegated to the United States by the Constitution, nor prohibited by it to the states are reserved to the states respectively, or to the people.

The Constitution as written is remarkably simple. The powers given explicitly to Congress are in Article I Section 8. These eighteen powers say, in summary, that Congress shall have the power to:

1.   Tax, with the provision that federal taxes shall be uniform in and among all states;
2.   Borrow, from anyone, on the credit of the new government;
3.   Regulate commerce with foreign countries, among the states, and with the Indian tribes;

4.   Make rules regarding naturalization and bankruptcy;
5.   Create money, regulate its value, and fix a standard of weights and measures;
6.   Provide punishment for counterfeiting;
7.   Establish post offices and post roads;
8.   Create patent and copyright laws;
9.   Create courts inferior to the U.S. Supreme Court;
10.   Define crimes and felonies committed on the high seas and to provide punishment for the same;
11.   Declare war and make "rules" regarding it;
12.   Raise and support armies, but with no single appropriation of money to remain in force for more than two years;
13.   Create and maintain a navy;
14.   Create martial law for the military services;
15.   Provide for militia to "suppress insurrections and repel invasions";
16.   Govern the militia employed by the United States, reserving to the states the appointment of officers;
17.   Exercise sovereign powers over the site of the federal government's installations;
18.   Make necessary laws to "carry into execution" the powers stated above.[1]

In addition to the powers given to Congress, the Constitution, in Article II, sets up the Executive Branch, and in Article III, sets up the Judiciary. Article IV contains the "Full Faith and Credit" provisions of the Constitution, ordering each state to recognize the laws and judicial practices of the other states.

The Constitution, as amended and interpreted, has now been the supreme law of the land, for two centuries. Also, the Constitution secured the rights of individuals to own property, settled and reserved the rights of the states and its citizens, and provided a consistent body of knowledge based on English common law. Consistent and calculable law is a requisite for the economic growth and development of an industrial nation and this body of law was provided in the United States Constitution.

THE LAND ORDINANCES OF 1785 AND 1787

One of the first tasks of the new Federal Government was to develop a policy as to the acquisition and the distribution of the vast amount of land that now belonged to the United States. Thomas Jefferson was given responsibility for developing the Land Ordinances of 1785 and 1787. Jefferson had been a student of modern theories of property rights. He realized that the sovereign sources of clear titles would begin with the national government. The government had inherited ownership and control of the land from the King of England. This was accomplished through the colonial charters and the surrender of ownership to that land by states such as Virginia, whose claims came from the British crown.

Jefferson's most important ideas about the land and its distribution can be summarized as follows:

- Tenure in the lands, acquired by private persons from the national government, should not be further subject to that government once titles were secured.

- The distribution should be orderly, with a scientific survey before sale and the boundaries marked by that survey, rather than by the "metes and bounds" of colonial times.

- The population occupying public lands would make those territories eligible to become new states, formed on an equal basis with the old states.

Jefferson viewed the national government's own tenure in the public lands to be fee simple, with the rights of ownership transferred to the private buyer upon sale or distribution of the land. The national government then stepped out, and the new owner of the land, in the language of Chapter 1, became the present or future state government. The land was then to belong to the state; taxes were due to the state, and the land should, in Jefferson's words, "Never after, in any case, revert to the United States." By this single act, the new states would be endowed with a future tax base, and property owners would be subject to their local governments.[2]

The Northwest Ordinance of 1787 embraced Jefferson's plan to divide the western lands into several roughly rectangular areas that would become states in due course. The Western territory below the Ohio River was organized in steps. Virginia consented to statehood for its territory of Kentucky, in 1792. North Carolina gave over its claims to Tennessee in 1790. The Southern territory, previously disputed with Spain, was organized as the Mississippi Territory in 1798, Georgia giving over her claim in 1804. Thus in a single decade, after peace in 1783, the entire territory between the Mississippi River and the Alleghenies was organized with constitutional rights and a guaranteed form of government. The foundation of future American capitalism, private ownership and control of productive resources, was thus created. Of the present fifty states, thirty-one came into existence under the organizing principles of the Northwest Ordinances. This was an incredible achievement from the minds and pens of Thomas Jefferson and our eighteenth century leaders.[3]

THE EVOLUTION OF POLITICAL THEORY

All societies have conservative elements within them, acting to preserve the institutions that those societies developed. Concurrently, the same societies have liberal elements within them, working to change or even eliminate those institutions. The terms liberal and conservative has become central to political debate in the western world ever since the monarchies of Europe began to be overthrown in the late eighteenth century.

The Age of The Enlightenment

Modern political liberalism began in the Age of Enlightenment, which provided the philosophical basis for both the French and American revolutions. Modern conservatism began as a response to liberal philosophy. For almost a thousand years, prior to the eighteenth century, Western Europe was divided into many kingdoms; each ruled by a monarch. The entire feudal system was hereditary; kings, nobles, and peasants were all born into a clearly defined class system.

This class system operated with the sanctions of the Church which was the glue that held the political structure of feudal Europe together. This alliance between the monarchs and the Church was the catalyst to a concept known as the "Divine Right of Kings." The European feudal system was essentially conservative with resistance to change built into it. The changes that did take place were the result of the gradual evolution of the institutions in the society. The most important of these changes was the rise of the new merchants who were positioned between the nobles and the peasants.

By the seventeenth century, the Age of Enlightenment had begun in Europe. The Enlightenment consisted of the individual efforts of many philosophers and scientists who changed the way people thought about reality, and about mankind. The philosophers of the time effectively replaced the reliance on the faith in God and the Church, as the ultimate authority on questions of reality, with the reliance on human reason. This concentration on the study of finding ways to promote human well-being, is the major link between the Enlightenment and modern liberal political thinking.

The Social Contract

The Enlightenment's questioning of faith as the supreme authority on social order was a clear threat to the monarchs of Western Europe. Since, in theory they ruled by divine right established by faith, if faith was replaced by human reasoning, by what right could monarchs continue to rule? One answer to this question was provided by English philosopher Thomas Hobbes. According to Hobbes, a strong form of central government was necessary because human beings tended to be selfish and even predatory. Some sovereign power had to be given the authority to make decisions and to enforce social order. For Hobbes, the best form that a government could take was a monarchy. This was an implied contract between the people and the monarch.

Hobbes theory was essentially a conservative one because it was both designed to justify the existing social order and it placed security above human rights in preserving that order. These two elements, a preference for maintaining the existing institutions and the overriding concern for the security of the nation, are basic to conservative political theory.

Another form of the theory of a social contract was developed by English philosopher, John Locke. He believed that men were essentially good and meant to be happy. Locke argued that a social contract was needed only because individuals couldn't judge for themselves the boundaries between their legitimate rights and the rights of others. Locke believed that what people thought, and consequently how they behaved, was strongly influenced by their environment. If man was unhappy or immoral, the fault must be in their environment which was perverting their basic nature.

The theories of John Locke and to a lesser extent Thomas Hobbes contained the basic elements of modern democracy. If all people were essentially equal, if they all had the same natural rights as stated by Locke, to Life, Liberty, and the Right to Property, then shouldn't they all have an equal vote in how they are governed? The masses would have to surrender some of their rights by agreeing to a social contract, but if they became unhappy with that contract; did they have the right to break it? Hobbes would say no. Locke would say yes to this question.

THE EMERGENCE OF POLITICAL PARTIES

The American Revolution was the logical culmination of much of the political and social theory of the Enlightenment. The revolution like the theory of a social contract was liberal in its ideals but essentially conservative in spirit. The new social contract drawn up after the American Revolution was the Constitution of the United States. The Constitution reflected two basic social concerns: the desire to assure that the new American government would never degenerate into tyranny, primarily a liberal concern, and the need to maintain order, which was essentially a conservative idea.

The issue of protecting the rights of individuals from the tyranny of the majority, clearly defines the differences between the liberal and conservative beliefs of the framers of the Constitution. Those like Alexander Hamilton and John Adams distrusted the unguided desire of the majority. Those of a more liberal belief, such as Thomas Jefferson, felt that the people had the right to exercise power over their government.

The founders initially believed that each political conflict that comes up could be resolved on its own merits. Eventually, however, ideology and self-interest replaced good intentions and political parties developed. When political parties did evolve they developed along either conservative or liberal lines. The first to emerge in the United States was the Federalist party, a conservative faction, led by Alexander Hamilton. The opponents of the Federalists called themselves simply the Anti-Federalist party. The Federalist party lost the election of 1804 to Thomas Jefferson and his renamed Democratic-Republican party. The Democratic-Republican party won the presidential elections of 1808, 1812, and 1818, and by 1820 the Federalists did not run a candidate for president. This for the time being ended the two-party system in the United States. In 1828 the two-party system was re-established with the emergence of the National-Republican party. This party, led by John Q. Adams, was created to face incumbent Andrew Jackson in the presidential election. The Jackson campaign catered to popular prejudices portraying the contest between democracy (represented by his Democratic-Republican party), and the more conservative aristocracy, as represented by John Q. Adams. Jackson won the election and was re-elected in 1832. The Democratic-Republican party, the party of both Jefferson and Jackson, is the forerunner of the modern Democratic party in the United States.

In the election of 1836, a new party the Whigs evolved in response to Jackson's perceived heavy handed tactics, especially his battle to defeat the Second U.S. Bank. The Whigs were named after the eighteenth century British party that tried to lessen the power of the crown. The Whigs were successful in only two presidential campaigns, electing William Henry Harrison in 1840, and Zachary Taylor in 1848. During the election of 1856, a new party, of northern Whigs and Democrats, combined to become the Republican party. The Republicans were a pro-tariff, conservative, nationalistic party that was founded to oppose the spread of slavery into the United State's territories. The first Republican president was Abraham Lincoln who was elected in 1860.

Politics, Government, and Business

In one major area, the question of government interference in the business economy, liberals and conservatives have, in effect, changed places. While Jefferson and the Democratic-Republicans favored a hands off policy, Hamilton and the Federalists felt that government should be directly involved in the nation's economy. The Federalists originally favored a strong national bank, a strong national currency, and government policies that promoted trade and commerce.

However, after the Civil War, businesses got bigger and were better able to promote and protect their own interests. During the last two decades of the nineteenth century, the federal government became concerned with the tendency of large businesses to create monopolies and eliminate competition. During this time, the federal government under the leadership of Republican president Theodore Roosevelt, began to exert more control over business by signing anti-trust legislation. However, the Democratic candidate for president in 1912, Woodrow Wilson, made the regulation of business an issue through an aggressive campaign calling for vigorous application of anti-trust laws against big business. This, conservatives felt, was hurting both business and the economy in general. Consequently, as the Democrats became more and more concerned with using government to control and regulate big business, Republicans became more and more concerned with keeping government out of business affairs. This perception, of the role of government in the affairs of business, continues to be a distinction between the modern day Democratic and Republican parties.

CHAPTER 6

FINANCE AND BANKING
(1800-1900)

"The whole community derives benefit from a bank. It facilitates the commerce of the country. It quickens the means of purchasing and paying for country produce and hastens on the exportation of it." —Thomas Paine

THE ROLE OF COMMERCIAL BANKS

Financial intermediaries play an important role in industrialized countries. The major function of a commercial bank is to gather the savings of many individuals and convert these funds into mortgage and business loans. Companies invest dollars in new plant and equipment and additions to inventory in order to increase the output of goods or services or to reduce the unit cost of producing these products. In modern times many of these investment dollars come from the savings of individuals. Banks collect these dollars in demand and time deposits and in turn make loans to corporations. In addition, individuals may choose to invest their dollars directly in corporations by buying their stocks and bonds through a stockbroker.

The key to a bank's profitability is making loans to individuals and firms at a rate of interest that is higher than the interest that they give savers on their deposits. Also, the interest rate charged must be sufficient to cover administrative costs and provide a margin of profit. This in banking is called the interest rate spread. Also, prudent banks try to match the maturities of their deposit liabilities with lending assets. For example, if the bulk of a bank's savings and demand deposits mature on an average of six months, the bank should limit the maturities of their lending portfolio to between six months and one year.

When a bank mismatches its maturities, that is has the bulk of its liabilities maturing in six months or less and the bulk of its assets maturing at one year or greater, it runs the risk of becoming illiquid. If depositors become worried that they may not be able to convert their deposits into currency, a run on the bank may occur. This would cause the bank to become insolvent and probably would force the bank to stop doing business. Therefore, a bank must practice prudent and sound lending practices if it wishes to increase the probability that it will stay in business in the long-run.

BIMETALLIC MONEY

In 1792 Congress chose the dollar as the official United States currency. Congress defined the dollar as containing either 371.25 grains of silver or 24.75 grains of gold or a relationship between the two metals of fifteen silver to one gold. The government offered to buy and sell unlimited amounts of gold and silver at the fifteen to one ratio. These purchases could be in either coin of bullion.

As long as this relationship held in the bullion markets, the system worked well. However, if the relative values of gold and silver as bullion differed from the fifteen to one ratio, people would exchange the overvalued metal for that which the U.S. mint undervalued.

Early in the nineteenth century, gold could be exchanged for sixteen times its weight in silver in the bullion markets. The result of this difference in the valuation of gold and silver as bullion versus the valuation of these metals as a medium of exchange was that U.S. gold coins disappeared from circulation. In 1834 Congress changed the mint relationship to sixteen silvers to one gold, but by this time the ratio overvalued gold. As a result of the changed relationship, silver coins became extremely scarce. The discovery of gold in California in 1848 only made the situation worse.[1]

When the United States defined the dollar as containing a specific amount of gold or silver, it determined the exchange rate between the dollar and foreign currencies, whose metallic content was also fixed. Dollars would exchange for British pound sterling in proportion to the rate that each currency could be exchanged for gold. Since gold could move freely between nations, there was only a limited extent to which the United States could both control its own monetary affairs and maintain fixed exchange rates.

BANKING BEFORE THE CIVIL WAR

Gold and silver coins were only part of the United States money supply. Most of the money that circulated was created by commercial banks. Prior to the Civil War, the use of bank checking accounts had become widespread, particularly in the Northeast and Mid-Atlantic states. In addition to checking deposits, banks could print notes that they could lend to customers. Today, in comparison, only federal reserve notes can circulate as U.S. currency. During the fifty years after 1800, the number of banks grew much faster than the rate of population, and bank assets, notes in circulation, and deposits grew even faster.

Since money's value depends on its scarcity, there are limits to a bank's ability to increase the money supply. Bank money has limited value if it is not convertible into legal tender. In the nineteenth century, legal tender meant gold or silver. Banks had to be able to exchange their notes and checking deposits for legal tender on demand from their customers. Under normal circumstances, only a small fraction of an individual bank's outstanding liabilities, would be presented for conversion to specie, on any given day. Thus, banks only had to retain about 10 to 30 percent of their notes or deposits in the form of gold or silver. The remaining deposits could be used to fund loans or to purchase securities.

If a bank's ability to convert its own money into specie was in doubt their notes would be accepted in trade at less than face value or at a discount. The discount would vary with the degree of uncertainty about the issuing bank's ability to redeem its obligations in full on demand. Information about the stability of banks generally became more difficult to obtain, when the issuing bank was located a great distance from the bank receiving the note. Therefore, most banks' notes were discounted at rates increasing with the distance from their point of origin.

ATTEMPTS TO REGULATE BANKS

Various attempts were made prior to the Civil War to regulate the state banking system. States often contributed to a bank's capital and did gain some control as stockholders. In general, banking laws specified the amount of capital that had to be subscribed by the bank's owners, limited the amount of notes that it could issue, and made some provision for inspections to insure compliance with these regulations. The extent of regulations and its enforcement was inconsistent, stricter where merchant communities were well established, and very lax in the rural areas. Often the regulation of banks was left up to the institutions themselves. Some self-regulation did occur in the eastern states but very little in the western states. An example of self-regulation was the Suffolk Banking system that attempted to regulate banks in the New England region of the country.

In 1820, the newly established Suffolk Bank in Boston offered to accept the notes of any rural bank in New England that would keep a permanent deposit of $5,000 over the funds required by the state clearinghouse. The Suffolk Bank also allowed rural banks to redeem their notes at the same rate of discount for which Suffolk had accepted them. Rural banks, that did not cooperate, found that the Suffolk bank would accumulate large quantities of their notes and present them, without notice, to the rural bank for redemption for specie. The Suffolk system caused the notes of all New England banks to circulate within the region at their face value, therefore eliminating the need to discount bank notes within the region. This made bank money a better medium of exchange and made trade run smoother within the system.[2]

New York State attempted to alleviate the propensity of small local banks to fail and therefore cause large losses to their depositors, through an institution similar to the modern Federal Deposit Insurance Corporation. In 1828, the state required that all banks in New York contribute 1.5 percent of their capital annually, up to a maximum of 3 percent, to a fund that would be able to make good the notes of failed banks whose assets were not sufficient to cover their outstanding notes. Banks were required to join the system as a condition for renewal of their corporate charters. Although the safety fund created by this legislature apparently was capable of protecting investors against the occasional failures of individual banks, it proved insufficient to deal with the bank collapses of the latter part of the 1830's.

Left to regulate themselves, most state banking systems had serious weaknesses. Regulation varied greatly between states. This resulted in the instability of the entire United States banking system because there was no source of additional reserves available for the entire system. If enough people began to fear that their bank notes or demand deposits could not be converted into gold or silver, a run on the bank took place.[3]

ATTEMPTS TO ESTABLISH A CENTRAL BANK

The major function of a central bank in industrialized countries is to regulate the nation's money supply. Ideally, central banks attempt to prevent rapid changes in the money supply. Their major tool for this purpose is the control over private bank reserves. Also, central banks serve as government depositories and disbursing agencies performing clearinghouse functions for the settlement of inter-bank debts. In the first half of the nineteenth century, no country had fully developed the central bank, but the United States had two banks that exhibited some central bank characteristics.

The First Bank of the United States

During the first half of the nineteenth century two United States banks were established by Congress. In 1791, Congress granted a federal charter to the First Bank of the United States. The Bank had branches and did business throughout the country and served as the government's depository. This structure enabled the Bank to return its deposits of the notes of other banks for prompt collection. This practice aggravated the smaller banks as it tended to restrict their lending or as we might say in modern times, it required the smaller banks to follow more prudent bank lending practices. The practice of restricting the lending of smaller banks was a continuous point of argument between Alexander Hamilton and Thomas Jefferson; Hamilton on the side of safe banking. The charter of the First Bank of the United States expired in 1811, and a bill to extend its charter for twenty more years was defeated in Congress by only one vote.[4]

The Second Bank of the United States

In 1816, Congress granted a new charter, to the Second Bank of the United States. The Bank was headquartered in Philadelphia, then the country's financial center, and like the First Bank of the United States, had branches throughout the country. The Bank served as the federal government's depository, receiving all payments to the government. The Bank also accepted deposits and made loans in the same manner as the country's other commercial banks. The first two presidents of the Bank were not strong leaders and as a consequence the Bank was not very well run. In 1823, Nicholas Biddle became president of the Bank. Under Biddle's leadership, the Bank assumed some of the roles that are characteristic of a central bank. For example, the Bank began to use its position as a net creditor to the state banks to control the amount of their note issues. As a result of this policy, the state banks were forced to limit their note issues to the growth of their reserves. This practice while good for the safety of the banking system, served to reduce the potential profit available to the state banks.

In addition to its other operations, the Bank could function as a lender of last resort. On occasion, the Bank made some loans of specie to state banks that were experiencing short term financial difficulty. Still, the Bank was first and foremost a profit making institution. Because of its profit motive, the Bank made loans with the first priority given to its own reserve position and its own profit potential. In addition, it occasionally increased its own reserves to meet a crisis by selling bonds to the public. This action when implemented by a central bank serves to reduce the money supply and therefore reduces business expansion. However, neither the First nor Second Bank of the United States could expand the money supply since they could not control the amount of reserves held by state banks.[5]

In 1832, President Andrew Jackson vetoed a bill passed by Congress to extend the Bank's charter for twenty more years. The Bank did obtain a state charter from Pennsylvania, and continued in operation until 1841. However, after 1841, federal deposits were withdrawn from the Bank. These deposits were then placed in banks owned by Jackson's political allies. Finally, after the financial panic of 1837, in which the government lost large amounts of dollars that were deposited in these state banks, the government's deposits were kept in an independent treasury system. The era of a federal bank came to an end in 1832, and the country from then on, operated under a state chartered banking system until the Federal Reserve System was created in 1913.

THE STATE BANKING SYSTEM

In 1838, Michigan and New York passed laws that greatly eased the previous banking restrictions. These banks were no longer required to obtain individual charters from the state legislature. Instead they could enter the banking business by depositing approved securities with the states' banking officials and by observing a few basic rules. Other states instituted their own rules, which became known as "Free Banking" laws. As a result of the reduction of bank regulations in many states, the number of state banks increased from 691 in 1843, to 1,520 in 1860.[6]

Although the history of banking is full of colorful tails about irresponsible practices, by 1860 it was commonly agreed between bankers and regulators that banks should keep reserves against all liabilities. The enforcement of state regulations began to improve, and some states even provided for periodic examinations. Therefore, it does not appear, based on modern studies, that free banking resulted in any serious damage and did not retard the economic growth in the new country from 1800 through 1860.[7]

THE ERA OF DUAL BANKING

Prior to the Civil War, there were many controversies over money and banking. These controversies usually revolved around the quantity theory of money and the operation of the state banking system. Many people still held the conviction that capital could be created and prices could be increased by expanding the money supply. During the war, the union government could no longer make payments of money in the form of silver or gold. The Union government had to choose between increasing taxes to pay for the war or to begin printing money. Congress, unwilling to increase taxes to pay for the war, authorized the issue of $450 million in paper money. This authorization was in the form of United States Notes. These notes, commonly called "Greenbacks" were declared by Congress to be "Legal Tender" that could be used for payment of all debts.

In 1863, Congress passed the National Banking Act to provide a uniform currency to eliminate the oversupply of state bank notes, and to create a market for government bonds. One of the major provisions of the Act was to establish a bond-secured national currency. The Act created the national bank structure under the supervision of the Comptroller of the Currency. To obtain a national charter, groups of businessmen were required to deposit a specific amount of United States bonds with the Comptroller. These bonds could then be used as collateral that allowed the national chartered banks to issue national bank notes. National banks were also required to maintain reserves against their deposits, originally set at 25 percent for city banks and 15 percent for country banks.

After the Civil War, Congress amended the National Banking Act by imposing a 10 percent tax against state bank notes. The result of this tax was to drive state bank notes out of existence effectively creating a system of national currency. In addition, the National Banking System changed the philosophy of commercial banking by emphasizing the "Real Bills Doctrine." This doctrine confirmed that commercial banks should make only short term self-liquidating loans to businesses. Under the National Banking System, loans were made against commercial paper (short term unsecured liabilities of businesses) and were theoretically self-liquidating. This practice helped banks to better match the maturities of their assets and liabilities. This practice tends to increase the liquidity of the banking system by providing the ability to weather any crisis caused by a withdrawal of deposits. When the maturities of a bank's assets and liabilities are matched, it enables the institution to liquidate their loan and securities portfolios in order to accommodate any run on the bank's deposits.

While the National Banking System brought about many improvements in commercial banking, it also had some major weaknesses. The banking system allowed the practice of pyramiding bank reserves in New York City. Pyramiding of reserves occurred as out-of-town banks piled up deposits in New York. When additional funds were needed in rural areas, these country banks rapidly drew down their deposits forcing the New York banks to call in their short term loans to brokers. This practice set in motion a chain reaction as brokers called in their margin loans to customers. The result was the reduction of the money supply during business contractions and the aggravation of financial panics.

Another weakness of the National Banking System was that it relied heavily on the real-bills doctrine, with its emphasis on commercial loans. This reliance on the real-bills doctrine, intensified tendencies toward boom and bust economic conditions. To add to this weakness, there was no central bank that could assist individual banks when they got into financial difficulty. In addition, there was no institution that could step in to stabilize the economy by discouraging speculative expansion during prosperity and softening the impact of deflation during panic and depression. Also, there was no national clearinghouse which continued the inefficient way in which check payments were made between different regions of the country.

In summary, the National Banking System made banking safer for national bank note holders and depositors; however, it made the currency less elastic (the supply of money does not expand or contract with the rise and fall of business activity) and capital funds less mobile. These weaknesses continued until the establishment of the Federal Reserve System in 1913.

INVESTMENT BANKING

During the late nineteenth century, American investment bankers also became more important. National banks were still reluctant to invest in industrial securities and a specialized business was needed to advise business leaders on the best ways to borrow money for long-term investment. Investment bankers began to market large security issues of common stock, preferred stock, and ordinary and debenture bonds, to finance the large business enterprises that were evolving at the end of the century. Markets for money and capital developed in all of the major cities during this period. However, New York City with its port, banks and proliferation of intermediaries, became the real center of all the nation's money and capital markets by the 1870's, and Wall Street centralized and dominated the country's finance. At first, a few industrial shares were listed in New York; Government bonds and shares issued by public utility companies and railroads, predominated the market. By the end of the century, industrialists, guided by Wall Street specialists, had easy access to the pooled resources of the country's savers, both directly and via the financial intermediaries. The country had a machine for the mobilization of capital, and expansion of it came through the use of the linked money and capital markets. By 1890, the New York Stock Exchange handled a total of 138 million shares with a value of almost $10 billion. Investment bankers were increasing the scope of their businesses and gradually reducing their dependence on the great banking houses of Europe. By the end of the century, the United States was no longer reliant on European capital funds. In fact, American investment bankers began to produce such great players as J.P. Morgan, Kuhn-Loeb, Brown Brothers, Harriman and Kidder-Peabody, who were becoming important players in financing the investment needs of the entire industrialized world.

CHAPTER 7

THE EVOLUTION OF CLASSICAL ECONOMICS

"Those organizations which are best fitted to their environment, or which change to fit themselves to their environment, will survive. The least fit will die out, leaving the strongest and best." —Herbert Spencer

THE THEORY OF MARGINAL UTILTIY

The primary concern of economics, throughout the nineteenth century, was with how prices, wages, rent, interest and profits, are determined. Ricardo had anchored the value of price of any manufactured product firmly on cost; the cost, in turn, was that of the labor going into the output under the least satisfactory circumstances of production. The price of the labor was only the cost of sustaining the laborer. The wages paid to labor were in equilibrium at the level sufficient to maintain their life. The difference, between the price of labor and the cost of labor, then accrued as rent to the landlord or as profit to the owners of the business.

This analysis was proper when the distribution was viewed from the point of positive economics. However, far too often, it was observed that profit was handsomely in excess of the outlays for wages. The distribution of profit to the owner was approved of if it was a result of their entrepreneurial ability. However, it was argued, that the unequal distribution of profit was due to the monopoly power, that was held by the capitalist, not the ability to manage the factors of production.

Another earlier flaw in the classical system was corrected as the century passed. During the second half of the nineteenth century economic analysis shifted from cost to supply as a determinant of price, and to demand as a determinant not only of price but also, of the factors of production. For example, there were attempts by economists to explain why some workers could command greater wages than others. The demand for workers was based on the supply of workers that had the particular skills that were necessary to operate the factories and machine tools available at the time. This development grew out of the efforts to solve the old and seemingly stubborn problem of why the most useful things like water, has a small price and why things with little practical use like diamonds commanded a far greater price.

During the last part of the nineteenth century, economists became preoccupied with solving the problem of value in use and value in exchange. In 1871 there was a breakthrough in explaining the question of value. In that year, William Stanley Jevons (1835-1882) in England and Karl Menger (1840-1921) in Austria, followed a few years later by John Bates Clark (1847-1938) in the United States (professors respectively at London, Vienna and Columbia Universities), recognized the role of marginal utility in determining price. Marginal utility was first explained as the proposition that the utility of any good or service diminishes, all else equal, with increasing availability. These economists held that it is the utility of the last and least wanted; the utility of the marginal unit, that sets the value of all goods and services.[1]

In fact, the marginal utility of a good was merely the first step to a further and final formulation of theory. The concept of marginality could be applied not only to demand but also for supply. Goods are produced at different levels of costs. Accordingly in industry as in agriculture, there is an omnipotent law of diminishing returns, or increasing cost at greater levels of production.

Because of the diminishing marginal utility to buyers, there is a collective reduction, on their part, to pay the listed price. In order for the producer to sell the remaining inventory of a product that had reached the level of diminishing marginal utility, the price of the product would have to be reduced. The result of this analysis was the downward sloping demand curve that stated that as marginal utility decreased, lowering prices in order to clear ever larger supplies from the market, would be necessary. Also, the cost of producing a product would increase as the productivity of the factors of production decreased. From the rising marginal costs of less efficient uses of the factors of production came the rising costs of additional supplies. The more of a good or service that is demanded, relative to the supply, the more that must be paid to producers to encourage them to produce that product. The determination that ever higher prices are needed to cover marginal costs and attract increased supplies to the market led to the discovery of the upward ascending supply curve. Thus the law of supply and demand was proposed with its supreme achievement at the intersection of the two curves; the price.

Also, there now appeared and was recognized as a major exception in the system, the monopoly. The monopolist extended production to where his more rapidly falling marginal return just covered the added costs. That was where profits were maximized. Production was at a theoretically smaller output than the competitive equilibrium. The monopolist could increase his profit by controlling supply and therefore keep prices artificially high. Accordingly, it was agreed that although the classical system generally was benign, monopoly was not. Monopoly established itself as the single great flaw in an otherwise thought to be perfect system.

UTILITARIANISM AND JEREMY BENTHAM (1784-1832)

One of the early defenses of the classical system came from outside the central current of economics. This was the Utilitarianism defense, which identified happiness or utility with that characteristic in any object, that tends to produce benefit, advantage, pleasure, good, happiness or similarly prevents mischief, pain, evil or unhappiness. In early nineteenth century England, nearly every intellectual wanted to follow the direction of the great physicist, Sir Isaac Newton, and attempt to discover precise answers to the basic economic, political and moral questions of the time. Smith, Ricardo, and Malthus wanted to be the Isaac Newton of economics, by discovering the laws of nature. Jeremy Bentham, the acknowledged leader of the Utilitarianism movement, sought to be the Isaac Newton of the moral universe.

According to Bentham's gospel, nature has two masters, pain and pleasure.[2] Since all human beings like pleasure and hate pain, they choose to do that which gives them pleasure. Bentham continues by stating that when choices affect others, people should choose the alternative that maximizes the total pleasure of all. "The greatest happiness for the greatest number," was the leading emphasis of the Utilitarian movement. Bentham even devised a method of quantifying the amount of pleasure and pain in a situation, called the "Felicific Calculus." In his system, any single experience could be measured by four basic factors: (1) intensity, (2) duration, (3) certainty, and (4) proximity.

Utilitarian theory as it applies to economics held that the maximization of pleasure or happiness could and indeed did come from the maximization of the production of goods, which was the unchallenged achievement of the industrial revolution. What encouraged production was useful or beneficial whether it resulted in incidental suffering for the lesser number or not; the basic rule was the provision of, "The greatest happiness for the greatest number." The unhappiness, even if acute, of the lesser number must be accepted as a matter of practical policy.

Bentham was also involved in politics. He and his followers carried on the battle for free speech and democracy. They fought the Stamp Act, which taxed periodicals, and opposed various restrictions on the right of assembly, and the Corn Laws. Bentham also denounced the barbaric English prison system, arguing that punishment should be used to deter crime, not to wreak vengeance on those convicted of a crime and sent to prison.

JOHN STUART MILL (1806-1873)

Among the visible problems of the classical system there was first, the appalling difference between the wages and resulting living standard of the workers and those of the employers or capitalist. Next there was the unequal distribution of power inherent in the system. The worker, adult or child, was subject to the discipline that came from dependence on the job, and many times for the next meal. These necessities the employer could give or withhold at will, and he often did. The unequal distribution of power was an obvious flaw in the classical system, a flaw that required a defense.

John Stuart Mill's writing and political career reflect an enlightened and expanded version of Utilitarianism. Mill held that the greatest happiness depends upon more than just pleasure. His publications enhanced Utilitarianism by invoking Platonic virtues of honor, dignity and self-development. This is the reason that Mill became an ardent advocate of public education.

In one of his earliest books, "On Logic," Mill developed a distinction between positive and normative economics. Positive economics, according to Mill, describes and predicts what actually takes place in the world. Normative economics advocates what should take place based on one's moral philosophy. This distinction was carried onto many other of Mill's later works.

In 1848, John Stuart Mill published his most famous work in economics that was entitled "Principles of Political Economy." For decades this work dominated the economics textbook market and was the principle textbook used in the major universities in England until 1919. In "Principles of Political Economy," Mill developed a comprehensive review of accepted economic doctrine and he added numerous improvements to existing theory. He wrote about the management of a firm; supply and demand as an equation rather than a ratio, and demand as a major factor in Ricardo's law of comparative advantage.[3] Mill firmly attributed the poverty of the working man to the immutable physical law of diminishing returns to labor and the relentless desire of the masses to reproduce themselves. The law of diminishing returns to labor states that as more and more workers are added to a fixed amount of capital there will come a point where the productivity of labor declines. Mill continues by writing that, "Little improvement can be expected in morality until the producing families are regarded with the same feelings as drunkenness or any other physical excess."

Mill also examined the value of providing relief to the poor. Mill wondered how society could give relief to the poor without dissuading them from obtaining work. Mill distinguished the able-bodied from the disabled, elderly, and the very young. Mill did not believe that society should cut its relief efforts for the disabled. However, he was not as lenient with those who were physically fit. He proposed that recipients of aid from the state, exchange their labor for welfare payments. Mill feared that if welfare was too easily doled out, generations of poor people would be born into families weaned of the work ethnic. In addition, Mill thought that higher welfare payments would only promote higher birth rates. Thus, Mill rejected socialist proposals for increasing relief benefits or wages for the masses.[4]

Ricardo, Malthus, and John Stuart Mill, still have a large amount of influence in the attitudes towards the problems of our large inner cities. Also, the critics of the welfare state can find a lot of ammunition in their theories. Requiring physically fit persons to perform work in return for welfare payments is in 1994, still a critical topic of concern for the American Congress.

Thus, in summary, John Stuart Mill both advertised dramatically the hardship that the Utilitarians accepted as necessary to progress and, as would many who followed him, appealed for patience and hope to withstand it. This remedy, like the knowledge that one was being sacrificed to the larger good, was never wholly satisfactory to those afflicted.

KARL MARX (1818-1883) AND THE GRAND ASSAULT

It is widely believed that Communism was born in the mind of Karl Marx in the middle of the nineteenth century. Also it is believed that Communism received its first definitive expression in 1848, when Marx and Frederick Engles published, "The Communist Manifesto." In 1848 there were no communist states in the world and no revolutionary governments of any sort. A few countries of Northeast Europe and the United States were industrializing rapidly, but there was no city in the world with a population greater than two million people, and no state; even Great Britain, in which a majority of the people did not live in the country and farmed for a living. While the skilled workers in the industrialized countries were beginning to form a middle class, over 90 percent of the World's population lived in poverty.

Into this world Karl Marx was born in 1818, in the Western German city of Treves. Treves was then a part of Prussia, the second most powerful of the independent German States. The Marx family was originally Jewish as both parents were descendants of rabbis. However, when Marx was six, his family was baptized as Lutherans, in order to save his father's career, in what was officially Lutheran Prussia.[5]

Marx's father wanted his son to become a lawyer like himself, and sent him through the best schools in Treves. In 1835, Marx was sent to the University of Bonn, and then in 1841 to the University of Berlin to study law.

In his years at the University of Berlin, some of Karl Marx's philosophy began to evolve. He came to believe that all of the various sciences and philosophies were part of one over-arching system, which when completed would give a true and total picture of the universe and man. The romantic philosophers of the time had transformed this faith, which they had inherited from their scientific predecessors. Marx believed that the core of such a science and philosophy was the growth, development, progress, and evolution of the world, human society, and the individual. He believed that nature and men evolve according to certain inexorable scientific laws, whose working can be embodied but not opposed by even the greatest of leaders.

Marx found the most thorough statement of these views in the works of the recently deceased philosopher, George Frederick Hegel. However, unlike Hegel, Marx came to believe that there was no God.[6] Marx became convinced that Europe was on the edge of reaction and revolution and that most of mankind was unhappy, held down by society, and cut off from its own true nature. Such convictions were a variety of radical Romanticism that the Germans called "Left Hagelianism."[7]

Having become a radical, Marx decided to give up his pursuit of the law and became a journalist in 1842, when he joined the staff of the "Rheinische Zeitung," a liberal newspaper in Cologne. However, the paper was closed down in 1843 by the Prussian police due to its radical editorials, mostly written by Marx.

During 1843 and 1844, Marx was acquiring yet another set of convictions. He read the works of Malthus, Ricardo and other British economists of the time. Marx accepted much of the classical economic analysis, but disagreed with their pessimism and their political judgments of the workingmen. Instead, Marx picked the industrial workingmen (for whom he adopted a term out of ancient Roman history, the Proletarian) as the key to the future development of society.

By the end of 1844, Marx had established his lifelong friendship with Frederick Engels. Engels was born of a Calvinist father in 1820 in Barmen, Prussia, which was south of the Ruhr. Young Engels had become converted to radicalism, in 1841, at the University of Berlin. During the middle of the 1840's, Marx and Engels produced a number of works where they depicted the ghastly condition of the growing working class. Also, they began to set forth their own version of a new social theory that they called "Communism," in the 1840's. Thus, since 1850, Communism has been considered to be a revolutionary form of Socialism.

Marx and Engels were atheist Socialists, who being far different from those who wanted to reform society by peaceful means, urged violent revolution to be followed by a brief dictatorship of the proletariat. In 1847, Marx and Engels were commissioned by the Communist League in London. The commission was to develop a theoretical and practical platform for the new Communist party. The result of this commission was the writing of the Communist Manifesto, which was published in February of 1848 in London. To this day the Communist Manifesto has survived as the first definitive statement of the Communist variety of Socialism and has become one of the most widely read and influential pamphlets in the history of the world.

The first chapter of the Communist Manifesto, pictured Europe as being in the middle of a tremendous struggle for control between the rising bourgeoisie and the developing proletariat. Marx defined the bourgeoisie as the people in the class of modern capitalists, owners of the means of social production and employers of wage labor.[8]

Chapter one begins by stating that "The history of all hither to existing society is the history of class struggles." Marx continues by stating that, "Society as a whole is more and more splitting up into two hostile camps; into two great classes directly facing each other, the bourgeoisie and proletariat. We see, therefore, how the modern bourgeoisie is itself the product of a long course of development, a series of revolutions in the modes of production and of exchange." According to Marx, "The bourgeoisie has at last, since the establishment of modern industry and of the world market, conquered for itself, in the modern representative state, exclusive political sway." Marx continues by saying, "The executive of the modern state is but a committee for managing the common affairs of the whole bourgeoisie."[9]

Marx did not question the productive achievements of the industrial system. What Marx did question was the vulnerable points in the capitalist system which he interpreted as the distribution of power, the highly unequal distribution of income, susceptibility to depression, and monopoly.

The Distribution of Power

The power in capitalism, according to Marx, resides with the capitalist; it is the natural attribute of the productive property he owns. The payments proceeding there from command the obedience and submission of people, who have no property and thus no alternative income. Nor is the power of the capitalist confined to the enterprise. He extends this power to the society and the State.

The Highly Unequal Distribution of Income.

The worker at the margin receives payment in wages reflecting his added contribution to the total revenue of the enterprise. That contribution diminishes as workers are added and the marginal wage sets the wage for all. However, those back from the margin, though paid the marginal wage, contribute more to earnings than their wage. They are in the infra-marginal, more fruitful stages of diminishing return. This is surplus value they create, and this surplus value accrues not to those who earn it but to the capitalist. It rightly belongs to the worker, but the Capitalist intervenes to appropriate it, i.e., steals the surplus value.

The Susceptibility of an Economy to Depression

The productive power of capitalism would press its goods relentlessly on markets, and as the labor supply became fully employed, wages would inevitably rise. The result would be a falling rate of profits, a loss and retrenching by the producing firms, and imbalance in the productive process. Balance would be restored only as diminished production, unemployment and falling wages allowed production to be profitable again. It was an important point for Marx that the system is stable only when wages are held down by a reserve of unemployed workers.

Monopoly

A flaw conceded by the Classical tradition. To the Classicists, monopoly was the exception to the competitive rule, and it presented no threat to the system as a whole. For Marx, monopoly was much more than a flaw; the increasing concentration of economic activity in the hands of ever fewer capitalists was an organic tendency of capitalism, one that proceeded with irresistible force.[10]

Thus, according to Marx, the economic system celebrated by the classical tradition would come to an end brought about by characteristics, some of the most important of which had already been identified by the Classical Economists themselves. However, capitalism is not dead yet for it has produced a middle class that indirectly owns some of the means of production through the stock markets. Some of Marx's defenders point to the growth of government in capitalist nations as the surprising savior of capitalism. Social welfare spending protects the capitalists from deeper depressions and revolution. Marx's defenders are probably right. However, we must remember, that Marx predicted that the political system would stay static, resistant to change and that inflexibility would destroy the entire system. In this respect as well as others, Marx will go down in history as a false prophet.

HERBERT SPENCER AND INDIVIDUALISM (1820-1903)

The rise of socialism and its cry for social justice required still another defense from the supporters of classical economics. Because Karl Marx's criticism of capitalism was based on Ricardo's labor theory of value, a theoretical defense of the system was needed.

One answer to Marx and capitalism was the nineteenth century philosophy of individualism, which developed as the ideology of the capitalist enterprise in the years after the Civil War, and endured until 1914. The basis for this new theory was a reinforced version of laissez faire, which defended the interest of the successful capitalist.

An English philosopher and economist Herbert Spencer, and an American sociologist, William Graham Sumner (1840-1910), were the leaders in the development of the philosophy of individualism. Spencer was an evolutionist even before Charles Darwin. In 1850, Spencer published "Social Statistics," where he argued that all social systems develop and change by a natural process that results in a maximization of individual welfare. This process of natural development stems from competition among individuals. Spencer held that any interference on the part of the government prevents full achievement of society's ideal goal.[11]

Spencer's early writings were followed by a ten-volume work entitled "Synthetic Philosophy," that sought to show that evolutionary progress occurred in all phenomena, in the biological world, in the human mind, in society, and in ethics. Where Darwin explained evolution in the terms of "Natural Selection," it was Herbert Spencer who coined the deathless phrase "Survival of the Fittest," as the source of economic and social progress. Spencer held that institutions conducted their business in such a way as to benefit the organization involved. "Those organizations which are best fitted to their environment, or which change to fit themselves to their environment, will survive. The least fit will die out, leaving the strongest and best."[12] According to Spencer the weakest individuals and the least useful social institutions gradually are eliminated. Since the individual member of society is the decision maker, the social organization that emerges from the process of change is more closely adapted to meeting the needs of the individual.

The ideas of Spencer led to a description of the ideal society, conceived as a static equilibrium between people and their surroundings, brought about by the full exercise of individual rights. The role of government was therefore limited to the protection of people and property and the enforcement of private contracts, nothing else.

One cannot avoid admiration for the comprehensive way in which Spencer and Social Darwinism served the defense of the system. Inequality and hardship were made socially benign and the mitigation of hardship was made socially acceptable. The fortunate and the affluent could have no sense of guilt, for they were the natural beneficiaries of their excellence, and nature had selected them as part of a relentless progress to an improved world.[13] Spencer's books sold hundreds of thousands of copies; his visit to New York in 1882 had some of the aspects of the coming of Saint Paul. A generation of American scholars echoed his thoughts.

Spencer's greatest follower in America was William Graham Sumner, an Episcopalian minister and economist at Yale University. Sumner's major work in the field of sociology was "Folk Ways," published in 1907. In this book Sumner examined social mores, which he defined as institutions and conventions that developed and continually change by process of adaptation to individual needs. If such institutions, according to Sumner, do not contribute to welfare and survival, they are gradually replaced by more effective methods, and the social system evolves into a higher and better form.

Sumner goes on to say that within the social system, individuals are also rising and falling. The person with ability, intelligence, and drive will rise to prominence by competing with all others. The lazy, ignorant, and weak will fall out of sight. The emergence of leading individuals brings progress, because these are the ones who innovate, who think, and who develop new ideas.

In a series of essays, most notably "The Concentration of Wealth: Its Economic Justification," Sumner applied his theory of society to questions of contemporary political and economic policy. Concentrated wealth, Sumner held, was justified because it was used to produce for others. The economic elite rose to the top only because they expanded activity and provided the goods and services that society demanded. In fact, Sumner proclaimed that "The millionaires are a product of natural selection. They get high wages and live in luxury, but the bargain is a good one for society."

Individualism was the evolutionary philosophy applied to the social system. It justified the wealth of the owners of production, on the ground that only social good could come from competition. It justified the unequal distribution of income on the ground that wealth existed only because it served others. It justified lack of social responsibility on the ground that anyone destroyed by competition could be considered "unfit," not capable of making a large enough contribution to the social order to survive.[14]

Rugged Individualism was a rigorous philosophy that associated success with right and failure with wrong, wealth with public service and poverty with uselessness. Thus the stage is now set for our understanding of the mind set of the industrial capitalist of the period and also, of the response of the workers and the less fortunate, who needless to say, never completely bought into this philosophy.

CHAPTER 8

THE INDUSTRIAL REVOLUTION (1800-1900)

"Not only is labor not dishonorable among such a people, but it is held in honor. In the United States, a wealthy man would think himself in bad repute if he employed his life solely in living." —Alexis de Tocqueville

THE EVOLUTION OF AMERICAN CITIES

Between 1790 and 1860, the land area of the United States tripled. However, during the same period the size of the population on the land increased at an even swifter pace. Urbanization increased in a sustained fashion from 1820 and continued until the 1870's. Urbanization resulted in the creation of a form of economic organization that was conducive to innovation. This was due to the increased opportunities for the exchange of information among persons living close to each other and living close to their place of work. In the new cities that were created, owners of both capital and labor could more easily make decisions that worked to their best economic interest. In a period in which communication over long distances was very difficult, cities were the only logical areas in which the marketplace was fully functional.

Urbanization also served as a medium for the circulation of information throughout the economy. Urbanization included not just a concentration of population but also a developing system of cities that enhanced the exchange of existing and new information and innovations. Also, the larger commercial seaports, particularly New York, served as central areas of information collection. The large seaports collected news from Europe, from other large American cities, and from smaller sized cities and in turn disseminated information throughout the entire urban system. By 1840, the nation had made major advances in the exchange of information, through the development of urbanization.

Urbanization did not proceed uniformly across the nation. Regional variations occurred in productivity and manufacturing, with the Northeast leading the way in industrialism. The regions with the highest income levels in 1840, New England and the Middle Atlantic States, also were leaders in urbanization and industrialization. The Southern States decline in per capita income, during the period, indicates that the cotton producing slave economy was unable to compete with the long-term growth potential of the Northern states. This was due to the manufacturing base that had already been established in the North.[4]

DISTRIBUTION OF INCOME AND WEALTH

A product of the first half of the nineteenth century was that the distribution of income and wealth was becoming less equal. The trend toward concentration of wealth was localized in the new urban areas, particularly in the largest northeastern cities. The growth of the urban population resulted in an increase in their numbers relative to the total population. The result of this relative growth was that the distribution of wealth, in the nation as a whole, was becoming more uneven. There were several factors behind the trend of concentration of income, in the northeast's large urban cities.[5]

Technology, Skills, and Immigration

Technology: The rate of technology change proceeded unevenly, both within the economy as a whole and within the urban sector in particular. Key factory based manufacturing industries led the way in creating productivity gains, with commerce, banking and transportation following. The pattern of technological change favored the intensive use of investment capital, such as machinery, and employment of people with the skills necessary to operate the new machinery. As the price of machines fell due to the many advances in the machine tool industry, the demand for skills, including management skills that were required to operate the machines grew rapidly. Consequently, the distribution of wealth among individuals became more concentrated in the hands of relatively fewer skilled individuals.

Unskilled Workers: They received lower incomes and spent a larger share of their earnings on basic goods that were produced less efficiently, such as fuel and food. As a consequence, the cost of living for most unskilled workers increased more rapidly than for skilled workers.

Immigration: During the 1840's and the 1850's the expansive flow of immigrants, who tended to be less skilled and less well informed about the marketplace than the native population, reduced even further the wages of the unskilled workers. In more modern terms, the demand for skilled workers increased relative to the supply. This resulted in an increased cost for skilled labor. However, the supply of unskilled workers increased relative to their demand. This reduced the price that the owners of capital would be willing pay to obtain their services.

GROWTH IN MANUFACTURING

Manufacturing led economic growth in nineteenth century America, even though early in the century manufacturing was mostly limited to a handful of states in the Northeast. The story of the development of industry rests on the success of American manufacturers in competing with the Western Europeans, particularly with the British. During the first half of the nineteenth century the British were riding on a more advanced wave of the industrial revolution, but American ingenuity would soon serve as a key ingredient gradually to close the gap.

Every young economy must devote most of its resources to agricultural production, for food is the basic necessity of life, and until a good supply is assured, manufactured goods must remain in the planning stage. However, the American people were determined to make their plans a reality. They were able and willing to use technology to supplement their labor and abundant raw materials. Nature had endowed America with ample supplies of most of the essential raw materials. There was plenty of iron and timber, and cotton could be cultivated on a large scale, but the entrepreneur found himself without the capital goods with which to process the raw materials. Gradually, the labor force, the land area, and capital were accumulated in amounts large enough to make a steady climb in the total manufacturing output possible. The mechanism that propelled the American factories toward increased output was technology development and improvement.

Technological progress means the application of analytic methods of science to the industrial arts. Anything that speeded up the process of invention, encouraged business entrepreneurs to experiment with new devices, or improved the skills of labor, accelerated technological change and industrial development. As the American economy advanced, numerous influences contributed to make this change progressively more rapid. The accumulation of capital, the creation of a workable money system, and the enlargement of the market area all served to stimulate to growth of manufacturing in America. However, changes in technology occurred gradually and continuously rather than sporadically. Almost every era in American history was rich in invention and innovation. Yet each period was dominated by a particular type of technological development: the early years, by the accumulation of machines and tools; the late nineteenth century, by the intensive development of bigger machines and better metals; the early twentieth century, by scientific management and research and development.

The American forte was not as the original inventor but as the innovators. American businessmen acquired technological processes from abroad and then experimented with them, often greatly improving on the original invention. The Europeans themselves were the first to recognize that the American approach was different from theirs. It was the Europeans, who coined the term the "American System." To the Europeans this term meant a system of mass production, of standardized interchangeable parts with heavy emphasis on utility, and a great disregard for aesthetics.[6]

The thrust of American technological development was toward the use of labor saving, capital-using innovations. Manufacturers in the United States learned how to use more capital per unit of labor than their British counterparts. The result of this propensity to substitute capital for labor, in ever increasingly innovative ways, was the enhancement of their own competitive position. The competitive success of American manufacturers also depended on the rapid technical advance in the development of machine tools. British engineers invented most of the basic machine tools, but Americans devised the most important new machine tools of the nineteenth century, most notably milling machines, grinding machines and the turret lathes. By the 1850's Americans had more specialized machine tools than those available in England, especially those used in woodworking and small arms' manufacturing.

However, the American superiority in machine tools was only one of the key ingredients toward the long-term goal of manufacturing superiority. In 1850, the English were still far ahead in most manufacturing fields, but what was most impressive was that a nation that was just getting off the economic ground should excel versus the British in any field.

In summary, American industry was able to compete with the British because of the relative cheapness of its raw materials. The availability of fertile land helped Americans become competitive by allowing them to compensate for the high costs of scarce labor and capital with the savings achieved on raw materials. Consequently, industries specializing in the processing of agricultural products thrived, with the cotton textile, lumbering, boot and shoe, flour milling and men's clothing industries leading the way. In addition, Americans competed with the British in the iron fabrication and especially the machinery industry as a result of their unique ability to take existing technology and adapt it to their own particular use. This is demonstrated by the output of America's leading industries in the year 1859 as follows:

Industry	Gross Value Added ($ in Millions)	Industry	Gross Value Added ($ in Millions)
1. Cotton Goods	$54.7	6. Iron Fabrication	$35.7
2. Lumbering	$53.6	7. Machinery	$32.6
3. Boot and Shoe	$49.2	8. Woolen Goods	$25.0
4. Flour and Meal	$40.1	9. Wagons	$23.7
5. Men's Clothing	$36.7	10. Leather	$22.8

Source: Secretary of the Interior, The Eighth Census, Manufacturers of the United States in 1860 (Washington, D.C.: U.S. Government Printing Office, 1865), pp. 733-742.

INTERNATIONAL TRADE

The international economy underwent a period of marked expansion during the nineteenth century and the American economy profited from participation in that growth. International expansion brought large amounts of foreign investment capital to the United States. Foreigners were willing to invest in America because of the possibility of the high returns that were available. The expansion of the world marketplace required the development of many institutions that are central to international economic growth. Nations had to develop capital markets that could provide the medium for increasing levels of international investment. Credit had been extended in international commerce for centuries, but only in the nineteenth century did firms appear whose primary function was judging the possible returns on a wide assortment of commercial activity. Following the rise of international bankers, such as the Rothchilds and the Baring Brothers, mobility of international funds increased. The American government also participated in the growth of international trade by sharply reducing tariffs in 1832.

America's development of its particular set of comparative advantages was reflected in the growth and structure of the nation's exports. The trend of exports was strongly upward throughout the period. After 1839, exports grew as rapidly as the national product. The result of this growth was an export level that amounted to 6 percent to 7 percent of the gross national product, during the period. However, the composition of American exports remained essentially the same from previous decades as agriculture and fiber products constituted most of the country's exports before the Civil War.

Manufacturing exports during the period consisted mostly of low quality cotton textiles. Raw cotton dominated the American exports throughout the period. Cotton had replaced the traditional colonial exports of tobacco, rice, lumber and naval stores as the leading export product. Exports of wheat and flour gained importance in the 1840's and 1850's, when the Irish potato famine, the Crimean War, and the repeal of the Corn Laws in 1846, increased European demands. Great Britain was the major importer of American goods.[7]

Despite the increasing export trade, the United States had an unfavorable balance of trade, with Europe, from the 1820's until the 1870's. With its balance of payments account in a negative position, America made up for the trading imbalance primarily through exporting gold and silver and the returns from service charges such as immigrant remittances and earnings from shipping. During the 1850's the excess of imports over exports was supported by the California mining boom, which allowed an outflow of almost $400 million in gold and silver from the United States. Thus, the new discovery of gold and silver in the West was a major contributor to the ability of all Americans to increase their consumption of foreign manufactured goods beyond their ability to export goods to Europe.

Trade, both international and domestic, promoted economic growth during the period before the Civil War, as it permitted a greater division of labor. Those institutional changes that widened trade encouraged greater regional and national productivity. Growing trade with Europe permitted Americans to rely more heavily on foreign producers for articles of consumption, enabled southern farmers to specialize in profitable cotton production, and provided a small but growing foreign market for American manufactured goods.[8]

However, internal commerce absorbed the vast bulk of Western and Northeastern production, and the specialization that resulted from this trade was more significant to the development and strengthening of industrialization in the United States than was the flourishing international trade.

THE GROWTH OF MASS PRODUCTION

Throughout most of American history, agriculture dominated the economy. After 1860 the economy continued to become industrialized and by the end of the nineteenth century production had shifted from the home to the factory and hand-crafted products were being replaced by factories with machines. One of the things that contributed to the overall growth of manufacturing was the natural increase in the factors of production. Gradually, the labor force, the land area, and capital expanded sufficiently enough to make a steady climb in total manufacturing output possible. At the same time, these factors of production were operating in a way that increased productivity in the entire economy, and especially in manufacturing. The tool that was used to increase production was the development of and the improvement in existing technology.

Technological progress includes the substitution of natural energy for human exertion. Improvements to technology can be used for the mechanization of industry, improvements in transportation and communications, and the development of mass production. The means of improving technology are through specialization and this is achieved through the division of labor. Technology improvement incorporates the application of human brain power and skill to improve physical property, factories, tools and equipment. As the American economy advanced, many things contributed to making this economic growth more rapid. The accumulation of capital, the creation of a workable state banking system, the growth of the mass market and the emergence of a more efficient transportation system were all large contributors to the growth of manufacturing during this period. However, of all the forces that were at work, three things were fundamental to the explanation of the economy's rapid growth during this period: the scarcity of labor, the expansion of education, and from the point of view of the business owner, the prospect of profit.

Technology and the Scarcity of Labor

One of the main reasons for the growth in technology was the scarcity of labor. It was through application of tools, machines and capital goods that the small labor force was able to produce more. Starting with a small population, compared to the land mass, the Civil War made the problem even worse by either killing or wounding more than one million of the country's most productive workers. However, America's population was young and the American culture encouraged the accumulation of material things. Because the population was not divided by social status, there were no peculiar class tastes or needs, anyone could buy goods provided they had the price.

For the most part American workers did not oppose the increased use of technology. The revolts against technology changes that took place in England during the last half of the nineteenth century had no counterpart in America. For in America where labor was scarce, machinery increased production that resulted in increased wages paid to the workers rather than to their unemployment.

The American value system based upon individualism, frowned upon leisure. It made work a fetish and production almost a religion. An often quoted English writer de Tocqueville, once said of the American system, "the notion of labor is presented to the mind of every side as necessary, natural, and honest condition of human existence. Not only is labor not dishonorable among such a people, but it is held in honor. In the United States, a wealthy man would think himself in bad repute if he employed his life solely in living." [1]

Education

Scientific information had been accumulated during the first half of the nineteenth century, but it was not yet a part of college instruction. As a result, scientific findings had not yet begun to filter down to industry. However, during the second half of the century engineering and mechanical education progressed at a rapid rate. In 1850 the Rensselaer Polytechnic Institute in New York became an engineering school. In 1862, the Federal Government through the Morrill act, started to subsidize state colleges. These colleges were created to teach agricultural and mechanical arts. In 1864, the National Academy of Sciences was founded and in 1865 scientific instructions began at the Massachusetts Institute of Technology. By the end of the century, 147 institutions were offering technical education.[2]

Technological progress was accelerated not only by the expansion of scientific education, but also by changes that occurred in the inventive process. This process began to move from the individual home or storefront into the laboratories of business organizations. The process of invention became more systematized, more disciplined, more collective and less individual. It became a profession, with a good share of it organized on a group basis and financed by business enterprise. As the process of invention shifted more towards the corporation, it became more efficient and more productive and more able to give the business owner better tools and products for mass production.

The Prospect of Profit

Technology and education are requisites of increased production, but the final ingredient was the business owner who assembled the factors of production. In America, the more enterprising businessmen recognized that there was profit to be made through mass production and they took ample advantage of these opportunities. Business enterprise accelerated the development of the new machinery by emphasizing both mass consumption and mass production. Without large-scale business the technological growth that occurred in America would not have taken place, because only large-scale business could afford to adopt the expensive machinery that technology produced. However, large-scale manufacturing brings with it large fixed costs. Therefore, mass consumption is necessary for mass production to exist. Early in American history businessmen realized that their opportunities relied on the expansion of mass consumption, and they set their goals accordingly. As early as the Jackson period, businessmen were suggesting that, a characteristic of American business, in the future, was to sell products to many customers at a low price, rather than at a high price, to just a few. Thus, it was a combination of labor scarcity, education, and entrepreneurial initiative that gave impetus to the growth and development of mass production in America.[3]

THE RISE OF THE INDUSTRIAL CAPITALIST

By 1870, transportation of goods improved in America as there was, by this time, over 50,000 miles of railroad in operation. The improvement in railroad transportation made it possible to ship large amounts of goods from more distant locations. For example, cattle from the Southwest could be driven to Kansas City for processing and then shipped by rail to the east coast. Also, in addition to the improvements in transportation, almost one-quarter of America's population was by that time living in cities. Mass production, mass marketing, and mass consumption was now possible. However, to take advantage of this new market potential, business required a system of enterprise that would include new techniques for expanding fixed assets, new methods off distribution, and new ways to finance large-scale business, and improved methods of supervising a large labor force. To fill this need, the industrial capitalist appeared.

The industrialist was primarily concerned with driving down unit cost through mass production and therefore increasing the supply of consumer goods. Indeed, operating in a vastly untapped market, the industrialist often took demand for granted. Often starting on a smaller scale as a business merchant, the industrialist of the late nineteenth century raised a large portion of their own capital, by plowing back earnings into the business. He distrusted the financial institutions of the era. As an individualistic owner, the industrialist believed in centralized authority and preferred to run a so-called one-man style of business. He regarded all office work, with the exception of accounting, with contempt. He maintained a paternalistic attitude toward his employees and paid almost no attention to public relations. He believed in individualism and the philosophy of Social Darwinism and that economic life was governed by the principle of "Survival of the Fittest." He distrusted government and politicians and in the hierarchy of social values, he argued that the interest of his business came first and that he had no responsibility to sacrifice the profit potential of his organization for the attainment of social goals.[4]

Between 1870 and 1890, many of the large businesses of the new industrialists were created. Charles

Pillsbury organized C.A. Pillsbury and General Henry
DuPont formed the Gunpowder Association in 1872.
Andrew Carnegie and his associates built the Edgar
Thomsom works to produce steel in 1873. Philip Armour
opened his meat packing plant in Chicago in 1875.
Wanamaker opened the Grand Depot in 1876 and the
partnership between Gustavus and Edwin Swift was
created in 1878. By 1879, the Standard Oil Company of
Ohio was formed by the brothers John and William
Rockefeller.

COMPETITION AND THE ATTEMPTS TO CONTROL PRICE

One of the results of increased mass production in
the United States during the last quarter of the
nineteenth century, was that production capacity was
increasing at a rate that was greater than demand. When
supply increases at a greater rate than demand for the
products produced, businessmen usually have to reduce
the price of their products in order to sell the quantity
produced. Thus the industrialists were confronted with a
new problem, one of excess capacity and the possibility of
ruthless price competition. The businessmen recognized
that price wars would benefit consumers at the expense of
the producers as they would result in losses in profit and
the potential of a large amount of business failures. The
strategy that was devised to avoid the potential of
business losses was to control the price of the products
produced.

The first attempt to control price competition was
through trade associations. In the 1850's, the so called
"Gentlemen's Agreements" began to appear regularly in
manufacturing companies. For more than twenty years,
businessmen tried to control price competition, through

these associations. However, not all of the participants in an association could be trusted to control their output. Members found it easy to evade the self-imposed restrictions and sooner or later one party was sure to sell their goods below the agreed-upon price. Controlling the price of goods in an industry required the cooperation of all members of the association; however, when even one of the member cheats, the whole system usually collapses.

It soon became clear to the industrial capitalist that the best way to control prices was to eliminate the competition by buying a controlling interest in rival companies in the same industry. This method of consolidation is known as a horizontal merger. The Gunpowder Association presents a good example of a horizontal merger. This association was controlled by General Henry DuPont, who owned a block of stock in each of the member companies, and the General used this power to control price competition within the association.

However, horizontal integration did not solve all of the business problems of the time for this provided little control over the supply of natural resources. The industrialist of this period solved this problem by integrating vertically. Vertical integration requires expanding forward to the customer through the purchase of wholesale or retail operations and backward to the producer of raw materials. The initial expansion was usually in the direction of the consumer as businessmen gradually took over the marketing of their products.

Two of the pioneers in building a marketing organization to integrate forward to the consumer were the McCormick Reaper Company and the Singer Sewing machine Company. McCormick began to sell agricultural products through commissioned agents and gradually this was built up to a franchise agent system. Edward Clark, the marketing brain in the Singer Company recognized that his company would have to demonstrate the sewing machine and provide instruction and service to customers. To provide these services, Singer established branch stores, 14 of them by 1859.[5]

The Standard Oil Company provides an example of a corporation that expanded both horizontally and vertically. In 1870 the Rockefeller Brothers and Henry M. Flagler reorganized their oil refining business under the name of Standard Oil (Ohio). This was because prices and profit margins on petroleum products were falling. This was due to over expansion of production. Rockefeller and his associates responded to this problem by establishing an aggressive and ruthless policy of horizontal integration by purchasing rival refineries, and also developed a long range plan for vertical integration. During the 1880's and 1890's, Standard Oil continued to buy small marketing businesses. The company also acquired the remaining minority interest in its marketing affiliates, organized new units, and accumulated miles of pipelines and fleets of oil tankers. Meanwhile, Standard Oil also began to purchase companies in the oil and gas production industry. By 1893 Standard Oil had become fully integrated from the oil well to the gas station. They controlled the supply of oil and therefore the price.[6]

EXPANSION OF INCORPORATION AND THE TRUST

The corporate form of organization was used in a small number of companies as far back as the colonial period. In early years, corporate charters were granted by special acts of legislation and limited liability was not available. However, state law gradually changed and limited liability to stockholders was common by 1850.[7] However, what made the corporate form of business even more important was that it suited the needs of expanding companies. Through the sale of stocks and bonds, businessmen began raising capital in much larger amounts then would have been possible through the proprietor of partnership forms of business. As a result of these advantages, the industrial capitalist resorted more and more to the corporate charter in the late nineteenth century. The experience of two industrial states, New Jersey and Ohio, can be used to illustrate the trend toward the use of the corporate structure. In 1870 these states issued almost 150 corporate charters to manufacturing companies. In 1883, the same states issued about 450 new corporate charters to manufacturers.

These early corporate charters were granted mostly to "Closed Corporations," whose stock was not bought and sold in the open market. The Carnegie steelworks was a typical example of the closed corporation. In the Carnegie organization, there were 25 stockholders, whose ownership ranged from less than 1 percent to over 58 percent. Under the terms of the corporate charter, stockholders could sell their shares only to the company. Moreover, the shares of any holder's stock, could be bought at book value if 75 percent of the stockholders voted that way.

Because of the limitations to raising capital inherent in the closed corporation, corporate lawyers and business owners soon created a new form of organization called the "Trust." This form of organization gave the corporation much more flexibility to expand its capital raising powers and at the same time gave control of the company to a small group of insiders.

A trust (often referred to as a cartel) by definition is a group of producers that attempt to maximize their profits by joining together to control output and thereby fixing prices. In the United States there has historically been a populist sensitivity that tends to associate large size with the potential for monopoly power. A trust is a combination of firms in which the companies haven't actually merged, but they act as a single unit usually for the purpose of controlling output and fixing prices. Therefore, trusts often acted as if they were monopolies.

Standard Oil provides a good example of the trust activities of the late 1800's. Standard Oil under John D. Rockefeller, demanded that the railroads pay it kickbacks on freight rates. These payments allowed Standard Oil to set lower prices for its products than other companies which had to pay the railroads the full price on freight. This arrangement enabled Standard Oil to sell its products at lower prices than its competitors. By 1882, Standard Oil had driven many of its competitors out of business. The company then created a trust and invited its remaining competitors to join or be forced out of business.

The trust innovation was mainly the idea of Standard Oil's legal advisor, Samuel C.T. Dodd. Under the 1882 agreement, 41 stockholders, in 40 different companies, turned over their stock to 9 trustees in exchange for $70 million in "Trust Certificates," that represented all the shares in 14 companies and most of the shares of 26 other organizations. Stockholders continued to receive dividends. In theory they owned the companies, but in practice they did not participate in the management of the firm and effectively did not have control over the trust.[8]

Once they had gained control of the majority of their competitors, Standard Oil used the monopoly power that it had gained to close down refineries, raise prices and limit the production of oil. The price of oil rose from a competitive level to a monopolistic level, and the consumer ended up paying a higher price for oil.

The Trust idea caught on very quickly, and trusts were soon formed in cottonseed oil, whiskey, distilling, sugar refining and other businesses. The device enabled a group of business owners to control many different companies in many different states thus giving them the ability to control pricing. Separately this practice was not permitted under existing corporate law, but by operating through the trust structure the law could be circumvented. It also enabled the industrialist to raise capital to support the huge investment in the fixed assets required for mass production without relinquishing any of their control over the organization. These trust certificates could be issued to the public and were traded on the major stock exchanges of the era.

However, the word "Trust" soon became synonymous in many people's minds with the word "Monopoly," and states began to take legal actions to dissolve them by antitrust proceedings. The most noticeable of these actions was in Ohio in 1892, when that state delivered a serious blow to the Standard Oil Trust, by ordering Standard Oil to withdraw from the trust.[9]

MONOPOLY AND THE GOVERNMENT

To understand the government's response to the large corporate combinations of this period, it is useful to first define monopoly in economic terms. Monopoly is a market structure in which there is a single supplier of a product. A monopolistic firm is the only supplier of a particular product. In addition, a monopoly firm must sell a product for which there are no close substitutes. For example, Standard Oil (Ohio) was able to form a monopoly position by eliminating competition through horizontal and vertical mergers, in a product (oil) where there was no close substitute.

ANTITRUST POLICY

The problem often faced by government policy makers is to determine whether a firm is acting in a way that fosters competition and to decide what to do when a firm's behavior reflects its intention to control prices, supply or in other ways, restricts competition. Antitrust policy is the term used to describe government policies and programs designed to control the growth of monopoly and prevent firms from engaging in undesirable business practices. The federal government's right to regulate business in the United States is based on the commerce clause of the Constitution. As previously discussed, Article 1, Section 8, of the Constitution, states that "Congress shall have power to regulate commerce with foreign nations, and among the several states, and with the Indian tribes." Three laws currently define the United States Government's approach to antitrust policy:

- Sherman Antitrust Act (1890)
  Section 1: outlaws contracts and conspiracies in restraint of Trade.
  Section 2: forbids monopolization and attempts to monopolize.

- Clayton Antitrust Act (1914)
  Section 2: bans price discrimination that substantially lessens competition or the ability to compete.
  Section 3: prohibits certain practices that might keep other firms from entering an industry or competing with an existing firm.

Section 7: outlaws mergers that substantially lessen competition.

- Federal Trade Commission Act (1914)
  Section 5: prohibits unfair methods of competition and unfair deceptive acts.[10]

Economic theory presents sufficient evidence against monopoly to justify the presumption that impairments to competition are harmful. Even classical economic theory conceded that monopoly was the one flaw in their otherwise, thought to be, perfect system. Determining if the firm's actions are beneficial for society, and, in addition, if large size is harmful to society, is the aim of our government's antitrust policy.

The United States government tries to distinguish between beneficial and harmful actions, by companies, through focusing on unreasonable monopolistic restraints. The first phase of antitrust policy in this country began in 1890 with the passage of the Sherman Act. The courts used the "Rule of Reason" for judging the individual firm's acts. On the basis of the rule of reason, to be illegal an action must be unreasonable in a competitive sense and the anti-competitive effects of the actions must be demonstrated.

The second phase in antitrust policy began in 1914 with the passage of the Clayton Antitrust Act and the Federal Trade Commission Act. At this time the courts began to use the "Per Se Rule" to judge individual firm's actions. Actions that were potentially monopolizing tactics were determined to be illegal under the per se rule. Currently the courts have returned to the looser rule of reason standard. Since the 1980's, collusion or price fixing, has been the only tactic deemed intrinsically illegal under the Antitrust Acts.[11]

The results of antitrust legislation in the United States have been mixed at best. If antitrust legislation was intended to establish a more competitive market structure, historically it has failed to accomplish this goal. With the exception of the dissolution of the Standard Oil Company and the American Tobacco Company in 1911, the Sherman Act and subsequent laws, has not changed the existing market structure. However, the Sherman Act clearly established the principle that competition was to be favored over monopoly. The prohibition of price-fixing, did not end attempts by firms to reduce competition, but the antitrust laws did reduce these attempts and limited their impact. As a result of these laws it was more difficult for firms to collude and practically impossible for them to prevent or punish cheating. As a result, price-fixing combinations became more difficult to create and less effective in operation.[12]

CHAPTER 9

NEOCLASSICAL ECONOMICS

"The institution of a leisure class is found in its best development at the higher stages of the barbarian culture. And the tribal rites of the latter have their counterpart in the dinners, dances and other entertainment's at the great houses in New York and Newport." —Thorstein Veblen.

ALFRED MARSHALL (1842-1924)

William Stanley Jevons contributed many important ideas about marginal utility, but it was Alfred Marshall who developed the idea of Marginalism into a practical economic theory. Alfred Marshall was born in 1842 in Bermondsey England. Marshall's father wanted him to attend Oxford University, where he could study Latin and prepare for the ministry. However, to his father's disappointment, Marshall did not hear a voice from God. Instead of a voice from God, Marshall heard cries of the poor, urging him to study economics. Up until the nineteenth century three educational disciplines reigned in English Universities: Theology, aimed at spiritual perfection; Law aimed at justice; and Medicine, aimed at physical soundness. Marshall offered a fourth great vocation, the study of economics. Throughout his life Marshall fought for economics as a separate field apart from politics, history and moral issues. In 1885, Marshall was appointed as the Chair in Political Economy, but it wasn't until 1903 that Cambridge University decided to establish a separate economics course.

In 1890 Marshall published his most famous work, "Principles of Economics," where in the beginning of his book he describes his basic belief "Natura Non Facit Saltum," Nature makes no sudden leaps. Whereas classical economists followed a Newtonian Scientific approach searching for laws of nature, Marshall emphasized a more evolutionary approach. For Marshall, the theories of Charles Darwin and biology, were more important than the physics of Isaac Newton. In this regard, Alfred Marshall's concepts about marginalism, are similar to the theory of evolution, if this theory was applied to economics. According to Marshall, the businessman and the consumer make no great leaps, but gradually attempt to improve their situations. Individuals, companies, and governments all conform to changing situations and changing prices. In the long run only those firms that can adapt to change, only those firms that are the fittest, survive.[1]

Marshall realized that like biological time, economic time, was not a constant. Marshall's way of dealing with time constraints was to create an ingenious system of analysis. While he was looking at one factor, he set aside all other into a "pound." He called the pound "Ceteris Paribus," meaning "other things being equal." Prior economists had already devised a ceteris paribus assumption, but Marshall derived an explicit method and constructed rigorous theories according to it. Today, microeconomics textbooks are still based on Marshall's method of analysis.

According to Marshall, economic events must be analyzed in conjunction with the time that is necessary for both consumers and producers to make adjustments. Marshall's analysis broke time into three different areas. First there was the very short run. This is the time period of just one day where only demand can fluctuate. This is because producers generally cannot adjust supply in such a short period. Next there was the short run. In the short run according to Marshall, producers can supply more of a product by hiring more labor and purchasing additional amounts of raw material. However, the short run does not last long enough to increase the capacity of existing equipment or to build additional manufacturing capacity. The third period Marshall called the long run. This was a period when producers have enough time to build new machinery and new factories, as well as to vary labor and materials. Also, in the long run, new producers could enter the industry; old and less efficient companies would be forced to leave and the surviving firms would earn profit margins that were normal for the industry. This analysis has a key implication for the long run growth of any economy. Government intervention can serve to increase or reduce economic activity in the short run, but in the long run the output of any economy can only increase through increases in productivity, i.e., output per man hour of work.

Marshall on Supply and Demand

Marshall did not agree with Ricardo's claim that the value of a product reflects the amount of labor it took to produce it. He thought that the supply and demand for a product were equally important. Based on the marginalist theory, economists had previously developed the downward-sloping demand curves, but Marshall developed the "Law of Demand," which stated that the greater the amount of products to be offered for sale, the smaller must be the price of those products. "The amount of a product demanded increases with a fall in the price, and diminishes with a rise in price."[2]

Marshall's analysis was based on the principle of "all other things being equal," but he knew that factors other than price entered into the analysis of demand. The most important of these factors were, consumer taste and preferences, customers disposable income, and the price of substitute goods. In modern terms, a change in quantity due to a change in price is depicted as a movement along a demand curve, whereas a change in factors other than price would be represented as a shift in the demand curve.

Marshall developed a similar framework for suppliers. As producers supply more of a product, the total costs of production will rise. Therefore, supply will rise only if the price paid to the producer increases. The producer will compare the additional cost of producing one more unit to the price he can obtain when selling that output. This, according to Marshall, is the reason that the supply curve slopes upward, whereas the demand curve slopes downward.[3]

Marshall held that, in the same way that the consumer compares the marginal utility of spending on various products, producers constantly compare the potential returns from spending. In this case, the producer is comparing the potential returns from investing in capital equipment versus labor. The business owner in order to be successful must engage in a constant balancing act among capital, labor and natural resources, i.e., between new and used equipment and between skilled and unskilled labor. For this reason Marshall came out strongly against unions that supported make-work projects and featherbedding, as their lack of productivity would only serve to reduce profits and in the long run hurt their members.

Marshall on Social Concerns

While Marshall's "Principle of Economics" tended to be theoretical, he insisted that economics must also be practical. Marshall frequently served on royal commissions and testified before parliament. He supported public education and a moderate redistribution of wealth, because it would heighten productivity and social welfare. However, he was not by any means a socialist and at one point called this philosophy the "greatest present danger." Just like philosophers and economists as far back as Aristotle, Marshall feared that collective ownership would "deaden the energies of mankind, and arrest economic progress; unless before its introduction the whole people had acquired an unselfish devotion to public good."

Marshall thought that the classical pessimists and the romantic Marxists were both wrong. The stationary state had not arrived. Population did not outstrip food as Malthus had predicted. Landlords did not reign. Although poverty still degraded a portion of the people, Marshall held that the "hope and poverty and ignorance may gradually be extinguished," and this philosophy was supported by the steady progress of the working class during the nineteenth century. The steam-engine had relieved them of much of their exhausting and degrading toil; wages had increased; education had been improved and the railway and the printing press had enabled members of the same trade in different parts of the country to communicate easily with one another.[4]

Alfred Marshall remained a professor at Cambridge until he was over eighty years old. John Maynard Keynes, who was his pupil, once praised the "old professor of Cambridge" as he wrote, "The master economist must, like Marshall, be a mathematician, historian, statesman and philosopher to some degree. He must study the present in light of the past for purposes of the future."[5]

AMERICAN CONTRIBUTIONS TO ECONOMIC THOUGHT

In the nineteenth century the United States was a world of improving land, life and well being. During that time the U.S. was a country of owner-operated farms. In the Southern states until the Civil War, wages were excluded from consideration because slavery, as in Aristotle's time, greatly focused attention on such ethical and moral issues as emancipation rather than on economic ones.

In the U.S. the discussion of economics was based on practical economic topics. These included the tariff, monopoly, the social behavior and defense of the very rich, and the diverse questions pertaining to banks and money. The American Economic Association, formed in 1885, was initially a protest against the highly conservative support accorded industrial capitalism by the accepted classical theory and the companion commitment to laissez faire. Only at the end of the nineteenth century did two distinctively American economic figures emerge: Henry George and Thorstein Veblen.

Henry George (1839-1897)

In his time and into the 1920's Henry George was the most widely read of American economic writers. His major work, first published in 1879, was entitled "Progress and Poverty." Henry George's principle idea centered on the accidental and unjust enrichment that came from the ownership of land and the further meaning this had for the financing of the modern state. From his vantage point of San Francisco, Henry George saw the lush enrichment of landowners: as the frontier moved forward, the population increased, and economic development proceeded. David Ricardo had previously witnessed that the tendency of a growing society to enrich the holders of its land would have an adverse affect on the capitalist. However, to Henry George, the resulting contrast between wealth and misery was intolerable.

From this observation followed the remedy he prescribed; it was to tax away the unearned gain in land values that did not derive from the effort or intelligence of the owner but came in effortless fashion from the general advance of population and industry. The revenues that were collected, George believed, would more than cover the operating expenses of the State; all other taxes would be redundant. Thus his great reform was given the name of, the "single tax."[6]

Needless to say, there were a very large number of wealthy landowners, who strongly motivated and politically powerful, were in opposition to the single tax idea. However, even today the beliefs of Henry George can be found in less formal conscious thought. The real estate developer or speculator encouraged by and encouraging an increase in land values, is, quite possibly, the least praised of American entrepreneurs.

Thorstein Veblen (1857-1929)

Of the early twentieth century economic writers, Thorstein Veblen is perhaps still the most notable. Just south of the small city of Northfield, Minnesota are 290 acres of land where Thorstein Veblen spent his childhood. From that background, Veblen went on to study at Johns Hopkins University and Yale, where among his principal mentors was William Graham Sumner.

Veblen established himself as a critic of the classical system, at first in a series of short papers published at the turn of the century. In these papers, Veblen argued that the central ideas of the classical system did not reflect a search for truth and realty; rather they were and are a celebration of approved belief. In Veblen's view economic institutions change; so does economic subject matter; there can be understanding only if one is in tune with change.[7]

A further Veblen contribution which was presented in "The Theory of Business Enterprise," published in 1904, identified a powerful conflict in the modern business organization between the engineers and scientists, who were professionals of great skill and productive potential, and the profit oriented businessmen. The businessmen, according to Veblen, keep the talents of the scientists and engineers under control and suppressed them as necessary in order to maintain prices and maximize profits. Today product managers and marketing people have continued this argument. Also, this argument can be extended to compare the propensity of many U.S. companies to manage in the short-term, i.e., from quarter to quarter, versus the Japanese propensity to manage for the long-term and to seek market share as their main goal.

From this view of the business firm Veblen developed his conclusion. If the business community could somehow release those who are technically and imaginatively proficient from the restraints imposed by the system, there would be unprecedented productivity and wealth in the economy.

Veblen's views on two other matters are also worthy of comment. First is his emphasis on the ordinary worker's concern for the quality of his performance, i.e., "I take pride in my work." This statement can be found in Veblen's "The Instinct of Workmanship," published in 1914. This attitude can be seen today in such things as:

- The Japanese team approach to management and process engineering.

- The new emphasis on service as a major part of a product.

Secondly, and in addition to his other contributions, Thorstein Veblen remains a resonant voice nearly a century after his most memorable book was published. This work was his superb examination of the manners and motives of the rich in "The Theory of the Leisure Class," published in 1899.

The two phrases that Veblen coined; "Conspicuous Leisure," and "Conspicuous Consumption," have permanently entered the American language and culture. They have affected the economic and social attitudes and behavior of countless thousands who have never heard of Veblen. As a consequence of Veblen's work, leisure for the affluent in the United States has come "to lack repute." No one is spared the question, "What do you do for a living?" Even more specifically, no forms of entertainment and no house, if sufficiently expensive or grand, are safe from   the   denigrating   description   "Conspicuous Consumption."[8]

Joseph A. Schumpeter (1883-1950)

During the early decades of the twentieth century the classical tradition, was now above any challenge in England. Also, because of the influence of such disciples as Harvard's Frank W. Taussig (1859-1940), classical economics was fully accepted in the United States. Prices adjusted to marginal costs; costs, including that of labor, adjusted downward as necessary to ensure the employment of available plant, materials, and above all, workers. Say's Law, which states that supply creates its own demand, was widely accepted.

Although Alfred Marshall ruled in these early years, his system did receive some influential amendments. Joseph Schumpeter added a major dimension to the Marshallian equilibrium. This came from the central figure of Schumpeter's system, the entrepreneur, who aided by bank credit, challenges the established equilibrium with a new product, a new process or a new type of productive organization. The tendency then is to a new equilibrium; a new stability in what Schumpeter saw as a circular flow with production moving in one direction, and the money to fund the production in the other. This new equilibrium would inevitably be disturbed and broken by the next innovator. Therefore, economic life would continue and expand; for this is the nature of economic development.

Joseph Schumpeter was born in Austria in 1883. He studied law at the University of Vienna and attended lectures by the leading economist of the day. These economists included some of the founders of the Austrian school of economics. The Austrian school traces its origins to Karl Menger and Friedrich von Wieser who worked in Vienna in the latter part of the nineteenth century. In the twentieth century the Austrian tradition was brought to the United States by Ludwig von Mises and Friedrich von Hayek among others. Today the Austrian school continues to have a strong following in the United States partly because of the theories of one of its close cousins, the Public Choice school of economics, which will be described in a later chapter.

In the view of the Austrian economists the spontaneous order of the marketplace is best viewed in terms of a market process that takes place continuously. The central player in the market process is the entrepreneur. It is the entrepreneur's efforts to move resources from less valued to more valued uses that is the source of profit for the capitalist.

In 1912 Schumpeter published his first book on economics entitled "The Theory of Economic Development." The book is about the way in which capitalism develops its propensity toward growth. The book starts with a description of a capitalist economy that lacks capital accumulation and growth is totally absent. Schumpeter's model pictures a society whose flow of production is perfectly static and absent of change, reproducing itself in a "circular flow" that never expands its ability to create wealth. Also, in the static flow of production, competition among the capitalists will remove all earnings that exceed their opportunity costs. In other words, economic profit would be zero with the economy in a static state. Workers would receive wages, landlords rent, and the capitalists would receive only their wages as managers.

Historically many economists had attempted to explain the source of profits in an economy. Schumpeter argued that profits did not arise from the exploitation of labor as Karl Marx had claimed, or from the "abstinence" of capitalists that was proposed by John Stuart Mill. Profits appeared in a static economy when the circular flow failed to follow its routinized course. From the starting point of the circular flow some new force is required to break the inertia and this force is the introduction of technological or organizational innovations into the circular flow. As a result of these innovations, a flow of income arises that does not come from the contributions of the workers or the resources of the capitalist.[9]

A new product that obtains an initial monopoly position in the marketplace or a new manufacturing process that reduces unit costs can result in a profit for the capitalist that is substantially greater than their opportunity costs. In economic terms the capitalist receives an economic rent for his innovation. An innovation requires an innovator who is responsible for combining the factors of production in new ways. Schumpeter held that innovators do not necessarily come from any social class. He took an old word from the economic lexicon and used it to describe these revolutionists of production and product innovation. He called them entrepreneurs. Entrepreneurs, according to Schumpeter and their innovating activity were the source of profit and growth in the capitalist system.[10]

THE THEORY OF MARKET STRUCTURE

The structure of a market is a term that refers to the conditions under which firms compete in it. The key traits of a market include the number and size of firms, the nature of the products, the ease of entry and exit from the market, and the information available to the competing companies.

Monopoly is a market structure in which there is a single supplier of a product. A monopolistic firm is the only supplier of a particular product. In addition, a monopoly firm must sell a product for which there are no close substitutes. The price of the product is set by the company. A monopoly is a price maker in the marketplace. An electric and gas utility is an example of a monopolistic firm.

Perfect competition is characterized by a large number of small firms, none with a significant share of the market; a product that is standardized, little or no barriers to either entry or exit from the business, and that all buyers and sellers have complete information about the price of the products, the inputs used to produce them and equal knowledge about industry production technology. A company in a purely competitive industry takes whatever price is established by the market. Purely competitively firms are price takers. Agricultural products are a good example of pure competition.

An oligopoly is a market structure with a few firms, at least some of which are large in relation to the size of the market. The product may be either standardized or differentiated; there may or may not be significant barriers to entry, and buyers and sellers do not have equal access to available information. The industry consists of both price makers and price takers as the firm with the largest market share often takes the lead in product pricing while the other companies follow the dominant firm. The automobile industry is an example of an oligopoly.

Monopolistic (differentiated) competition resembles perfect competition in that there are many small firms with easy entry and exit, but under this market structure, the various firms' products are differentiated from one another. Firms in this market structure invest additional amounts of money into expanding the features of their products to add value for their customers. Also these companies usually spend large amounts on advertising to create a favorable image of their products with potential distributors and retail customers. Companies that can successfully differentiate their products in the eyes of the consumers are price makers as they can usually charge a premium for their output. The restaurant industry is an example of monopolistic competition.

The Trend Toward Oligopoly in Manufacturing

In 1933 two economists working separately developed the theory of oligopoly. They were Edward H. Chamberlin (1899-1967) of Harvard and Joan Robinson (1903-1983) of Cambridge. Chamberlin and Robinson both argued that between the general case of competition in the classical system and the exceptional case of monopoly, there was an array of intermediate possibilities. The most important case as an intermediate between pure competition and monopoly, was that of small numbers of participants in the same industry. This market structure they called oligopoly, which is a term that promptly entered the language of economics. The American automobile, petroleum, steel, chemical, rubber tire, machine tool and farm equipment industries, with a few giants in each industry, are cases in point.[11]

The intelligent oligopolist would, in setting his price, give thoughtful consideration to what would be most advantageous for all; so would the others in their industry. Therefore, the price and profit that would be arrived at by an oligopolist, would be somewhere between that of pure competition and monopoly.

The concept of oligopoly, was considered a lesser threat to competition than that of the monopoly, and therefore, entered classical thought without any great difficulty. The large modern corporate sector of the economic system, where oligopoly ruled, was the dominant sector, and, monopoly or not, one could not declare it illegal. Also, while oligopoly was, in principle socially unjust, in actual performance, it aroused no great consumer resentment. While economists might argue that oligopoly was wrong in principle; in practice, it produced a whole spectrum of new and lower cost products. Therefore, economists came to view oligopoly with theoretical concern, but they dismissed the necessity for practical action in dealing with it. Although monopoly was still considered the one great flaw in the system, oligopoly was accepted as a common business practice.

PRODUCTIVITY AND COMMUNISM

Just as the latter half of the nineteenth century saw the growth of formalized education for engineers, the twentieth century witnessed a great acceleration of formalized education for businessmen. Between 1900 and 1910 alone, 240 volumes of business management books were published, and in 1908, Harvard University founded its Graduate School of Business Administration.[12]

Therefore, what effectively ended the long run potential threat to Capitalism from Communism or more moderate forms of Socialism, was the increase in the productivity of the workers. Increased output for man-hour meant increased profit for the owners of business. However, increased productivity through training created skilled knowledgeable workers who could command more wages. Also, labor unions began to gather some strength during the twentieth century which gave the workers the ability to control the supply of skilled labor. The result of these changes was an increase in the amount of the price received for a unit of production that went to the worker. In summary, there eventually was no need for a revolt because the skilled worker was becoming the Bourgeois, the middle class or in today's economy, the favorite target of the tax collector.

CHAPTER 10

SCIENTIFIC MANAGEMENT, MASS PRODUCTION AND WORLD WAR I

"We were going to build one model. The chassis would be exactly the same for all cars. Any customer can have a car painted any color he wants so long as it is black." —Henry Ford

THE PRODUCTIVITY REVOLUTION

According to Peter Drucker, Capitalism has gone through three distinctive phases; the Industrial Revolution, the Productivity Revolution and the Management Revolution. Within one hundred years, from 1750 to 1900, capitalism and technology conquered the globe which led to the creation of a civilized world. What made capitalism different from previous transformations was its speed of diffusion and its global reach across cultures, classes, and geography. This speed and scope converted capitalism into a system of consistent technical advances called the industrial revolution.

This transformation was driven by a change in the meaning and the use of information. Historically knowledge had always been applied for the purpose of intellectual pursuit, i.e., to the process of being. What made the industrial revolution different is that information was applied to making things, i.e., knowledge was applied to tools, processes and products. This change in the use of knowledge created the industrial revolution.

In its second phase, starting at the beginning of the twentieth century, knowledge gained a new meaning as it began to be applied to the work itself. This ushered in the Productivity Revolution, which in seventy-five years converted Marx's proletarian into a middle-class with an income level that was close to the upper class.[1]

FREDERICK TAYLOR (1856-1915)

History has proven Karl Marx to be a false prophet, in fact, the very opposite of what he predicted has happened. However, in the late nineteenth century many of his contemporaries shared his view of capitalism, even if they did not share his prediction of the outcome. Even those who spoke out most strongly against Marx's views accepted his analysis of the inherent contradictions of capitalism. Some of the industrialists, such as J.P. Morgan, were convinced that the military would keep the proletarian in check. Almost every intellectual of the late nineteenth century shared with Marx the conviction that capitalist society was a society of inevitable class conflict. However, as we have encountered throughout the history of economics, something developed to overcome the "inevitable contradictions of capitalism," the "alienation" and "immiseration" of the laboring class. The answer according to Peter Drucker, one of America's most prolific modern day writers, was the Productivity Revolution.[2]

The Productivity Revolution began in America in 1881 when Frederick Winslow Taylor first applied knowledge to the study of work, the analysis of work, and the engineering of work. This new field of study was soon to be called Scientific Management; a term that was first used in 1910 at hearings before the International Commerce Commission.

Scientific management represented the utilization of research as an approach to the solution of management problems. Scientific management stressed standardization of product and process; better organization, coordination and control of workers, materials, and machines. It also meant rigid production planning in factories, time and motion studies, incentive plans and selection and training of workers.

What got Taylor to start on the study of work was his shock at the mutual and growing hatred between capitalists and workers, which had begun to dominate economic discussion in the late nineteenth century. Taylor saw in these class conflicts what Marx and others saw, but he also saw what they failed to see; that the conflict was unnecessary. Taylor then set out to make workers more productive so that they would earn increased wages. Taylor's motivation was not efficiency in production or the creation of more wealth for the owners. His main motivation was the creation of a society in which owners and workers, capitalists and proletarians, could share a common interest in productivity and could build a harmonious relationship on the application of knowledge to work.[3]

In the 1880's, Taylor began to make his initial experiments. At that time he was employed as the assistant foreman in the machine shop of the Midvale Steel Company. Taylor started by studying each job in order to ascertain scientifically the "one best way" of performing it. After determining the best way to do a job, he developed a set of rules for each worker to follow. Taylor's initial goal was to measure and specify a proper day's work for each operation. On the basis of this goal, he began to experiment by controlling all the variables in the actual production process in order to discover the most productive working conditions for one group of workers in one particular task.

Taylor almost immediately achieved success with his method as output began to increase without any additional effort on the part of the workers. After succeeding in increasing the productivity of a single group of workers, Taylor began to broaden his horizon. He perceived that jobs in all work places could be standardized and that operations behind the worker could be coordinated in order to facilitate the flow of work. This standardization meant that the output for each job could be measured against a predetermined benchmark and that operational flows could be coordinated so that men and machines would no longer be inactive between job operations. To implement his theory, Taylor instituted special training in order to secure the most effective performance and coordination of all operations at each work station. Thus planning, preparation, training and cooperation was added to measurement and standardization as elements of managerial technique. [4]

In its initial stages scientific management, as developed by Taylor, was basically concerned with the production function. However, after World War I, the movement broadened and began to aim for more rational utilization of all the elements in the factors of production, i.e., materials, labor and machinery. The various problems of management were approached analytically and studied in more detail than ever before. Business enterprise began paying more attention to functions such as sales forecasting, cost accounting, statistical quality control, budgeting and personnel administration.

PRODUCTIVITY AND THE AUTOMOBILE

One of the major changes brought about by the productivity revolution was its effect on people. The industrial revolution concentrated on improving productivity by substituting machines for labor. The productivity revolution concentrated on making people themselves more productive. Many industries would serve as an example of the increase in manufacturing growth, but no case offers a better illustration of the sweep, the dynamics and the effects of industrialization and technological development than the history of the American automobile industry.

The automotive industry began in the late nineteenth century, and within a single generation, expanded into a giant of mass production. To describe how this change was accomplished is to describe the basics of industrialization; the factors that made industrialization possible, the long lasting process of invention, the fulfillment of mass production, the development of scientific management and the adaptation of these changes to the business enterprise.

The basis for the gasoline-driven automobile came in 1876, when a German inventor patented the four-cycle engine. Gottfried Daimler applied the new technology to motorcycles in 1885 and Karl Benz built a motor car in the same year. The United States adopted the contributions made to the automobile by foreigners, modified them and added the "American System" of mass production. Shortly after the turn of the century, America became by far the largest producer of automobiles. The vast area of the United States lent itself ideally to the use of the automobile, and a road system would soon be developed to take advantage of this new method of transportation. The American middle class was greater in number than that of any European nation. This offered the potential supplier of automobiles a mass market especially if the price could be brought in line with the purchasing power of this group. Also, the raw materials necessary for automotive manufacturing either were available in the United States or could be purchased abroad.[5]

The initial phase of this industry is analogous to a household industry with automobiles being produced in an individual's garage or small business establishment, and usually by a mechanic. Ransom E. Olds was the first man to attempt to manufacture rather than build automobiles. Olds believed that the principles used in manufacturing carriages could be applied to automobiles. This meant buying automotive parts in quantity and assembling them into a finished product. In 1899, Olds opened an automotive assembly plant in Detroit. However, after one year in Detroit, Olds moved to Lansing, Michigan, and in 1901 he began mass producing a $650 Oldsmobile by buying parts in quantity and assembling them on a moving assembly line. Olds was the first person in the automobile industry to use the division of labor, the first to use the moving assembly line, and the first to bring the materials to the worker instead of the worker to the materials. With this new process of assembly, Olds sold 5,000 cars in 1904.

By 1903, the pioneer work in mass production had been accomplished. The assembly line, interchangeable parts, precision instruments, machine tools, material routing, and machine layout had all been developed. The automobile industry was ready to expand into mass production.[6]

At the turn of the century, substantial progress was being made in incorporating mass production methods into the production of engines, bodies, and parts. Ransom Olds bought most of his engines from the Leland Faulconer Manufacturing Company in these years. The company's owner, Henry M. Leland believed that manufacturing a standardized engine with interchangeable parts was possible and practical. In 1903, Leland took over the Henry Ford Company and began to manufacture the Cadillac. This was the first automobile that adopted interchangeable parts successfully.

While Olds and Leland were the pioneers in introducing mass production methods in the automobile industry, Henry Ford carried mass production much further. Ford's great contribution was the emphasis he placed on a combination of timeliness and accuracy through such improvements as standardization, the moving assembly line, material handling, and the careful timing of the manufacturing process. By 1908, most automobile manufacturers were producing high-priced cars. Ford decided that there was a greater opportunity for profit in the mass production of low-priced cars. As an example of his philosophy, Ford once said, " We were going to build one model. The chassis would be exactly the same for all cars," and he continued, "Any customer can have a car painted any color he wants so long as it is black."[7]

Ford began to manufacture the Model-T, which was a completely standardized automobile that retailed well within the price range of the middle class worker. Ford's Model-T completely dominated the market in these early years, but competition was beginning to develop. W.C. Durant had bought the Buick Company in 1904 and, in 1908, he combined Buick, Olds, Cadillac and several other manufacturers into a holding company which he named "General Motors." The competition between Ford and General Motors was intense, but at first Ford prevailed. In 1915 the Ford motor company produced 35 percent of the nation's total output of 880,000 motor vehicles, and by 1923, he produced 57 percent of the four million cars and trucks that were sold.

Led by Ford, the automobile business embarked upon the most spectacular mass production operation in history. This was the heroic age, the era of the industrial capitalist and an untapped market, a period of rapid plant expansion, extensive technological innovation, and substantial increases in productivity. In less than 20 years, the automobile industry emerged from nowhere to become by far America's leading industry. Only 200,000 automobiles were registered in 1908; however, by 1927, there were over 23 million.[8]

By 1923, it was apparent that the heroic age of the automobile business was clearly ending. Durant's strategy was to increase production to the point of growth for growths' sake. Ford was obsessed with production, to the exclusion of all other aspects of the business. Each, it was said, ran his company in a state of anarchy. However, by the early 1920's the style of management began to change as Alfred P. Sloan, Jr. took over the direction of General Motors, revised its objectives and reorganized its structure and administration. Sloan enlisted his executives in a real partnership. The entrepreneurial decision makers in General Motors were concerned with long-run objectives rather than the day-to-day activity of the firm. The whole managerial hierarchy attempted to approach problems in a systematic, orderly fashion. In summary, Sloan was the first industrialist to bring management techniques to the automotive industry. Ford had nothing but contempt for this new style of

management, but the times were changing and Ford was
not keeping up with the changes.

Twenty years of high-volume production in the
automotive industry had ravished the virgin market that
Ford had originally envisioned. At first automobiles had
been price elastic, that is total revenue would increase
when prices were decreased as a result of an even larger
increase in demand. However, the evolution of the used-
car market, development of installment credit, and a
market that was becoming saturated began to make
prices inelastic. When the price becomes inelastic,
corporations must adjust their strategy to emphasize the
differences in product features and the quality. Product
differentiation through advertising and promotion, and
credits become more important in a market structure that
had become what economists refer to as "Monopolistic
Competition." As the industry matured, it became much
more concentrated. During the period of 1903 through
1926, there were almost 180 companies that produced
cars. Only 11 companies survived the entire period. Thus,
by the end of the decade, the automotive industry was
well on its way to becoming the country's largest
oligopoly.

THE FIRST LARGE MERGER WAVE (1898-1906)

The years around the turn of the nineteenth
century marked a period of business consolidation that
was considerably different from the previous decades.
Business firms continued to grow at a fast pace, but they
increased their size more through mergers than internal
growth. Many more corporations went public in these
years and new methods were developed for dealing with
the competition. By the outbreak of World War I, the
large, bureaucratic, and oligopolistic corporation, had

become the dominant institution in the marketplace. By the beginning of the twentieth century the importance of the industrial capitalist was reduced and their type of business system could clearly not continue without a serious modification. By 1900, most of the flamboyant, owner-entrepreneurs who were the catalysts for the growth that began in the 1870's, had retired from active business life.[9]

The old industrial capitalist was slowly being replaced by the new business managers and steps were being taken to change the existing corporate structure and to overcome some of its weaknesses. Frequently the catalyst for this change was the investment banker of the era. These bankers had previously participated in the railroad and textile businesses, but as the nineteenth century came to an end, that intervention became more frequent. The investment bankers brought with them a management philosophy that was quite different from the industrialist. The investment bankers spread their influence over many industries instead of concentrating on just one industry. As a result, investment bankers were more interested in financial policy than in any other aspect of business activity. These bankers were, in a sense, portfolio managers who were not interested in production or distribution techniques.

Because the bankers and industrialists were so different, they tended to dislike and distrust each other. For example, J.P. Morgan is said to have once stated that Carnegie was a dangerous man who had demoralized the steel industry. For his part, Carnegie abhorred promoters and is said to have boasted that he could operate a steel business better than a lot of "stock-jobbers" who paid more attention to security manipulation than to steel making. However, whether the industrial capitalist liked the investment bankers was almost immaterial as far as economic growth was concerned, for the bankers controlled very large amounts of funds and with these dollars they acted as the catalytic agent in the development and growth of large business concerns in the early 1900's.

In American history, mergers occurred in three great waves; the first between 1898 and 1906, the second in the 1920's and the third following World War II and into the 1970's. The first of these merger waves, however, was the most important of the three to American economic history. All of the giant corporations that appeared in the early 1900's were for the most part a result of these mergers. During these years, more than 3,200 mergers took place in the manufacturing and mining industries and twenty-two firms including such names as United States Steel, American Tobacco, American Smelting and Refining and American Can, grew to massive size as a result of merger.[10]

Overall, business mergers were the result of the same basic causes that had produced vertical combinations in the previous decades. The major objective of these mergers was to gain control over the market and to eliminate competition. By 1900, concentration had gone far enough to alter the basic structure of the market. Sporadic price cutting still occurred, but, overall, prices were beginning to conform to the goals of the new business leaders. That is, prices were not set high enough to encourage competitors to expand or new firms to enter the market, and prices were not low enough to set off a destructive price war.

Businessmen also used mergers in an attempt to stop declining profit margins. These business leaders often assumed that large-scale enterprises created by mergers could gain substantial economies that were not available to smaller businesses. It was commonly believed

that the economies of mass production were endless.
These "economies of scale," as economists called them,
could be achieved both in production and administration.
The large firm had decided advantages in buying raw
materials and in distribution of goods. The advantages
achieved through economies of scale resulted in large
companies having lower unit costs than smaller
competitors.

Today, after the third wave of mergers and
consolidations, we have learned that being bigger does
not always mean operating more efficiently. Most
probably, the initial growth of business firms in this era,
lowered the unit costs of production. However, once an
individual plant had passed its optimum size, further
opportunities to reduce unit cost, were not available. The
multiple plant organizational structure sometimes
enabled firms to achieve further economies, but this too
would end as firms, as well as the individual plants,
passed beyond the point of diminishing returns.

Some businessmen who participated in these
mergers were empire builders whose purpose was growth
for growths sake. Others were motivated by the prospect
of making financial profits on security transactions, but
when economic logic took a back seat to financial analysis
or growth, mergers often turned out disastrously. In fact,
about half of the major mergers that were completed
during this period, ended in failure. The reason for many
of these failures is that the companies were put together
as conglomerates not as diversified companies. The
common link, in most conglomerates, is financial
performance. In other words, there is no "synergy"
between the separate companies within the organization.
Once the economies of scale are depleted, there is no
common bond between the units that make up the
conglomerate. For example, if a conglomerate made up of

two companies, was to each show a profit of $100, then the combined profit will be $200. In a diversified company where synergy exists, common functions such as selling, advertising, and research and development can often be combined in a way that will result in the profit of the entire company being greater than the contribution of its individual parts. Therefore, with diminishing returns from production and the lack of synergy between the individual units, the act of combining these companies into a conglomerate, serves no economic purpose. This is the basic reason that in the early 1900's, so many of these business combinations failed.

WORLD WAR I AND THE INTERNATIONAL ECONOMY

Compared with the Civil War, considerably more armaments, munitions, and armored vehicles were used in World War I. Because it was far more mechanized than the Civil War, World War I required a greater industrial effort and much more government planning. New industries had to be created, old industries converted, and new facilities were built to provide the necessary tools of war. The federal government for the first time engaged in economic planning and set up elaborate controls to regulate the economy. The whole civilian population was affected to a far greater extent than in any previous war in American history.

When war broke out in Europe in 1914, it was almost a surprise to the nations involved. A conflict between the industrial countries of Europe was thought to be extremely improbable or at worst, if one did occur, it would be short. This was because the costs of a worldwide war would be too great. However, even the most pessimistic forecasts of the length and cost of World War

I, was apparently drastically underestimated. One of the major awakenings brought about by the hostilities was the realization that the belligerents at one time were the other's best customers. The war shattered the network of international trade and monetary agreements that were critical to Europe's industrial development.

The Germans had originally planned to defeat the French before they could receive aid from Britain and Russia. However, this strategy failed because Russia mobilized much faster than the Germans expected. Consequently, the war in Western Europe became a bloody stalemate. The war soon became a conflict of endurance. The nation that could sustain its military efforts longest would have the best chance of winning the war. Once this was determined, the European belligerents attempted to divert their productive capacities towards producing more military equipment and destroying their enemy's military efforts.

All of the combating nations soon found their ability to produce was inadequate for both consumer requirements and the war's enormous demands. By 1916, the British Naval blockade became so effective that trade between Germany and North America was almost nonexistent. However, as the war needs rose, the allied nations (Britain, France and Russia), began looking to the United States (the only major industrial nation that was not at war), for economic assistance. By 1916, the flood of orders from the Allies began to overwhelm even the American productive capacity. The United States Administration was hesitant to assist the European Allies at first as Woodrow Wilson wished to remain neutral. However, Wilson eventually relaxed his opposition and let American manufacturers respond to the European demand. American exports began to rapidly increase to meet the European demand and to supply traditional

European export markets such as Latin America. From 1914 to 1917, total United States exports to Europe, in current dollars, rose from $1,486 million to $4,062 million, an increase of 173 percent, while imports from Europe during the same period actually declined. This created a large negative merchandise balance of trade between the United States and Europe.

Financing World War I

In international trade and finance, a negative balance of trade must be financed through what is known as a country's international capital account. A negative balance of payments can only be financed through the reduction of a country's assets or by borrowing. Europe had traditionally made up its deficit in direct trade with the United States by running surpluses with nations from which America was a net importer. However, by 1916, this method of financing their trade deficit was no longer available. Europe had few goods to export to any region because most of their production capacity was devoted to the war effort. Therefore, to finance their imports, the Allies had to liquidate their American assets by shipping gold to the United States and selling their portfolios of American securities. As their assets became depleted, the Allies turned to the only means left to finance their imports, to borrow from America.

To finance their imports from America, British and French bonds were sold directly to private citizens in the United States. The firm of J.P. Morgan & Co. was active in purchasing war material on behalf of the French and British governments. In total, the Allies sold their holdings of United States securities worth $4 billion, shipped over $1 billion in gold, and borrowed almost $5 billion from private sources in America, to finance the war. After America entered the war, the U.S. government loaned the Allies another $9.5 billion. From a large-scale debtor through most of the nineteenth century, the United States had been transformed, in just a few years, into the world's largest international creditor.[11]

The Wars Impact on the American Farmer

Because European demands for meat and grain were increasing, American farmers had to increase their agricultural production. The high demand for agriculture products was supplemented by government guaranteed prices after the United States entered the war in April of 1917. The combination of increased demand and higher farm prices encouraged farmers to expand production by putting less productive land to use. Farmers also purchased additional amounts of machinery that enabled them to produce more with less labor. A great deal of this expansion was financed by borrowing, which appeared to be a safe investment, while farm prices were rising. However, increases in real production in farming require time and agricultural production had shown only slight increases before 1918, but prices for most farm products had nearly doubled since 1914.[12]

World War I brought the farmer unprecedented prosperity, despite the fact that he had greatly expanded production. However, the farmer's new prosperity could only last as long as prices of agricultural products remained high. The additional cost of new machinery, placing less productive land into use and the interest on borrowed funds resulted in a large increase in farm production costs. An industry can only continue to operate in this way as long as demand is strong and prices are high.

Immediately following World War I, European demand for agricultural products fell substantially as they resumed their own production. Domestically, consumers began to spend a smaller percentage of their income on food as more durable goods became available. In the face of declining demand, farmers were unwilling or unable to reduce production sufficiently enough to prevent prices from falling drastically. Thus, the combination of high fixed costs, reduced demand and low prices, resulted in some serious problems for the farmers after World War I.

April 1917, The United States Enters the War

After 1916, the United States industry was operating at almost full capacity. Therefore, increased output of military goods could only be achieved by diverting resources from the production of consumer goods to the production of military goods. The task was further complicated by the diversion of labor into the armed forces. The prewar military strength of the United States had been about 165,000 men, but by 1918, the Army and Navy alone expanded to nearly three million.[10] This military expansion required almost 7 percent of the American labor force. Unemployment in the United States had almost vanished by 1918. This was because a large portion of the labor force was now employed by the military, and the demand for goods and services from the Allies had substantially increased.

Since the demands of the American and Allied military and those of the civilian population, far exceeded the available production capacity, a system of priorities was necessary. To meet this requirement, a series of government boards was established. Because of the strain of a huge increase in traffic traveling mostly to the east coast, the Federal government took over the management and operation of all United States railroads. Food purchases for the Allies were consolidated under the Food Administration with Herbert Hoover in charge. The Shipping Board and the Emergency Fleet Corporation took over the building of merchant ships and coordinated maritime traffic.

In total, the Wilson administration created several thousand Federal agencies in order to coordinate the war effort. The job of tying together the work of all these agencies was given to the War Industries Board, under the direction of Bernard Baruch. The War Industries Board made some progress in standardizing designs of tools and persuading some defense contractors to accept these modifications. However, the War Industries Board had two major problems in developing an effective plan for coordinating the war effort. First, there was little information available on the war needs as the United States had never fought in a major war on European soil, and secondly, there was a lack of industrial capacity to meet the war needs. Even when priorities were established, they were difficult to maintain, because the War Industries Board had no authority over prices, and many customers were far more concerned over output than prices. This was not a situation that encouraged producers to voluntarily comply with the Board by controlling prices for there was almost unlimited demand for their products.

In general, the success of the War Industries Board in controlling prices and allocating resources was at best only moderate. However, their success in achieving cooperation between the firms in some industries would be a factor in the trade association movement of the 1920's.

The United States After World War I

When World War I ended, the United States had to assume a new global position. This new position was as the financial and the industrial leader of the world. However, the United States was totally unprepared for this was a role. In addition, the United States had accumulated some wartime legacies of its own; for example, inflation, over capacity in agriculture, shipbuilding, and the coal industry, plus a large war induced public debt. Yet in 1919, none of these problems seemed serious to most Americans especially when compared with the problems of the Europeans. However, signs were beginning to appear that the United States was almost as unprepared for their new role as the leader of the industrial world as they were prepared to enter a world war in 1916.

CHAPTER 11

THE ROARING TWENTIES - PROSPERITY AND DEPRESSION

"The depression must be allowed to run its course. Recovery was something that always came by itself and our analysis leads us to believe that recovery is sound only if it does come of itself." —Joseph Schumpeter

THE CHANGING CORPORATE STRUCTURE

In the nineteenth century, both the internal business structure and its external environment were relatively simple. Most businesses, with the exception of the railroads, were small and were run by an owner-manager. Labor unions were weak and almost non-existent for non-skilled workers and government was friendly. In the twentieth century, the ownership of the large corporation changed and became increasingly more widely dispersed. The professional manager began to replace the entrepreneur and the investment banker as the person in control of large corporate enterprise. This, in turn, resulted in a whole series of new corporate problems such as the separation of ownership from control, the corporate hierarchy and the corporate bureaucracy.

The behavior of the marketplace was also very different in the twentieth century. The market changed because population growth slowed and consumers demanded more diversification in the products they purchased, and in the method of financing the purchases. In response to the changing market demands, corporations had to develop a whole new bag of selling tricks. Departments were developed in major companies with the responsibility of marketing products to consumers. Corporations began to intensify their advertising campaigns in an attempt to convince potential consumers of the quality of their products. They began to search for markets overseas. They created new products through research and development, and they diversified by branching out into entirely new businesses. Competition became more of a struggle between marketing departments to differentiate their products based on real or perceived differences and less emphasis was placed on pricing. Internally, the centralized organization of the industrial capitalist gave way to the decentralized organization of the career manager.[1]

By the 1920's, most large firms were still centrally organized and still dealt in a single product. However, to protect themselves against future business cycles and changing consumer demand, many businesses began to diversify. Some pioneering business owners began to recognize that diversification required an entirely different kind of managerial approach. The DuPont Company's reaction to the trend towards diversification can be used to illustrate how strategy and structure changed in this very successful firm.

Following World War I, DuPont's managers felt that further expansion in their main product explosives was not attractive because of decreased demand. The company, therefore, began to diversify its investments, which included the purchase of a substantial share of General Motors stock, and it began to manufacture and market new products through existing departments such as chemicals, paints, celluloid, dyestuff, and synthetic fibers. However, it was soon discovered that their existing department structure could not be used efficiently to produce and market many different products.

To resolve this problem, in 1921 DuPont adopted a new structure of five autonomous divisions, which were cellulose, paint, purolin, dyestuff and explosives. Each of these new divisions was run by a general manager, with its own staff and with the responsibility for day-to-day operations. This placed the responsibility of production and marketing at the division level. The central office was then given the responsibility of developing strategy for managing the firm in the long run.

During the 1920's, the second merger wave began. There were several differences between the mergers of the 1920's and those of the 1890's. In the 1890's, mergers were between very large corporations within the same industry. The goal of these mergers was monopoly. In the 1920's, mergers were usually between middle size companies and the goal was oligopoly. A second difference was that, in the 1920's, bank mergers, in addition to the mergers that had already taken place in manufacturing, mining and transportation, became popular. Finally, mergers for the purpose of diversification became one of the dominant reasons for combining corporations. In summary during the 1920's, the entrepreneur in large corporate business was replaced by the professional manager. Diversification into new products and markets became the dominant reason for corporate mergers, and the major form of corporate business became the oligopoly.

THE NEW CENTRAL BANK - FEDERAL RESERVE SYSTEM

In the early part of the twentieth century money was still seen in these years as a largely neutral intermediary that facilitated the exchange process. Also, the Central Bank, the most elegant example being the Bank of England, was able to control any unduly liberal lending and deposit creation activities that might jeopardize the ability of the individual banks to redeem their deposits in gold. If lending and the resulting money creation seemed too liberal, government bonds from the portfolio of the Central Bank could be sold to reduce the money stock.

In 1913, after nearly 80 years, it had become possible to face down populist suspicion in the United States and establish a Central bank. The Federal Reserve Act of 1913, created the Federal Reserve System of twelve banks that were geographically placed throughout the country. Control over the system was given to the Board of Governors of the Federal Reserve System that was located in Washington, DC.

At first the Federal Reserve Board was primarily an administrative agency with little control over the system's operations. Even the power to rediscount was not centrally controlled but was dispersed throughout the 12 district banks. The original purpose of congress in creating the Federal Reserve System seems to have been to improve the commercial banking machinery, rather than to exercise a major influence over the economy. However, within a few years after its inception, the Federal Reserve System began to abandon its passive role as a mere helpmate for the commercial banks and took on a more active role in guiding the economy. During the 1920's the Federal Reserve developed another extremely important tool to help regulate the money supply and therefore, in theory, the growth of the economy. This tool was in the form of open market operations. When member banks did not find it necessary to borrow from the Fed because of the low level of business borrowing, the System, in order to maintain its revenue, began to buy government securities and found that this tactic had an important impact on member bank reserves. At first, each district bank carried on its own open market operations; but under the leadership of Benjamin Strong, the Governor of the New York Federal Reserve Bank, a committee was formed in April of 1923 to coordinate the activities of all the district banks. By 1923, the Federal Reserve had begun to develop a theory to control credit and the money supply. The general aim of the new policy was to provide credit freely enough to encourage business expansion, but not freely enough to encourage speculation.[2]

THE PRIMARY CAUSES OF THE GREAT DEPRESSION

Historians have searched with little success for that one thing that caused the depression of 1929. Blame has been placed on the distortions caused by World War I, the problems of the farmers, the overproduction of consumer durable goods, the stock market crash of 1929 and the inappropriate policies of the federal government. However, the real cause of the great depression is most probably a combination of all of the above events. Therefore, each of these occurrences will be examined separately, while at the same time keeping in mind that it was a series of situations that contributed to the length and severity of the depression.

The Distortions Caused by World War I

After World War I, the major problem that faced the American economy was inflation. The federal government did very little to plan for this situation and failed to act effectively to control inflation. The stored up demand for consumer goods and the increased expenditures for new construction created an economic boom after the war. However, the combination of new technology and new management techniques in manufacturing increased production to a rate that was greater than the current demand. The result of this over production was a buildup in manufacturing inventories that led to a mild downturn starting in January of 1920. The Federal Reserve acted to the mild contraction by reducing the growth of the money supply. This was the wrong policy as a reduction of the money supply leads to a reduction of the demand for consumer durable goods and a reduction in business investment in new plant and equipment. The result of the business contraction and the policies of the Federal Reserve was a sharp reduction in prices. Production declined especially in the fall of 1920 and as a result of this reduction in output, nearly 10 percent of the labor force was unemployed at the bottom of this depression.

The depression bottomed out in July of 1921, some eighteen months after it had begun. Sales began to pick up and manufacturers began once again to build up their inventories. The recovery gathered strength and continued through the 1920's, with only minor pauses in 1924 and 1927.[3]

Although the American contribution to World War I was large both in financial and human costs, it was far less than the European belligerents. However, what was more important in the long run to the American economy were the structural changes that were brought about by the war. The most significant of these changes was the dramatic enhancement of America's position in the international economy. The war pushed America to a position of dominance so swiftly that serious international instability resulted. America was placed in the position of the world's leading economy, a position that it was totally unprepared to handle.

The Problems in Agriculture

For the farmers, favorable conditions had persisted for almost two decades, from the turn of the century through 1919. On the basis of past events, farmers began to expect continued strong demand for their products and rising prices. After World War I, American farmers, expecting continued prosperity made large investments in farmland. In so doing, farmers were behaving much like large scale manufacturers with large investments in additional, often marginal land, and machinery. This continuing investment in fixed assets caused farmers to become extremely vulnerable to a reduction in prices. Individual farmers control only a small percent of the marketplace for agricultural products. Therefore, they do not, for all practical purposes, have any influence over the price of farm products. Therefore, the only way they can maintain a level of income high enough to cover a large investment in fixed costs, is to increase production. The reason for this is based on the simple business formula of (Revenue = Price x Quantity). If the farmer has no control over price, then the only other option available to him is to increase quantity, or in this case production. However, if all farmers increased production at the same time, this will lead to an over supply of farm products, which in turn will result in prices being reduced even further.

In June of 1920, farm prices began to drop sharply and with it the dreams and fortunes of many farmers. Those farmers who had expanded production and increased their land holdings during the periods of prosperity now found themselves heavily in debt and in many instances were not able to cover fixed expenses. During the remainder of the 1920's, farm prices continued well below what they were at the turn of the century. This resulted in a reduction of purchasing power of farmers to about three-quarters of what they had experienced during World War I. Consequently, agriculture's share of the national income was also in decline. In summary, the American farmer was in a state of depression long before the great depression began, and they never recovered before suffering further blows in the 1930's.

Overproduction of Consumer Durable Goods

The 1920's was a time when consumers shifted their household demands dramatically to the purchase of durable goods on credit. During the 1920's a host of new electrical household gadgets appeared. To purchase the new consumer durable goods, Americans began to use installment-plan buying, instead of saving for future purchases. However, when consumers buy items on credit, it increases the overall expense of the purchase because interest payments are added to the cost of the product. Buying on credit shifts consumption from the future to the present and at the same time reduces the consumers long term buying power. For example, the extended use of installment-plan buying in the 1920's was so great that 75 percent of automobiles, 70 percent of furniture and 80 percent of household appliances were purchased on credit. A permanent new "American Way of Life" was born, financed by innovations in the country's financial institutions and a desire by consumers to enjoy now and pay later.

In addition to installment plan purchases, there was a housing boom during the 1920's. Mass production of automobiles brought their price within the range of the middle class worker and the improved roads led the way to the development of the suburbs. This led to a large increase in residential construction outside of the cities. The great building boom of the 1920's raised total income generated from construction by almost 80 percent. The value of new construction permits rose by almost 190 percent between 1919 and 1926. However, building construction in both residential and non-residential units is subject to long cycles of growth. A.F. Burns and Wesley C. Mitchell in the publication "Measuring Business Cycles," concluded that building cycles are regular, predictable and usually last, in America, from 18 to 22 years. When the construction boom stopped in 1926, it was not halted by rising building costs, demand simply dried up. It was not the case that the country was suffering from an excess of housing, but, given the existing distribution of family incomes, demand was exhausted.[4]

During the 1920's, as previously discussed, there was another wave of mergers that resulted in even more concentration in business. This concentration led to increased market power and a tendency for manufacturers to keep prices at a level that increased corporate profits but reduced consumer purchasing power. This resulted in an income distribution that was highly in favor of corporate executives, at the expense of the middle class workers. This along with the reduction in the rate of population growth was the reason that consumer demand for durable goods began to decline in the summer of 1929. However, the manufacturing sector did not react to the reduced consumer demand by decreasing production. This resulted in a large stockpile of inventories, which in turn, led to a reduction in economic growth, in the summer of 1929. A downturn in economic activity had begun. However, the reduction in growth, from the loss in demand in both the construction and consumer durable goods industries, would probably have resulted in a downturn that was similar in size and magnitude to the depression of 1921.

The Stock Market Crash of 1929

Since the latter part of 1927, the stock market prices had been seriously inflated. When choosing a corporate stock, an investor can use two different types of analysis; a fundamental analysis of the company's potential growth or a technical analysis based on charting the company's or market's past growth. During the latter part of the 1920's, the investing public began to ignore the fundamentals and began to bet on the future growth of the stock market based strictly on a technical analysis. In other words, investors feeling confident about the current level of stock market prices, became convinced that they would continue to increase in the future. However, there were at least three sources of weakness in the stock market that made it vulnerable to a potentially large correction.[5]

The first weakness was the makeup of the investment public and the method used to finance the purchase of stocks. Most of the additional money that was coming into the stock market was from those individuals and organizations that were new to the market. Their interest was not long term capital gains, but short term profits. Although some of the new investment originated in the commercial banking system, a greater portion of the investment was from foreign banking agencies, corporations with large cash balances, brokers, and individuals searching for short term profits. Adding to this potential problem was the method in which the stocks were purchased. Individual investors could invest on margin; that is they would borrow up to 90 percent of the price of the stock, in order to make the purchase. This method of funding a purchase is called financial leverage. Financial leverage will benefit the investor as long as the price of the stock increases at a rate greater than the interest paid on the loan. However, if the price of the stock goes down, financial leverage will greatly increase the size of the loss.

In addition, stock purchases on margin usually contain a call feature. The broker borrows the money that is lent to an investor from a bank with the provision that the bank can demand payment of the loan by the broker on very short notice. Also, the broker's loan to the investor requires that the purchaser of stock, on margin, maintain a certain portion of the price of the security, in an account with the broker. The market value of the stock is used by the broker as collateral for the loan to the investor. If the price of a stock goes down, the broker will request that the investor place more cash in the broker's account. Therefore, when an investor purchases stock on margin, he risks the loss of market value and the loss of cash, if the price of the stock goes down. In fact, if there is a major reduction in the value of all traded corporate stock, everyone involved in the margin purchase loses; the investor loses value and cash, the broker cannot pay off its loans with its banks and the banks must reduce their assets and equity by the amount of any loans that have to be written off.

A second source of weakness was a new financial institution called the investment trust. The investment trusts were similar in nature to our modern day mutual funds. They were non-operating companies that purchased stocks for their own account and offered its own stock to the small investor. Because of the newness of the investment trust, they were not subject to government regulation. Furthermore, these trusts relied heavily on debt financing. This made their own stocks very attractive in a bull market, but very risky in a down market. Consequently, these highly leveraged investment trusts were vulnerable to any hint of weakness in the market. The trusts contributed to the burst of unmatched growth in the late 1920's and, in the process, made the market even more top-heavy. In addition, because many of the investment trusts were owned and promoted by commercial banks, the stock market crash was a contributing factor to the coming crisis in the banking industry.

A final source of weakness was the activities of the stock market "insiders" and the lack of regulation of this group of investors. These insiders were usually made up of groups of exchange members who represented syndicates of large investors. They would choose a particular stock and bid up its price without regard to the fundamental earnings capacity of the company. Once the price of the stock rose significantly, the insiders would sell the stock short (betting that the price of the stock would go down) before the price returned to its natural value. The lack of regulation of brokerage firms allowed the insiders to feed the bull market of 1927-1929, which added a further measure of instability to the market. Also, lack of regulation jeopardized the capital of many investors who had been duped by the insiders and their brokers.

The stock market, during the late 1920's, had become the symbol of the nation's prosperity and economic strength. Also, the stock market was the embodiment, of the faith of millions, in the ability of corporations to sustain that well-being. When the stock market crashed all the frenzy that had stretched out over two years in sending stocks up was concentrated in a few incredible weeks, beating prices down. On Tuesday, October 29, 1929, an avalanche of selling crushed the stock exchanges. Goldman Sachs, a highly regarded investment trust, lost almost half of its market value on this day. In a single day, the increase in the value of traded stocks of the entire preceding year had been wiped out and millions of individual investors who, based on their previous paper gains, thought they were well off, were faced with the reality of being poor.

When the bubble burst in October of 1929, Americans' optimism changed and they became pessimistic about the future. The impact of the crash was to sharpen and prolong the crisis of confidence that grew worse as the depression dragged on between 1929 and 1933. The depression became self-perpetuating. The longer it continued, the more dismal were the prospects for recovery. The stock market crash contributed to the length and severity of the depression by providing tangible proof of the weakness of the American economy.

Monetary Policy and The Federal Reserve

Monetary policy reached the height of its prestige during the 1920's. Many economists believed that the Federal Reserve System, with its ability to expand and contract the money supply, greatly reduced the potential for depression. During the 1920's, the Federal Reserve lowered the rediscount rate (the rate charged to commercial banks on loans from the Fed), and brought government securities in the open market during the mild recession of 1924 and 1927. These actions by the Federal Reserve tend to encourage economic expansion by increasing the money supply and lowering interest rates. However, during 1928 and 1929, the Federal Reserve instituted a tight money supply in an attempt to reduce the speculative boom in the stock market. The Federal Reserve executed its tight money policy by raising the rediscount rate to 5 percent in 1928 and to 6 percent in 1929. At the same time, the Federal Reserve reduced its holdings of government securities from $620 to $145. However, the Federal Reserve's action to tighten the money supply was badly timed. Changes in monetary policy have a lagging effect on growth as they have to filter their way through the banking system. Therefore, the Federal Reserve's tight money policy, that was implemented in late 1928 and 1929, probably started to affect economic activity in the summer or fall of 1929. Thus, the tight money policy that was designed to break the back of the stock market boom, probably accomplished that purpose, but in doing so, most certainly helped to push the economy into a depression.

As soon as the depression began, the Federal Reserve reversed its tight money policy and began to supply additional reserves to the banking system by buying government securities in the open market, increasing its holdings from about $450 million in late 1929 to $1.9 billion in late 1932. At the same time, in order to encourage borrowing, the Federal Reserve lowered its rediscount rate to 1.5 percent. However, by 1932 any act by the Federal Reserve to encourage borrowing was practically useless, as the economy was in such bad shape that there was almost no demand for bank loans.

Overall, the basic problem with the Federal Reserve was the bad timing of their monetary policy. However, in October of 1931, frightened by a drain on the gold supply, The Federal Reserve raised the rediscount rate from 1.5 percent to 3.5 percent, to protect the gold reserve. From this action to reduce the flow of gold out of the country, the Federal Reserve severely limited the ability of the nation's banking system to meet domestic demands for currency by making borrowing much more expensive. This action to tighten the money supply was taken in an economic environment in which there was almost no demand for loans. In total, as a result of the Federal Reserves policies, the stock of money fell by almost one third, from August 1929 to March 1933, when the economy reached the trough of the great depression.

When the money supply is reduced significantly, national income can only be sustained at the current level if the velocity of money increases, i.e., consumers would have to spend their money faster. However, Americans responded to the depression by deferring spending and withdrawing their deposits from their banks. The increased preference for holding their savings in cash was a result of the expectation that prices would continue to fall and because consumers did not believe that banks could guarantee the safety of their deposits.

The combination of poorly conceived and poorly executed monetary policy and the lack of public confidence turned financial panics into serious banking crises in October 1930, March 1931, and January of 1933. The heavy withdrawal of deposits in each crisis produced a wave of bank failures. The failures reinforced public distrust of banks, causing each crisis to become worse than its predecessor. The problem continued to become progressively worse until in March of 1933, the bank holiday and the Emergency Banking Act caused all banks to close for at least one week to protect the system from massive deposit withdrawals.[6]

Fiscal Policy and the Hoover Administration

The federal government's policies were no more effective than those of the Federal Reserve during the early years of the depression. The framework of international trade collapsed as most nations, now caught up in a world wide depression, attempted to export their unemployment by raising tariffs. The United States through the Smooth-Hawley Tariff of 1930, raised its import rates and extended the range of dutiable imports to levels comparable to the high tariff era which existed before 1900. However, this strategy only served to increase worldwide unemployment, because if all major trading nations increase their tariff, no country can gain in the long run, and the economic efficiency of international comparative advantage is lost to all countries.

As for the administration, President Hoover believed that the federal government was obligated to maintain a balanced budget and that to allow revenues to fall short of expenditures for any prolonged period was a prescription for national bankruptcy. Hoover, also believed that relief payment to the unemployed without some form of work expectation, would ruin the moral fiber of the recipients.

The immediate reaction of the Hoover administration to the depression was a cut in taxes and an increase in spending on public works projects. However, the budget surplus of 1929, soon became a deficit. The administration's response to the federal deficit was to reduce spending, but the deficits continued, and in 1932 a large tax increase was enacted. Since higher taxes could only reduce an already inadequate volume of private spending, this policy was misguided. Nevertheless, it was supported by both houses of congress.[7]

In summary, there was probably no one singular culprit that was responsible for the great depression of 1929. The depression was the result of a series of events, each adding to the length and magnitude of America's longest and most devastating economic downturn.

CHAPTER 12

THE GREAT DEPRESSION AND
THE NEW DEAL (1929-1939)

"The only thing we have to fear is fear itself." —Franklin Delano Roosevelt

CLASSICAL ECONOMICS AND DEPRESSION

A singular and significant feature of the classical system was the lack of a theory of depression. The equilibrium to which the economy adjusted itself was one of full employment. This was the result to which movements in wages and prices inevitably led.

From the classical theory there could not be a remedy for a depression, if depression had been ruled out by the theory. Consequently, when the great depression struck after the stock market crash in October of 1929, economists stood aside. This was something to be waited out.

Through what remained the presidency of Herbert Hoover, until March of 1933, the economic policy of the United States followed the classical design. Recovery was expected and compulsively predicted. There was no need for action to advance the inevitable. Herbert Hoover was, in fact, in complete accord with the accepted economic ideas of his time.

However, in 1933, there was a full fledged depression that had three undeniable features as follows:

- The first was the relentless deflation in prices, with its bankrupting effect on industry and agriculture. This was especially severe on any industry that had high fixed costs.

- The second feature was unemployment. By 1933 the unemployment rate was over one quarter of the working population.

- The third was the hardship depression brought for especially vulnerable groups of the old, the young, and those in poor health.

FRANKLIN D. ROOSEVELT AND THE NEW DEAL

When Franklin D. Roosevelt became president in March of 1933, the first broad line of his policy addressed the problem of prices; the second sought to aid the unemployed by providing them with jobs; and the third attempted to mitigate the hardships of the vulnerable. In this last line of policy was the idea of the Welfare State, which had come earlier to Europe and was by this time on its way to the United States. However, Roosevelt did not develop a new approach to stimulating a depressed economy in a vacuum. Roosevelt received assistance from a new breed of economic advisors who were not restrained by classical beliefs.

In Roosevelt's gubernatorial (New York) years, a small group of scholars rallied to support him. The economic advisors among these new scholars were from Columbia University and were part of a group of Roosevelt's advisors, who were often referred to as the "brain trust." Two members of the Roosevelt brain trust, Rex Tugwell and Adolf Berle, were figures of particular distinction. Rex Tugwell was a key participant in developing strategy for Roosevelt's presidential election and later served in the administration. With his academic credentials, Tugwell was in a good position to persuade Roosevelt that he could break with the classical tradition.

The second economic figure in the brain trust was Adolf Berle, who like Tugwell, was a professor at Columbia University. A lawyer, not an economist, by profession, Berle was the author, along with Gardner C. Means, a young economist at Columbia, of an attack on the classical system of economic analysis.

The Berle and Means publication was entitled "The Modern Corporation and Private Property." It was about the management and control of the large enterprise. Their book described the current concentration of business in America. According to Berle and Means, the professional managers were now extensively in control of the modern business enterprise and their objective was often self-enrichment. This is a subject that has been previously noted as one of the reasons why major industries in the 1920's produced more than could reasonably be sold.

In the imperfect or monopolistic competition of Joan Robinson and Edward Chamberlin, the capitalist or entrepreneur still ruled and profits were still maximized. The results were not socially optimal, but they could be adapted to classical thought. The views of Berle and Means could not.

Following Roosevelt's election to the presidency, Rex Tugwell and Gardner Means immediately took government posts. Berle joined the ranks a little later. By the time Roosevelt came to office, prices had been in a devastating three year slump, and from across the country there were appeals for government action to reverse the trend. One of the first reactions by the Roosevelt administration was an attempt to stabilize the economy. These actions took the form of declaring a bank holiday in March of 1933, suspension of gold payments to increase exports, and policies developed to stabilize prices.

ACTIONS TO STABILIZE THE ECONOMY

Stabilizing the Banking Industry

By 1921, there were over 31,000 separate commercial banks in the United States. That number was reduced considerably because over 14,800 of these banks had failed by 1934. In 1932, there was a decline in the rate of bank failures from the previous year, but as 1933 began, pessimism started to set in and a new wave of bank failures threatened the collapse of the entire system. When the depression began, demand deposits held with commercial banks or savings and loan associations, were not insured by the federal government. Because they feared a loss of deposits if their bank failed, large numbers of people were going, into banks and demanding their deposits. In a fractional banking system, such as ours, deposits are put to work making loans. This results in a balance sheet where deposits are vastly in excess of actual currency. Banking is based on the theory that all depositors will not want to withdraw their funds at the same time. However, if a majority of a bank's depositors demanded an immediate withdrawal of funds, the bank would become insolvent and therefore, would be required to stop doing business.

By March 4, of 1933, a run on the nation's banks caused such a financial panic that most of the banks in all thirty-eight states were forced to close. On March 6, 1933, President Roosevelt declared a "Bank Holiday," which specifically forbid the nations' banks to make any payments in cash. The major purpose of closing the banks was to give them the opportunity to liquidate some of their assets, especially government securities. The Federal Reserve banks attempted to assist the commercial banks with their liquidity problems by issuing more Federal Reserve notes against the government bonds that were held by the banks. The banks were audited by government inspectors who were instructed to take an optimistic view of the current values of bank assets.

As banks were found to be in satisfactory condition, they were issued licenses by the treasury and then allowed to reopen. About 2,000 banks never reopened their doors after the holiday; however, public confidence in the banking industry was restored and the outflow of currency was halted. Cash actually started to flow into the banks, and the wave of bank failures was over. As the banks began to reopen, the government began to take steps to improve the quality of their assets. Large volumes of bank loan assets were sold to federal government agencies such as the Reconstruction Finance Corporation, the Home Owners' Loan Corporation, and the Federal Farm Mortgage Corporation. These agencies also made loans to commercial banks, and purchased some of their debt and equity issues.

While all of the changes to the banking industry outlined above were important, the most important and enduring improvement, was the creation of the Federal

Deposit Insurance Corporation and the Federal Savings and Loan Insurance Corporation. These two federal agencies provided the commercial banks and savings and loan associations with federally backed insurance against individual bank deposits. All members of the Federal Reserve System were required to join the Federal Deposit Insurance Corporation, and nearly all of the state chartered banks became members on a voluntary basis. The result was a major improvement in the stability of the commercial banking system. Bank runs all but disappeared because depositors were assured of the safety of their deposits.[1]

The Suspension of Gold Payments

In the first days of the New Deal, Roosevelt ordered the suspension of gold payments by the banks and forbade the hoarding of gold. This action suspended the gold standard in the United States. Also, the order prohibited the holding of gold, in anticipation of its appreciation in dollars. Although commodity prices stirred upward briefly in the summer of 1933, there was nothing in the president's action that added to purchasing power and demand.

In the autumn of 1933 the administration began to offer progressively higher prices for newly mined gold, which was brought to the treasury to be traded into dollars. The dollar fell on the foreign markets as foreign currencies, which were still on the gold standard, could now be exchanged for more dollars. This resulted in a depreciation of the dollar. As a result of the cheaper American money there were some improvements in exports. However, the results of this action to stimulate export was minimal as the United States in the 1930's was basically a domestic economy.

ACTIONS TO RAISE PRICES

The first action to increase prices was a direct one that took place through the National Industrial Recovery Act. Under the provisions of this act, sellers were brought together to agree on minimum prices. They, in turn, were required to allow labor to bargain collectively and in good faith. Oligopoly, not competition, was now recognized as the industrial norm. Therefore, it was thought, that individual firms could strongly influence their own prices. The National Industrial Recovery Act provided the organizational framework of this program by instituting over 700 industrial codes that sought to stabilize production, employment, and prices. By agreement, the firms joining in an NRA code acted to arrest the downward spiral of prices. Market competition to reduce price was proclaimed by the NRA to be against the public interest, and monopoly; the conceded flaw in the classical system, was proclaimed acceptable. In fact, the NRA codes sought to create a monopoly pricing structure. At first, the ambitious effort at industrial coordination appeared to work; production, employment, and income grew during much of 1933. However, planning as a solution to the recovery problem, never got a long-run test because the political difficulties of reconciling the conflicting interests of large manufacturers, small businessmen, and labor served seriously to reduce the effectiveness of the NRA. Then, on May 27, 1935, the Supreme Court invalidated the code making provisions of the National Recovery Act, thus bringing the experiment to an abrupt end.

The second major effort at price enhancement occurred in agriculture. Beginning in the last century, the United States government and the states, through land grant colleges and universities, had been supporting agricultural experiment and education. In the United States Department of Agriculture in Washington, there was a large and intellectually active center of research in the highly regarded Bureau of Agricultural Economics.

The Bureau of Agricultural Economics, in its examination of farm prices, agricultural credit, farm markets and farm management, was highly pragmatic. This method of operation was, at the time, necessary to assure funding from Congress. Because of their practical orientation, these economists were not committed to the classical system. From the 1920's on, the principle concern of the Bureau was with economic problems, particularly the low prices paid to the farmers. Various scholars from Minnesota, Massachusetts, Montana, and California began an intense discussion of how to raise farm prices. Government, not just the marketplace, it was thought, should have a role in determining farm prices.

With the arrival of Roosevelt in 1933, the agricultural economists also came to Washington. Under their   direction,   the   Agricultural   Adjustment Administration (The Triple A) was born. One major provision of this act was a policy that sets minimum prices for most agricultural products,   reduced farm production, and provided for the storage of any production that exceeded the established limit.

ACTIONS TO IMPROVE EMPLOYMENT

Most of Roosevelt's "New Deal" programs were aimed at treating the symptoms of the depression and not at finding a cure. While the cause of the depression was greatly reduced demand, for both industrial and consumer goods and services, the result was severe unemployment. The Roosevelt administration, unlike the Hoover administration, accepted responsibility for easing the plight of the unemployed. In May of 1933, the Federal Emergency Relief Administration, with Harry Hopkins as its director, officially came into existence. The purpose of the FERA was to assist the unemployed. The federal government decided that federal efforts to aid the unemployed would be concentrated on finding jobs. The Federal Emergency Relief Administration was empowered to make grants to the states to support their work relief efforts. Such FERA programs as the Civil Works Administration, the Works Progress Administration, and the Civilian Conservation Corps provided several million people with jobs each year.[2]

While some of these programs were said to be mere excuses to provide income to the unemployed, the basic concept was a response to the obvious hardships caused by the depression. The programs for the most part were designed to provide employment and income; however, many times the resulting products were not of a material consideration. The exception to this was the Public Works Administration. The responsibility of the PWA was not just to create jobs but to invest in public infrastructure, such as roads and dams. The primary emphasis of the PWA, under Secretary of the Interior Harold Ickes, was on the importance of the projects themselves. Every effort was made to complete these projects as efficiently as possible, regardless of the employment effects.

Although the PWA provided about seven hundred thousand jobs in 1936, this was far below the nearly five million employed under FERA programs at their maximum in 1934. However, many important and lasting improvements to our infrastructure such as the Hoover Dam on the Colorado River, was a direct result of the projects completed under the Federal Emergency Relief Administration. In total, during the depression years, federally funded employment programs, were directly

responsible for creating more than eight million jobs.
While FERA projects were not a cure for the headache of
unemployment, for those employed by the program, it was
certainly a great aspirin.

ACTIONS TO RELIEVE THE HARDSHIPS OF THE DEPRESSION

One of the most significant responses to the Great
Depression in the United States was the creation of the
welfare state. It would be the creation of the welfare state
that would most endure from the Roosevelt
administration. However, the welfare state was not
conceived in America. The welfare state was born in
Germany of Count Otto Von Bismarck (1815-1898). In the
Prussian and German tradition, the state was competent,
beneficent and highly prestigious. In 1884 and 1887,
welfare legislation was passed in the Reichstag. The
legislation provided for accident, sickness, old-age, and
disability insurance.

A more comprehensive step in this process came in
Britain twenty-five years after Bismarck's great
initiative. Under the sponsorship of Lloyd George, the
Chancellor of the Exchequer, legislation was passed in
1911 that provided for sickness and invalidism insurance
and then unemployment insurance. A non-contributory
system of old-age pensions had previously been written
into law. In a very real sense, the success of Lloyd George
in 1910 and 1911 paved the way for the American action
a quarter of a century later. John R. Commons, of the
University of Wisconsin, is the American companion to
Bismarck and Lloyd George on the development of the
welfare state.

John Commons' greatest achievement was in
assembling and leading a group of colleagues who set out

in a highly practical way to redress the evident social problems of the time. Their initiative began with the Wisconsin State Government in Madison. The Wisconsin Plan included a pioneer state civil service law, the effective regulation of public utility rates (a monopoly), a limit on usurious interest charges, support to the trade unions, and a state income tax. Also, an unemployment compensation system was developed in 1932. This had a penetrating effect on economic and political attitudes. This was the most important contribution to the federal legislation on the subject of welfare reforms, that came 3 years later.[3]

The Social Security Act

The Social Security Act of 1935 provided three types of relief from the hardship caused by the depression. First, there was direct aid to those unable to work: the old, handicapped, and dependent children. Secondly, it provided a system of accumulating income for retired workers; and finally, the act provided for unemployment insurance. The portion of the social security program that provided direct money payments to the needy was the forerunner of our current welfare system. The Social Security Act was the first explicit recognition in the United States that, in a market economy, there may be persons unable to provide for themselves.

The Social Security Act, which provided pensions for retired workers, was to be financed by taxes on both individual incomes and employers' payrolls. The contributions to fund worker pensions were to be shared equally between the employers and employees. However, since a payroll tax increases production costs, this expense would eventually be passed on to the consumer

in higher prices. Social Security, however, did remove
some of the hardships of old age. No longer was it
necessary for people to work until they were almost dead.
Prior to the Social Security Act the elderly who lacked
adequate savings, often wiped out by the depression,
faced a rather poor assortment of choices. They could
depend on their children or turn to the public authorities
for support. The Social Security Act provided a system of
forced savings, with a federal government guarantee that
the potential benefits could not be taken away by future
depressions.

Another part of the Social Security Act was a
system designed to provide income to the unemployed. A
tax was levied on employers' payrolls and used to
establish a fund from which payments could be made to
those out of work. The length of time over which
payments would be dispensed was limited for the purpose
of providing incentives for the unemployed to seek work.
The plan was designed to encourage each state to set up
its own program and to ensure conformity among the
various state programs.

The principle that the Social Security (old-age
pensions) accounts must be sustained by their own tax
levies has remained nearly unchallenged ever since. The
response from classical economists to the Social Security
Act was relatively mild. Unemployment and economic
disabilities of age did exist; perhaps these flaws should be
remedied. The old-age pensions paid their own way; they
were an Insurance, not a radical thing.

In total, the changes made by the Roosevelt
administration during the depression years, in the basic
workings of the American economy, were modest. The
emphasis was largely on saving the market system,
rather than replacing it with a socialist system. The
United States has always taken its social reforms the way

the frontier took religion or   the way its younger population took a dose of castor oil. America continued to attack the symptoms of business cycles, usually in large doses, and only long after the need for a cure had become overwhelmingly clear.[4]

CHAPTER 13

KEYNESIAN ECONOMICS

"In the long run we are all dead." —John Maynard Keynes

ECONOMICS IN ANTICIPATION OF KEYNES

In 1936, the fourth year of the Roosevelt administration's "New Deal," a very temporary recovery developed. However, 17 percent of the American labor force was still unemployed, and real gross national product was only 95 percent of the 1929 level. In 1937, there was another sharp slump. Since there was already a depression, a new name had to be found, and it was called a recession. Classical economic theory continued relentlessly to predict an eventual recovery from the depression. However, by this time a large portion of the population was beginning to wonder if the economy would ever return to normal. What was needed was a new theory to explain why the economy was not adjusting to lower wages and lower interest rates and therefore, returning to a level of full employment as the classical economists had promised. The public, in general, was just running out of patience. A new economic theory was required to explain the current circumstances. The new economic theory was developed by the distinguished British economist John Maynard Keynes in his 1936 publication, "The General Theory of Employment, Interest and Money." The essentials of Keynes' case were designed to release the fiscal policies of the British treasury and the Roosevelt administration from its classical economic constraints. The modern economy, Keynes held, does not necessarily find its equilibrium at full employment; it can find it with unemployment, i.e., the underemployment equilibrium.[1]

According to Keynes, it is not necessary to wait for the economy to self adjust to a depression. The government can, and should, take steps to overcome a shortage of aggregate demand. In a depression the desire of the federal government to balance their budget must give way to the need to stimulate aggregate demand. However, there were economists, who, by their actions, expressed the need for government intervention to stimulate demand well before Keynes. The most notable was the case of Sweden. Here for two generations, an alert group of economists took part in critical discussions of economic ideas as they were related to public affairs.

The independent minded Swedish scholars were men   such   as   Gunnar   Myrdal,   Bertil   Ohlin,   Erik Lundberg, and Dag Hammarskjold. Dag Hammarskjold was later appointed to be the Secretary General of the United Nations. While these men all had full knowledge of the classical theory, they were more concerned with the practical problems of the Swedish economy. Instead on being constrained by a theory that just was not working, they advocated the deliberate use of the government budget to sustain demand and employment. The worldwide depression of the 1930's led the Stockholm economists to abandon hope that actions of the Central Bank to lower interest rates would materially expand investment expenditure and, therefore, aggregate demand. Instead, they held that in good times the public budget should be balanced, but in depression the budget should be unbalanced deliberately so that the excess of expenditure over income would sustain demand and employment. All of this was being done in Stockholm in the 1930's, well in advance of Keynes. By the middle of the decade, word of developments in Sweden was finding its way to Britain and to the United States. Sweden, with its now well developed social welfare system, was being pictured as the "Middle Way" between the classical economic system and Socialism and Communism.[2]

Finally, in anticipation of Keynes, there was a highly practical application of government deficit spending going on in the United States. Through most of the 1930's, the federal government ran a substantial deficit. Beginning in 1933, this was increased by expending for direct relief, public works, and other public forms of employment. This type of employment was managed through such agencies as the Federal Emergency Relief Administration, the Public Works Administration, and the Works Progress Administration. By 1936, the federal revenue receipts were only 59 percent of government expenditures. The deficit was four and two tenths of a percentage of the current gross national product. The hardships brought about by the depression had already made what Keynes was to urge necessary.

JOHN MAYNARD KEYNES: THE MAN BEHIND THE THEORY

Early advocacy of Keynesian policy included strong attempts at persuasion by Keynes. However, none of this earlier effort ranked in importance with the publication of "The General Theory," as his book began to be known, in 1936. It was, as Keynes had intended it to be, a lethal blow at the classical conclusions as to demand, production and employment and the resulting policy. Say's Law was dead, and a new theory developed by John Maynard Keynes had arrived to take its place.

The General Theory, owed much of its acceptance to the Great Depression and to the failure of classical economics to contend with the problems brought about by that unsettling event. However, the acceptance that this book received owed much to Keynes' ability and reputation. No economist is ever more highly regarded than he regards himself or followed with more certainty than that which he himself manifests. The affect that The General Theory had in changing economic analysis owed much to the background, reputation and prestige of its author.

John Maynard Keynes (1883 - 1945)

John Maynard Keynes was born in 1883 into a Puritanical Victorian home. John Neville Keynes, his father, was a well-known economist at Cambridge University; but Keynes, unlike his parents, had little use for puritan values. Keynes attended King's College at Cambridge where he developed friendships and liaisons with other intellectuals and was invited to join the university's most select and secretive society, the Apostles. Later, Keynes and many of the other Apostles, formed the Bloomsbury Group, whose Anti-Victorian, and Bohemian attitudes powerfully affected the evolution of British culture.[3]

Keynes originally attended Cambridge to study mathematics. His introduction to economics was through Alfred Marshall's "The Principles of Economics." After a brief departure from Cambridge, Keynes returned to accept Marshall's offer as a lecturer in economics. In his early years at Cambridge, his economic beliefs did not extend far beyond those of Marshall and the classical tradition. During the 1920's, Keynes continued to teach, edit, write, and advise the British government. He corresponded with most of the prominent politicians, academicians, and artists of his time. A lot of skill and a little bit of luck assisted him as he accumulated a fortune trading in stocks and commodities. There is a question that is often asked of economists, which is; "If you know so much why aren't you rich?" Only David Ricardo would rank higher than Keynes in becoming rich and most other economists would flunk this test miserably.

Keynes on Savings and Investment

In economics, Keynes originally focused mostly on monetary policy, especially in his "Treatise on Money," published in 1930. The Treatise tied together much of Keynes' earlier work on investment, with some new discussion of the connection between savings and investment. The Treatise examined the question of what made the economy operate so unevenly. The question had received the attention of economists for decades. Malthus had considered that savings could somehow result in a general economic glut, but most other early nineteenth century economists rejected the idea. In the world of Ricardo and Mill, virtually the only people who could save were the wealthy and their savings were usually invested in their own businesses. Therefore, saving was properly called accumulation for it represented the amassing of a sum of money and the immediate use of those funds in purchasing new capital equipment.

After the American Civil War, the structure of the American and European economies changed. The distribution of wealth improved as those who had the technical skills required to operate the new factory machines could demand higher wages. At the same time, business organizations became larger and were increasingly searching beyond their owners for more investment capital. Commercial banks also entered the equation by performing the function of funneling consumer savings into business investment. Hence savings and investment became divorced from each other as they became separate operations carried out by different groups of people. However, this separation of savings and investing often led to economic problems because the funneling of savings into investment is not automatic. Business firms usually need savings to fund the expansion of their operations. This is because business cash flows are not sufficient to provide it with enough capital to build a new factory or to purchase an expensive piece of equipment. Consumer saving is not spending, because it reduces national income. If businesses invest the savings of consumers the economy usually grows; however, if these savings are not invested it could lead to depression. The Treatise was a masterful analysis of this seesaw of savings and investment and its potential effect on economic stability.

The Fall of Classical Economics

The early 1930's brought challenges to economics so perplexing that Keynes soon began to realize that he could not rest on his previous publications. From 1929 to 1933 in the United States, Adam Smith's invisible hand of the free market kicked prosperity in the backside. Unemployment went from 3 percent to 25 percent, national income was reduced by almost half and the economy came to a screeching halt. The popular song writer Yip Harburg echoed the frustration and disparity of the nation in his song "Brother, Can You Spare a Dime?"

The British treasury and the American government, especially under Hoover, prescribed patience and promised recovery in the long run. However, Keynes blasted the treasury view as he wrote in his "Tract on Monetary Reform." What is the point of having such a government? "In the long run we are all dead." Keynes justified the advice he gave to politicians in his 1936 masterpiece. The General Theory smashed the classical theory of economics and presented a new framework for a new field of study to be called macroeconomics.[4]

THE ECONOMICS OF JOHN MAYNARD KEYNES

In the General Theory, Keynes denounces the classical model of a self adjusting economy. According to Keynes, the most nincompoopish belief was in Say's Law that, as previously discussed, states that the production of goods and services generates enough income to workers and suppliers for all the products to be purchased. However, if someone believes in Say's Law, according to Keynes, they cannot believe in long-term unemployment or depressions. The simultaneous occurrence of a self adjusting   mechanism   to   prevent   long-term unemployment, and the great depression of 1929 is, by definition, mutually exclusive. Only a schizophrenic could believe in both. Even Keynes would not accuse his colleagues of being schizophrenics. He gave them the benefit of the doubt and called them stupid.[5]

Keynes developed a two-pronged attack against the prime positions of the classical system. According to Keynes, the self adjusting system of classical economics did not work because there was no link between savings and investment and wages were not flexible. On the subject of savings and investment, Keynes held that consumers and businesses save and invest for entirely different reasons. Households save for many different reasons, but what determines how much they are able to save is their disposable income. Interest rates have very little to do with the amount that consumers save. Businesses may invest more if interest rates are low because some projects may become profitable with low interest rates. However, a business invests in fixed assets based on future expectations. If a business believes that there is no market for its products, they will not invest to increase production capacity. This business decision will be made without regard to the rate of interest.

If household savings exceed business investment, a decline in aggregate demand will result. Business inventories will increase and production will decrease as a result of reduced demand for the company's products. Companies will react to the reduced demand by reducing the size of their work force, leading to even less consumption. As income falls, consumers, especially those out of work, will start to liquidate their savings. Savings will eventually drop enough to equal investment, but not necessarily at full employment.

The central ideas of Keynes' theory are that the decisive problem of economics is how the levels of output and employment are determined. Keynes argued that there is a direct relationship between income and savings. As consumer disposable incomes increase, savings increase, and as incomes decrease, the portion of total income saved decreases. Keynes assumed that each time a consumer gets an additional dollar of income they have two choices; they can spend or save the income. Keynes calls the part spent the marginal propensity to consume, and the part saved the marginal propensity to save. When analyzing the U.S. gross domestic product, it becomes apparent that the largest portion of expenditure, i.e., 67 percent of total GDP in 1992, is personal consumption. Therefore, if incomes are reduced, as a result of a reduction in employment, consumption will also fall. In addition, since households make up the largest portion of total expenditures, a reduction of consumer expenditures will have the greatest effect on aggregate demand.

Businesses also buy goods and services. By investing in fixed assets and additions to inventory, businesses account for another substantial part of aggregate demand, i.e., 14.5 percent of GDP in 1992. However, the most important reason that businesses change their investment plans is their future profit expectations. Businessmen do not change their investment plans in response to short run changes in interest rates, and they especially do not increase their investment in production capacity when there is a reduced demand for their products.

Therefore, in order for an economy to operate to its potential production capacity with full employment, households must provide consumption and businesses must expand their investment in fixed assets and inventory. The expansion must be adequate for sales of goods to be brought into equilibrium with the amount of items produced. Thus, if people were to spend all of their income, the marginal propensity to consume would be one. If all income is consumed, then the economy would function according to the classical economist self adjusting model. However, since people save some of their income, business investment must make up for the lack of personal consumption. If business investment does not equal savings, output will be greater than sales, inventories build, and employers will lay off workers. Therefore, according to Keynes, depressions are caused by a drastic reduction in demand and one of the main culprits is savings.

In addition to his views of the relationship between savings and investment, Keynes did not agree with the classical theory on the flexibility of wages and prices. When unemployment occurred in the classical context, the accepted cause was wages that were too high or too rigid. With Keynes, this was no longer so; what was true for the individual employer was not true for all. If all employers   were to lower wages in a time of unemployment, the flow of purchasing power, the aggregate of effective demand, would diminish. The result of this reduced purchasing power would be that consumers would not have enough income to buy the products produced. Therefore, unemployment could not be blamed on high wages or on the supply controlling effects of labor unions. Unemployment is a result of decreasing aggregate demand. Thus, according to Keynes, the equilibrium situation in the economy is not necessarily at full employment; it can be at different and even severe levels of unemployment. This new theory by Keynes became known as the Underemployment Equilibrium.

The Keynesian Solution

In the past, critics of the capitalist system angrily pointed their finger at the robber barons. Keynes suggested that consumers who insist on increasing their savings, especially in times of recession, do more harm than the nefarious industrialist. In addition, this wicked deed of savings has a tendency to compound itself through what Keynes called the "Multiplier." This theory states that an increase or decrease in spending has an affect on the economy that is greater than the original change in expenditures. This multiplier affect occurs because as money is spent on goods and services, those who receive the revenue now have additional income, part of which they spend.

Keynes provided a simple formula to calculate the multiplier with the key being the marginal propensity to consume:

Multiplier = 1/[1-MPC] or 1/MPS

According to Keynes, the higher the degree of consumption, the higher the multiplier affect would be. On the basis of this formula, Keynes concluded that small reductions in investment may severely pressure the economy as a whole. Also, if deficient demand is the cause of a recession, the cure must be to stimulate more spending. However, if the MPC is known, spending can be injected into the economy, which will multiply throughout and end the recession by filling the original gap between output and consumption.[6]

Keynes estimated the United States multiplier to be about 2.5 times, and based on this estimate, he advocated massivefederal spending programs. His recommendations were made in letters written directly to

Roosevelt as well as publishing articles in magazines. According to Keynes, the United States could stimulate its economy directly through government spending projects. However, the amount of the injection could be less than the shortfall of consumer and business spending. For example, with a multiplier of 2.5, if the difference between the potential output and the actual output of an economy was $1 billion, the government would only have to inject $400 million in new expenditures to fill the output gap. Therefore, Keynes urged Roosevelt to raise the level of government spending. This meant that the federal government would have to run a deliberate deficit in order to pull the economy out of a depression. This alone would break the underemployment equilibrium, by increasing aggregate demand, through investing the savings of the private sector. It was a powerful affirmation of the wisdom of what was already being accomplished by the Roosevelt administration in order to relieve the hardships caused by the depression.

Keynes and Mars the God of War

For the Keynesian system World War II had major consequences. First, it brought a younger breed of economists into positions of power in Washington. Secondly, World War II demonstrated beyond comparison the power of Keynesian economics. In addition, these young Keynesian economists had the support of such established authority as Alvin Hansen, who came to the Federal Reserve Board, and John Maynard Keynes, who arrived from England to represent the British government.

The final contribution of World War II to the propagation of Keynes' beliefs was that it showed what his economics could accomplish through fiscal policy. Fiscal policy was defined as the actions of the federal government in changing expenditures and tax collections for the purpose of stimulating or slowing down an economy. From 1939 to 1944, the wartime peak, gross national product in constant dollars (1972 dollars adjusted for inflation), increased from $320 billion to $569 billion. Personal consumption expenditures increased from $220 to $255 billion. Unemployment was approximately 17.2 percent of the civilian labor force in 1939; in 1944 it was a nominal 1.2 percent. Overall, in the last full year of the war, Americans were living better than ever before. This was the result of the upward pressure of public demand on the economy. The federal government purchases of goods and services, in these years, increased from $22.8 billion in 1939 to $269.7 billion in 1944. No one could seriously doubt that Mars the God of War, had demonstrated how fiscal policy, could be used to stimulate an economy.

Also, World War II had a great and everlasting effect on the tax system of the United States. Taxes, by modern standards, had been insignificant before 1941. In 1939, federal revenues were just under $5 billion; by 1945, they were in excess of $44 billion. With the war, and in justification of these taxes, came the notion of an approach to the equity of sacrifice: the poor would pay with their military service or their toil; the affluent, especially the non-serving rich, would pay with their taxes. The principle of a strongly progressive tax, effectively an income redistribution, is still a major topic of political debate in the 1990's.

As the World War II had affirmed Keynes, so it had dealt a heavy blow to classical laissez faire. In the economics profession a new view of government and a new reliance on its intervention would be one of the major economic consequences of the war.[7]

KEYNES AFTER KEYNES

After the war the Keynesian economists retained their power in Washington and had found allies in the business world. Full employment would no longer be considered the autonomous consequence of the competitive economy. Keynes proved that the underemployment equilibrium was possible, and in the future it would be the responsibility of the federal government to ensure full employment.

In January of 1945, with the end of the war in sight, four senators, Robert F. Wagner of New York, James E. Murray of Montana, Elbert Thomas of Utah and Joseph O'Mahoney of Wyoming, sponsored a bill that was designed to guarantee full employment. However, because of strong reaction by business interest, the bill as originally written could not be passed. Full employment was therefore reduced to a goal of high employment. The Employment Act was finally passed by congress and signed by President Truman in 1946. The bill stated that it now was the recognized responsibility of the federal government to provide an environment where those able, willing, and seeking to work, could find employment.

In addition, the Employment Act of 1946 created the Council of Economic Advisors to consult with the president on measures to enhance employment and economic policy. The passage of the employment Act of 1946, with its provision for a council of economic advisors, was very important to the history of economics. It established economics firmly in the center of modern American administration.[8]

The quarter century following the end of World War II, was very good in economic performance. In only three of these twenty-five years did the American gross domestic product fail to increase. Reinforcing domestic expenditures in the United States was an inflow of purchasing power from abroad as the country had a strongly favorable trade balance. After World War II, the United States was the only major industrial power that remained intact. This put America in a position of economic leadership that had no comparison in the twentieth century.

The World War II demands required a sizable advance in the growth of the economy and an enormous transfer of resources from peacetime to wartime needs. The average level of federal expenditure from 1942 through 1945 amounted to roughly one half of the net national product. The federal government, in contrast to its performance during World War I, made a determined effort to control inflation. Roosevelt initiated a program of price controls and rationing in January of 1942 and the Truman administration maintained it until June of 1946. The primary vehicle for implementing price control was the Office of Price Administration (OPA). As a result of the efforts of the OPA, price increases averaged only 6.4 percent, from 1939 to 1948. This was the result of an effective enforcement campaign, the popularity of the general war effort, and the unusual willingness with which Americans accepted price controls and rationing.

One of the curiosities of the postwar expansion was that it defied a restrictive government fiscal policy. The curtailment of government expenditures that began in 1946 continued throughout 1948, with expenditures declining to about one third of what they had been in 1945. However, government tax receipts decreased by less than 10 percent. This resulted in a government surplus of $8.4 billion by 1948.

After World War II, there was a great deal of concern in the United States that the nation would return to the depression of the 1930's. However, during the war two major things occurred to prevent a continued depression. First, there was the elimination of unemployment, and secondly, an expansion of the total number of persons employed. The war effort required a tremendous expansion of the production of military equipment. With the bulk of the young men recruited to fight the war, it was necessary to recruit millions of women to work in the factories that produced military equipment. In addition, government rationing programs restricted the supply of consumer goods that were available to purchase. This pattern of increased revenue and reduced products to purchase resulted in a large increase in savings. The end of World War II brought with it a release of pent-up consumer demand following the lifting of wartime restrictions, especially with regard to consumer durable goods and housing. The combination of pent-up consumer demand and the lifting of wartime restrictions resulted in a large increase in consumer demand that eliminated any possibility of a renewed depression. Because of the large accumulation of money and other highly liquid assets to support this demand, the public would have spent a great deal more on peacetime goods and services had the government not run a surplus.

Another expansive force was the increase in the stock of money, which grew at a rate of slightly more than 4 percent per year between January 1946 and August 1948. The weakness of policy during the late 1940's and the 1950's was more in the management of fiscal policy than in the use of monetary mechanisms. The Federal Reserve Board maintained a rather consistent posture throughout the period, in effect, working to keep the nation's money stock growing at a reasonable stable rate, one upon which other institutions and individuals could depend.

In 1964, There was a deliberate attempt to use Keynesian economics to prevent the economy from entering into a recession. It was the tax reduction of that year. This idea to stimulate demand was begun earlier by President Kennedy, and signed into law after Kennedy's death by President Lyndon Johnson. The highest rate on the personal income tax was reduced to 70 percent. Also, there was a reduction in other lower income brackets and the basic rate on the corporate income tax was reduced. This tax reduction was deliberately designed to expand consumer purchasing power which would stimulate aggregate demand and avoid a budget surplus at full employment. Also, the Federal Reserve accommodated fiscal policy by instituting a moderately simulative monetary policy. The results of the federal government's use of fiscal policy to stimulate the economy, was that the unemployment rate declined from 6.7 percent in 1961 to 3.8 percent in 1966. The first attempt by the federal government to use fiscal policy to increase aggregate demand and therefore, to reduce unemployment was a success and resulted in only a slight increase in the rate of inflation.

CHAPTER 14

ECONOMIC MEASUREMENT
AND FORECASTING

"Forecasting is very difficult, especially if it's about the future." —Edgar Fielder.

NATIONAL INCOME ACCOUNTING

Once the concept of macroeconomics was developed by John Maynard Keynes in the "General Theory," it became essential to create a terminology to describe its aggregate elements. During the 1940's, many of those who had been converted to Keynesian economics set out to develop a terminology and to measure the entire system of final output in the United States. Their work was the starting point for what today is called National Income Accounting. Simon Kuznets and Richard Stone received a Nobel Prize in Economics for their efforts to define a set of rules and definitions for measuring total economic activity.

National income accounting provides a way of measuring the total output of an economy over a designated period. The Department of Commerce, which gathers the necessary statistics, provides a measurement of economic activity each quarter called the Gross Domestic Product (GDP). GDP is widely reported in the media each quarter as an annualized figure. For example, if GDP grew by 1 percent in the first quarter of 1996, this would equate to a projected growth of 4 percent for the entire year. In national income accounting, aggregate economic production is broken down into two kinds of output, consumption and investment.

Consumption consists of goods and services bought by households for their personal use, such as new cars, and household goods and services. These various goods and services are often referred to as consumer goods. Investment goods are those purchased by business firms to start or to increase their production, by individuals to purchase new homes and by the government to build public infrastructures such as highways and bridges.

Accounting by definition is based on certain identities. For example, in a business, revenue must equal the total cost of producing plus a profit or in some cases a loss. All costs and revenue are kept track of through the use of double entry bookkeeping. In the national income accounts, whenever things are produced, income goes to the people who participated in the production of those goods and services. In other words, individual wealth is created by the production of goods and services. In financial accounting terms, for every use of funds in producing a product, there must be a source for those funds. In the national income accounts, we can define GDP as expenditures as a use of funds and GDP as income as a source of funds. GDP as expenditures, is divided into four main categories: Consumption expenditures, gross private investment, government purchases, and net exports.

GDP as Expenditures

Consumption expenditures are the total of all goods and services that are purchased by households during the course of a single year. This category is further broken down into durable and non-durable goods. Durable goods are those products that last for periods greater than one year; for example, automobiles and household furniture. Non-durable goods are those that usually last for a period of less than one year. Consumption expenditures are by far the largest category of GDP.

Gross private investment expenditures are made by businesses and households for capital goods. When economists use the term investment, they refer to the nation's stock of capital assets. Financial assets such as corporate stocks and bonds are not considered capital assets. Gross private investment is broken down into two sub-categories called, fixed investment and changes in business inventory. Fixed investment is by far the largest portion of investment and includes investment in residential buildings, buildings used by business and government, and equipment such as machinery and computers. Inventory investment is the change in the aggregate value of the current stocks of finished goods that businesses have produced and have not yet sold.

Government purchases are divided into federal expenditures and state and local government purchases. Government purchases involve consumption and fixed investment as they can buy both bridges, highways, and pay their employees. The state and local government purchases combined are greater than the federal governments. However, the budget of the federal government is much larger than their total purchases. For example, for fiscal year 1996, total federal expenditures were about $1.597 trillion and total purchases were $523 billion. The reason is that the largest part of the federal budget involves transfer payments or entitlements. Transfer payments take money from some Americans and transfer it to others, for example, from tax payers to Medicare recipients. However, the government does not spend the money on purchases and therefore transfer payments are not part of the GDP.[1]

Net exports are the final value of all goods and services that are sold to foreign individuals, businesses and governments less the amount of goods and services that are purchased from foreign sources. If we sell more goods and services abroad than we buy there is a positive balance of trade and as in recent years, if we buy more than we sell, a negative net export figure is entered into the GDP accounts.

GDP as Income

Domestic income is the total income earned by the residents and businesses in a country. However, the United States' federal government does not report domestic income in the GDP accounts. The government instead reports national income. National income is the total income earned by the citizens and businesses of a country. Since GDP is based on domestic income an adjustment to account for the foreign income that is paid and received must be made to reconcile the two methods of accounting. To move from domestic income to national income, you must add the difference between investment income received from abroad minus the income earned by foreigners. This adjustment to domestic income is called the net foreign factor and is necessary to convert gross domestic product to gross national product so that national income and expenditures can be compared.

National income consists of, compensation paid to employees, rents paid to individuals, interest payments paid by businesses to individuals, and business profits. Compensation paid to employees consists of wages and fringe benefits paid to individuals, adjusted for government income taxes, social security and unemployment insurance deductions. Compensation to employees makes up the largest category of GDP as income.

Rents are the income that is received by individuals for letting other people use their property. Rents received by business firms are not considered here because they are a part of the income and therefore the profit of businesses.

Interest payments are the income that businesses pay to households that have purchased financial assets from the firms. The largest providers of interest payments to households are the financial institutions that hold individual demand and time deposits.

Profits are the amounts left over after a business makes payments to the factors of production. Corporate profits are either paid out to shareholders in the form of dividends or held by the corporation as retained earnings. However, both dividends and retained earnings are owned by stockholders. Therefore, for national income accounting purposes, both are considered to be household income.[2]

To equate national income to gross national product, two additional adjustments must be made. The GDP as income accounts reflect net investment and GDP as expenditures show gross investment. To reconcile the two accounts, depreciation expenditures must be subtracted from gross investment. Also, GDP as expenditure contains indirect business taxes. Indirect business taxes include retail sales taxes, excise taxes, business property taxes, customs duties and license fees. These are all expenses of doing business, but they are not income flows to the factors of production and therefore, is not considered as part the of GDP as income accounts.

The table 14-1 is a source and use of funds statement for the year 1996. This statement shows in detail how the two accounts are reconciled. However, in calculating GDP using two different methods, there are bound to be some slight differences. These differences are reconciled by an account that is called statistical discrepancies. These discrepancies are caused by the different methods that the Department of Commerce uses to calculate GDP.

BUSINESS FLUCTUATIONS

In order to make the mass amounts of historical economic data useful it is helpful to categorize the various forms of fluctuations and to develop techniques of analyzing them. Economists usually classify business fluctuations by the trend, cycles, and seasonal variations. Each of these fluctuations is a result of a different class of factors, and discovering the nature of these causes is important to economic forecasting.

Seasonal variations occur because of changes in business conditions from one season of the year to the next. A seasonal variation exists when there is a regular pattern of variation in the series and this change occurs over a period of time that is usually one year.

Table 14-1
National Income Accounting Source and Use of Funds
Statement 1996 (Dollars in Billions)

Source of Funds		Use of Funds	
GDP as Income	$	GDP as Expense	$
-----------------------	---------	-----------------------	--------
Wage and Benefits	$4,449	Durable goods	$ 632
Rental Income	$ 127	Non-Durable	$1,545
Interest Income	$ 403	Services	$2,975
	---------		--------
Household Income	$4,979	Consumer Exp.	$5,152
		Residential Inv.	$ 311
Corporate Profits	$ 654	Business Inv.	$ 791
Non-Corp. Profits	$ 518	Inventory Change	$ 15
	--------		--------
Business Income	$ 1,172	Investment Exp.	$1,117
National Income	$6,151	Govt. Purchases	
		Federal	$ 523
		State & Local	$ 883
Adjustments			--------
		Total Govt. Pur.	$1,406
Depreciation Exp.	$ 858		
Indirect Bus. Tax	$ 633	Exports	$ 855
Net Foreign Factor	$ -9	Imports	$ 954
Statistical Error	$ -57		
	---------		--------
Total Adjustments	$1,425	Net Exports	$ (99)
Total Sources	$7,576	Total Uses	$7,576
	=====		=====

Source: Survey of Current Business: April, 1997.

The trend is the persistent underlying movement that has taken place in a series of data over a period long enough to cover several business cycles. The long-term trend in the real gross domestic product (GDP adjusted for inflation), has been gradually rising at a fairly constant rate. Economic growth is the result of increasing the quantity and/or the quality of a country's factors of production. For example, in order to increase the size of the labor force either the population must grow and/or the quality of the labor force must improve.

A business cycle is the movement of some aggregate measure of economic activity upward or downward over time. The length of time of the cyclical movements will vary, and the magnitude of the movement upward or downward will differ over time. A business cycle can be divided into four phases as the economy fluctuates around the long-term growth trend. The peak of the cycle is the point which real output reaches a maximum. The period during which real output falls is known as the contraction phase. At the end of the contraction, real output reaches a minimum known as the trough of the cycle. After the trough, real output begins to grow again and the economy enters an expansion that lasts until a new peak is reached.

Joseph Schumpeter drew on the work of other economists and concluded that there were three distinct cycle lengths. He named the cycles after the economist that was most associated with these cycles. The Kondratieff cycles consisted of long waves averaging fifty-four years and oscillated around the economic trend. The second of these cycles, Schumpeter called Juglar cycles. These cycles oscillate around the Kondratieff waves and are nine to ten years in duration. Schumpeter named the third cycle, Kitchin cycles which lasted about forty months. The forty month cycle approximates the average length of most post World War II short term business cycles. The principle reason for the Kitchin cycles is the accumulation and eventual reduction of business inventories as aggregate demand changes. However, longer cycles are affected more by the level of investment in long-term fixed capital and business innovations.

Innovations, according to Schumpeter, can be put into five classes, which require the introduction into the economic system of one or more of the following:

• New products, capital goods or consumer goods.

• New methods of producing goods or services.

• New markets for commodities.

• The exploration of newly discovered sources of raw materials.

• New means of organizing business activity.

According to Schumpeter, the first Kondratieff wave started in the late 1780's and was associated with the industrial revolution and the development of steam power, iron and cotton textile mills. The second wave started in the late 1840's as a result of the expansion of the railroads. This expansion of railroad transportation created opportunities for mass marketing. The third Kondratieff cycle, started around the turn of the twentieth century. This cycle marked the introduction of electricity into the homes and factories and with the mass assembly of automobiles.[3]

In modern times, we can make a good case for the fourth Kondratieff wave in the invention of the jet airplane and the microcomputer. The invention of the microprocessor in 1971 by Intel has changed the organization of every business from the small establishment to the giant multinational corporation. The jet airplane brought with it tourism, which by the 1960's was the largest single industry in the world and made multinational giants out of several American corporations.

An examination of economic history reveals periods of great prosperity, often lasting a decade or more, followed by equally long periods of very slow, zero or even negative growth. The most accepted explanation of this phenomenon is that technology and innovation opens up a whole level of opportunities for economic growth. Therefore, improving technology as a result of capital investment and innovation must be considered when developing an economic or business forecast.

ECONOMICS AND BUSINESS FORECASTING

Prior to 1970, economics was basically used to explain current events. There was, for all practical purposes, no attempt to forecast economic events into the future. However, there were two developments in this period that changed the future value and use of economic data. The first was the Input/output analysis of Wassily W. Leontief. The Leontief tables showed the value of what each industry and subsections of each industry sold to each other and received from each other. The resulting great complex, showed how any given change is distributed through the economic system. For example, what an increase in automobile production would mean in extra sales to the steel industry.[4]

The second development was a product of the great engineering advances in data storage. This was the development of the econometric or computer models of the economy. Going beyond Keynes, and Leontief, these economic models seek to emulate the effects of all major changes in the economic system. Changes in public expenditures, taxes, interest rates, wages, profits, industrial production by individual industries, and housing construction were captured. With this data the changes that were measured were associated with other changes that were occurring throughout the economy.

From the models came forecasts and more specific information relevant to corporate decisions. Each day, business executives and government officials, make decisions that require assumptions about the future. The modern large business enterprise must plan. Planning always involves the future. The forecasts help establish probable magnitudes of demand for a firm's products and keep decisions within the range of plausibility.

However, when preparing a forecast, the business or government planner would be wise to use the rules of forecasting that were first developed by Edgar Fiedler.[5]

- Forecasting is very difficult, especially if it's about the future.

- The moment you forecast you know that you are going to be wrong: you don't know when and in which direction.

- The forecasters best defense is a good offense, so; if you have to forecast, forecast often.

- But if you're ever right, never let 'em forget it!

CHAPTER 15

INFLATION AND MONETARISM

"His [Keynes] disciples, as disciples will, went much farther than the master. The view became widespread that money does not matter." —Milton Friedman

THE ECONOMICS OF INFLATION

Gross Domestic Product can be defined as the aggregates of all revenue that is received for the sale of goods and services that are produced in an economy in one year. In addition, GDP can be represented using the simple equation of "R = P x Q," where:

R = Total Revenue = GDP,
P = Aggregate prices of all goods and services,
Q = Aggregate quantity of all goods and services produced.

Nominal GDP is the total value of goods and services reported at current prices. Real GDP is the term that economists use to describe the total amount of goods and services produced, adjusted for price level changes, i.e., nominal GDP = P x Q, and real GDP = Q.

For example, between 1987, the year currently used by economists as the base year, the U.S. gross domestic product, measured in nominal terms, increased from $4.540 to $5.951 trillion, an increase of $1.411 or 31 percent. However, a major portion of the dollar value of GDP reflected an increase in the prices at which goods and services were actually sold. For comparison, the Department of Commerce sets the base year, in this case 1987, at 100. The GDP deflator is then used to adjust nominal GDP to real GDP. The GDP deflator is used to adjust gross domestic product to account for the effects of inflation because it is the most broadly based measure of price changes in the U.S. economy. For 1992, the GDP deflator was 1.209 or 20.9 percent higher than it was in 1987. To adjust nominal GDP to Real GDP, nominal GDP is divided by the GDP price deflator as follows:

Description	($ in Trillions)	
Nominal GDP	$5.951	
------------------ = Real GDP	--------- = $4,922	
GDP Deflator	1.209	

Therefore, the increase in GDP from 1987 through 1992 can be broken down into its two fundamental elements as follows:

Increase due to	$ (Trillions)	% Increase
Price (P)	$1.029	22.7
Quantity (Q)	$ 382	8.3
	---------	------
Total Increase	$1.411	31.0

During this five-year period, GDP increased by an average of 6.2 percent. The average increase due to price changes was 4.5 percent, while the increase in real output only averaged 1.7 percent.

Inflation is defined by economists as a long-term sustained increase in the general level of prices. The most often used measures of changes in the price level are the GDP deflator, the producer price index and the consumer price index. The GDP deflator, used in the above example, is a weighted average of the prices of all final goods and services produced in the economy in one year. The producer price index is a ratio of a composite of prices based on a sample of goods and services bought by business firms. Economists use the PPI as an early indication of the future direction of inflation. This is because many of the producer prices are those of the raw materials used as inputs in the production of consumer goods.

The most widely reported measure of inflation is the consumer price index. The CPI is often used to index wages in labor contracts and is also used by the federal government to decide the yearly increase in social security payments and the salaries paid to many government workers. To determine the CPI, the government records the prices of approximately 90,000 different consumer purchases in seven different groups each month. The major groups of consumer purchases are entertainment, medical care, housing, food and beverage, transportation, apparel, and other goods and services. The data is collected and compiled by the U.S. Department of Labor Statistics that has about 680 workers and 360 part-time collectors who survey prices in eighty-five cities. The annual budget for developing the CPI on a monthly basis is about $35 million.

THE ROOTS OF INFLATION IN AMERICA

The result of the simultaneous use of expansive fiscal and monetary policies that was started in 1964, was the achievement of an exceptionally low rate of unemployment. However, the low unemployment rate came at the expense of future price increases. At the beginning of 1966, unemployment moved below 4 percent for the first time since 1957 and remained below that level until the first quarter of 1970. However, the increasing aggregate demand that reduced unemployment, also placed pressure on the economy's production capability. The combination of increased consumer disposable income and the expansion of the money supply created a situation where there was more marginal money available to spend than products available for purchase. This occurrence of "too much money chasing too few goods," as economists called it, accelerated the rate of price increases and created a widespread anticipation of further price increases. This created a psychology of inflation among American businesses who became more concerned with increases in revenue than with controlling operating expenses. The attitude of many producers and even commercial banks was that, if they could pass along price increases to consumers, why should they worry about controlling costs.

In the Keynes system deflation and unemployment called for higher public expenditure and lower taxes, which were politically acceptable actions. Price inflation, on the other hand, called for lower government expenditure and higher taxes, which were far from politically agreeable. Therefore, the economics of John Maynard Keynes, while acceptable in theory, was not effective in controlling inflation. Keynesian policy was a one-way street, an avenue that presented a politically pleasant remedy for curing a recession, but a politically unpalatable solution to the problem of inflation. After 1966 the rate of inflation began to accelerate; it went up more than 6 percentage points between 1969 and 1970, nearly 8 percent between 1972 and 1973 and nearly 14 percent from 1974 to 1975. In 1975 the phrase "double digit inflation," was introduced to American economic terminology.

A further and yet more serious problem in all the industrial countries was the new form of inflation. This was price and wage increases coming from the interaction in the modern economy and its large corporate organizations. With industrial concentration, corporations had achieved a very substantial measure of control over their prices. Also, trade unions, by controlling the supply of labor to large manufacturing corporations, had achieved substantial authority over the wages and associated benefits paid to their members. From the interaction of these entities came a new and powerful inflationary force. This was the upward pressure of wage settlements on prices, and the upward pull of living costs on wages. This was the interacting dynamic that came to be called the "wage-price spiral."[1]

In 1965, with the economy running at nearly full capacity, President Lyndon Johnson instituted his "Great Society" social welfare program. At the same time America had begun a military involvement in the civil war between North and South Vietnam. However, based on excessively optimistic forecasts of military and domestic expenses, the total cost of this joint program was badly underestimated. The Johnson administration began to realize that taxes would have to be raised to prevent further inflation. However, no tax increase was enacted until 1968, when inflation was already well established.

The new taxes were introduced as a surcharge rather then a part of the permanent tax tables. The reaction of consumers to a temporary increase in tax rates was a decrease in savings. The decrease in savings increased the marginal propensity to consume which offset the effects of the tax increase. This change in consumer spending habits made the tax increase totally ineffective.

Policies of the Nixon and Ford Administrations

In 1969, Richard Nixon became the thirty-seventh president of the United States. The Nixon administration found it necessary to maintain the tax surcharge throughout 1969, and then the surcharge was removed in stages. After all, politicians do not like to give up increased taxes. Meanwhile, the Federal Reserve began to implement policy designed to tighten the money supply. The result of the Feds policy was a sharp reduction in the growth of the nation's money supply and an end to the economic expansion that had begun in 1962. By 1970, a recession had replaced the long economic expansion in the United States and recessions bring about an event that often puts fear in the heart of politicians, i.e., unemployment.

A combination of 6 percent unemployment and 5 percent inflation created a real problem for politicians about to launch a reelection campaign. The problem for the administration was how to reduce unemployment and inflation at the same time. Remember, both monetary and fiscal policies, which are designed to effect recession or inflation, work on one side of the problem at a time. President Nixon's answer to this dual problem was the announcement of a "New Economic Policy." The most important part of the new economic policy was an immediate freeze on all wages and prices. Although the price controls received widespread political support when they were announced, they proved mostly ineffective. Employers and workers quickly found ways to limit the effect of these controls. Many goods that were normally sold domestically were exported to avoid the price controls. Companies found ways to avoid the wage controls by promoting key employees or by changing job titles.

The result of the first peacetime attempt to establish wage and price controls was, for the most part, a failure. The controls were designed to cure inflation by treating its symptoms, while at the same time other government policies exacerbated the causes of the inflation. Most wage and price controls were dropped in mid-1973. However, since the factors that cause inflation had not been addressed, the result was an increase in inflation after the controls were lifted. Finally, beginning at the end of 1973, there came the large increase in oil prices, the results of the cartel action of the Oil Producing States (OPEC). Between 1972 and 1981, the index of prices of household fuels in the United States climbed from 118.5 (1967=100) to 675.9, an increase of almost 600 percent.

In 1975, President Gerald Ford called into conference some of the country's better known economists to prescribe for inflation (There was a 13.5 percent increase in the consumer price index in that year). The full group agreed on only one remedy: government should remove any impediments to market competition. For practical effect, this was no better than the president's own prescription, which was the wearing of buttons inscribed with the insignia (WIN - Whip Inflation Now). The Keynes system of using fiscal policy while theoretically logical, was in practice of limited value. Congress was not going to vote to increase taxes or to reduce expenditures to decrease inflation. This is because most congressmen run for office on a platform emphasizing the amount of increased government programs that they can obtain for their district. The way that politicians get elected to office in the United States, was found to be mutually exclusive with the requirements of Keynes economics, during periods of inflation. Consequently, there remained only one viable course of action: to use monetary policy to control inflation.[2]

MONETARY POLICY

In 1979, President Jimmy Carter appointed Paul Volcker as the Chairman of the Federal Reserve System. Under Volcker, the Federal Reserve began a policy that was determined to control inflation. However, before we examine the effects of this new policy, it would be beneficial to explain just how monetary policy works and to illustrate how the Fed uses its monetary tools to implement the policy.

Monetary policy operates against inflation by raising interest rates. As interest rates increase, consumer durable goods such as new homes and automobiles become too expensive to purchase and business organizations reduce investment spending as the expected return on investment for new projects does not meet the companies' minimum return on investment requirements. This, in turn, reduces bank lending, the resulting deposit of funds and the creation of money.

Monetary Policy and the Federal Reserve System

Monetary policy is executed by the Federal Reserve System in the United States. The Federal Reserve System is divided into twelve district banks that are directed by

a nine-person board of directors with three coming from
commercial banks, three from non-banking business
interest and three appointed by the Federal Reserve
Board. The Federal Open Market Committee is the
official policy making body of the Federal Reserve
System. The committee is made up of the seven members
of the Board plus five of the twelve district bank
presidents. Since the New York Federal Reserve Bank
actually carries out monetary policy, the president of the
Federal Reserve Bank of New York, is a permanent
member of the committee.

The major responsibility of the Federal Open
Market Committee is to set monetary policy goals that, in
theory, would lead to long-term economic growth and
stable prices. The Fed controls the money supply, which
in turn, affects the nation's gross domestic product and
the level of prices. The Federal Open Market Committee
sets monetary targets and then implements them through
the Federal Reserve Bank of New York. Each FOMC
directive outlines the conduct of monetary policy over a
six to eight weeks period.

The Federal Reserve controls the money supply by
changing the reserves of its member banks. There are
three ways that Federal Reserve action can affect the
money supply. These tools are an adjustment to banks
reserve requirements, changes in the Federal Reserve
Discount Rate and Open Market Operations. These tools
work as follows:

Reserve Requirement

The Fed requires banks to hold a fraction of their
deposits on reserve. This fraction is the required reserve
and was last changed in 1992 to 10 percent of demand
deposits. Legal reserves are the sum of a bank's vault

cash and deposits in the Federal Reserve Bank. When legal reserves equal required reserves, the bank has no excess reserves and can make no new loans. If the Fed lowers the reserve requirement, as it did in 1992 from 12 to 10 percent on transaction accounts, a portion of what was previously required reserves becomes excess reserves. Excess reserves can be used by commercial banks to make loans and in turn, to expand the money supply. Also, if the Fed wants to fight inflation, it can increase reserve requirements which will reduce excess reserves and reduce the money supply.

Discount Rate

The Discount rate is the interest the Fed charges its member banks who borrow directly from the Federal Reserve. When the Fed raises the discount rate, it raises the cost of borrowing. This action reduces the amount of reserves borrowed by member banks. If the Fed reduces the discount rate the excess reserves at commercial banks will tend to increase. This, however, is not a very effective tool for controlling the money supply, for banks usually borrow from the Fed only to satisfy seasonal needs and as a last resort.

Open Market Operations

This is the major tool of monetary policy. If the Fed wants to Increase bank reserves, the Federal Open Market Committee issues a directive to the bond trading desk at the New York Fed, to buy bonds. The bonds are purchased from private bond dealers. The dealers are paid with checks drawn on the Federal Reserve, which then are deposited in the dealers' accounts at commercial banks. As bank deposits and reserves increase, banks are able to make new loans. To the extent that the banks use these new reserves to make loans, the money supply expands. If the Fed wants to decrease the money supply, it sells bonds.

The expansion of the money supply depends on the amount of new purchases of securities by the Fed and the banking system's willingness to make new loans. If the banks choose to use excess reserves to buy securities for their own portfolio, then the money supply is not increased.

Also, when the Fed talks of controlling the money supply, they are not just referring to cash in consumers' pockets. The Fed defines money in terms of M1 and M2. M1 is called the money stock and is defined as Federal Reserve notes in circulation plus transaction deposits. Transaction deposits are made up mostly of demand deposits kept with commercial banks. M2 is defined as M1 plus short term liquid assets that cannot be used directly as a medium of exchange but can be easily converted into cash or checkable deposits. The money supply, referred to as M2, includes M1 plus money market demand deposits at banks, money market mutual fund accounts, savings accounts and certificates of deposit that are under one hundred thousand dollars. When the Federal Reserve announces that they are targeting the money supply they are referring to the monetary items in M2. What the Fed normally targets is a range of yearly growth of the money supply, for example, between 4 and 8 percent per year.

Monetary Policy and Inflation

As the 1970's passed, inflation persisted. The administration of President Jimmy Carter initiated a strong monetarist action. During the early 1980's another word was added to the economist's vocabulary, "Stagflation," that describes a stagnant economy in association with continuing inflation. In the early 1980's, interest rates were brought to unprecedented levels, in the United States. This resulted in the unwanted combination of double-digit inflation and double digit interest rates. Double digit interest rates curtailed demand for new housing construction and for automobiles and other credit supported purchases. In 1982 and 1983, they brought a sharp restriction in business investment expenditure. The sharp reduction in business investment resulted in a large increase in unemployment, i.e., 10.7 percent in late 1982. Further, the high interest rates brought in a strong flow of foreign funds, which bid up the value of the dollar, curtailed American exports, and strongly encouraged imports, especially from Japan. The overall result of the use of monetary policy to curtail inflation was the deepest economic recession since the Great Depression of the 1930's.

However, by the end of 1984, the consumer price index was nearly stable. Inflation had been substantially reduced. Monetary policy had worked to control inflation, by producing a severe economic slump. However, there remained a serious question as to whether the cure was any less painful than the condition remedied.[3]

MILTON FRIEDMAN AND MONETARISM

Many economists believe that the equation of exchange provides important insights into the way the economy functions and the way monetary policy can affect price levels in the long run. Monetarism is a theory of long-term macroeconomic equilibrium based on the equation of exchange. According to the equation of exchange, shifts in the velocity of money are reasonably predictable. The equation of exchange was first introduced into economics in 1911, by Irving Fisher of Yale University. The most popular version of the equation of exchange is the "Quantity Theory of Money" with its simple equation of MV=PQ. The M in this equation represents the money stock and the V is the velocity of money. The velocity of money is defined as the amount of times money is spent during the course of one year. The P in the equation represents the general price level and the Q is the amount of goods and services actually produced by an economy in one year. Therefore, according to the equation, the stock of money multiplied by the number of times money turns over equals the dollar value of all goods and services produced in that year.

Monetary Economics

The basis for the monetarist theory is as follows:

• Velocity of money is constant or at least predictable.

• The amount of goods and services that can be produced in the short run is fixed because organizations require time to increase their production capability.

• Increases in the supply of money, in the long-run, will only result in an offsetting increase in price levels. The quantity theory essentially eliminates velocity and quantity from the equation, and concludes that any change in the money stock will be felt only in the price level.

Monetarists usually agree that short term changes in the supply of money can affect economic activity. For example, the Federal Reserve can increase the money supply that will lower interest rates. In times of recession, the lower interest rates will stimulate additional consumer purchases of durable goods and increases in business spending. The reason for the increased spending is because many consumer items that are purchased on credit become more affordable with lower interest rates.

Also, business projects that did not provide an acceptable rate of return under assumptions of high interest rates, may be approved when the cost of funding the proposed projects is reduced. There is one other key ingredient that determines whether monetary policy will be effective. Monetary economics works through the extension of bank credit. Therefore, the commercial banking systems must be willing to make loans if monetary policy is to have any influence on economic growth.

While monetarists concede that the Federal Reserve System can affect economic growth, they argue that these benefits are only short-term. In the long-term, they hold, changes in the money supply can only change price levels. Assuming the velocity of money is constant, the classical quantity theory of money implies that, over the long-run, rapid inflation can be caused by growth of the money stock, if that growth is in excess of the long-term growth rate of the gross domestic product. This implies that monetary policy can keep inflation under control over the long-run by making sure the growth rate of the money stock does not exceed the growth rate of an economy's ability to produce.

Milton Friedman

Milton Friedman was a diligent advocate of the policy that was to fill the post-Keynesian void. Friedman was the leading American exponent of the classical competitive market, which he claimed still exists, except as it suffered from ill-advised government intrusion. He is a powerful opponent of government regulation and government in general. According to Friedman, the key to a healthy, stable economy is for the money supply to expand, at a constant rate, in accordance with the growth of an economy's production capability. He is a believer in laissez faire capitalism and a fan of Adam Smith. For his work, he received the Nobel Prize in Economics in 1976. Friedman's books include "A Monetary History of the United States, Capitalism and Freedom, and Free to Choose." Friedman taught at the University of Chicago for 30 years. He retired in 1977 and currently works out of the Hoover Institute at Stanford University.

In a series of studies Friedman rescued the quantity theory of money from the attacks of Keynesian economists. In 1956, Friedman published a set of essays that were designed to test the quantity theory. According to Friedman, demand for money and in turn the velocity of money is stable. The demand for money depends on long-term factors such as health, education, and individual income expectations. Since consumers do not vary their long run expectations very often, the amount of times each year that they spend their money does not vary widely. In other words, velocity remains constant in the long-run. Consumers will not let a bad week or month or even a year alter their spending patterns. They will simply use up some of their savings.[4]

To test his theory of long-run stable velocity of money, Friedman, with Anna J. Schwartz, published "A Monetary History of the United States, 1867-1960." This publication pointed out that between the years 1929 and 1933, the quantity of money available in the United States, had plunged by one-third. According to Friedman and Schwartz, one of the major causes of the Great Depression was the refusal of the Federal Reserve to provide liquidity to the nation's banks when panic stricken depositors demanded a redemption of their deposits. In summary, Friedman claimed that poor policy execution by the Federal Reserve has accompanied every severe recession and every significant inflation that occurred in the twentieth century.

In addition to explaining the power of money and breathing new life into the quantity theory, Friedman attempted to challenge Keynes' claim that government spending could spur the economy. However, to prove this point, monetarist had to show that the Keynesian expenditure multiplier did not exist. Monetarist, when analyzing the Keynesian prescription for stimulating an economy, ask one simple question: Where does the money come from? If the money supply remains constant and the government increases its expenditures, then either consumers or businesses must spend less. Therefore, increased government spending must take the place of business or consumer spending. Economists refer to the replacement of consumer and business expenditures with government spending as the "Crowding Out" effect.

Keynesians do not deny that crowding out takes place. However, they propose that crowding out does not completely offset government spending, especially during a recession. Therefore, the debate between the monetarist and Keynesians revolves around the question of the size of the multiplier and whether it is consistent during different levels of economic growth and recession. Data Resources Corporation has developed a large computer model of gross domestic product and its many components. According to the DRI model, the multiplier is estimated to be about 1.6 the first year of the increased government expenditures and steadily dropping after that.[5]

By the late 1970's, the monetarists were no longer receiving the butt of jokes from the economics' profession. Many of the views of Melton Friedman and the monetarist were being recognized. Central Banks throughout the world began to closely monitor their country's money supply. Main-stream economists absorbed many of the monetarists views and began to shed their insistence on the use of fiscal policy alone. An even congress was rescued, as the Federal Reserve provided them with a set of tools for fighting inflation without the difficult task of having to reduce their spending habits.

CHAPTER 16

THE FEDERAL DEFICIT

*"I saw a startling sight today, a politician with his hands
in his own pockets." —Mark Twain*

THE TWIN DEFICITS

During the severe recession of the early 1980's in
the United States the production of goods and services
declined over a broad range. With the exception of
adequate housing, no one was thought to suffer because of
what was not produced. All suffering was identified with
the interruption in the flow of income, i.e., with the loss of
employment. That, not prices or the unequal distribution
of income, is demonstrably the prime social anxiety of our
time. In the modern industrial economy production is of
first importance not for the goods it produces but for the
employment and income it produces. Economics in the
1980's concerns itself with the elements of national
income (wages, rents, interest and profits), more than
national product. Say's Law has, for all   practical
purposes, been reversed. That is demand creates its own
supply.

Unemployment, in the past, has been seen as a macroeconomic problem. Unemployment was something caused or remedied by the overall design and management of fiscal and monetary policy. This also will cease to be so; increasingly it will be seen that unemployment arises from the non optimal performance and the changing competitive position of particular industries. In the United States, coal mining, steel making, automobile, and textile and apparel manufacturing are examples of industries that are losing market share to foreign competitors. While macroeconomic policies can increase or decrease general unemployment, they cannot remedy it, given the specifics of these industries.

Money spent abroad for goods and services and travel by American residents in excess of what foreigners were spending in the United States had an economic effect precisely opposite from the expansive public deficit of the Reagan administration. The Keynesian effect on the budget deficit was thus offset in the 1980's by the negative effect of the large trade deficit. The result was a very modest stimulating effect from the largest budget deficit ever created by man.

The Trade Deficit

The world may change, but the need for economics to explain the change remains. The world of the 1990's and beyond will be almost as different from the world of the 1950's as the industrial revolution was from merchant capitalism. The United States has gone from a point where they were world's largest creditor after World War II to the world's largest debtor in the 1990's. From 1988 through 1991 the United States has run a huge trade deficit with Japan and the "Little Tigers" of Asia. For example:

Table 16-1

U.S. - Asian Trade ($ in Millions)

Trade Deficit With:	1988	1989	1990	1991
Hong Kong	4,552	6,235	2,648	1,142
Japan	52,070	49,002	41,070	43,386
Singapore	3,943	1,597	1,821	1,153
South Korea	8,899	6,264	4,094	1,514
Taiwan	12,647	13,003	11,185	9,841
Thailand	1,254	2,086	2,303	2,369
Total Deficit	$83,365	$75,387	$63,121	$59,405

Source: Bureau of the Census.

As a comparison, the net exports, for the United States in the year 1989, was a negative $112.0 billion. Of this total, $75.4 billion or 67 percent of the trade deficit was with the above Asian Countries.

However, before we attempt to evaluate the potential problems of a continuing international trade deficit, explaining the international balance of payments accounts, would be helpful.

The domestic components of gross domestic product as expenditures, have already been addressed. However, to complete an analysis of gross domestic product, one final component must be added. This is referred to as net exports in the GDP as expenditures accounts. For example, in 1996 gross domestic product, showed the following amounts:

1996 GDP AS EXPENSE BY COMPONENT	DOLLAR AMOUNT (in billions $)
Personal Consumption Expenditures	$5,152
Gross Private Domestic Investment	1,117
Government Purchases	1,406
Net Exports	-99

Total GDP	$7,576

The net export's component of GDP is derived from a country's balance of payments account. The balance of payments is a record of a country's trade in goods, services, and financial assets with the rest of the world. There are two basic categories in the balance of payments account; the current account and the capital account.

The current account is the sum of the balances in the merchandise, services, net investment and net transfer receipts accounts. The merchandise account records all transactions involving goods. U.S. exports of goods are merchandise credits; U.S. imports or foreign goods are merchandise debits. The services account includes travel and tourism, royalties, transportation costs, and insurance premiums. The sum of the total merchandise and services accounts is equal to the GDP net exports. One of the largest components of the current account is the return on investments. The income earned from investments in foreign countries is a source of funds and the income paid on foreign-owned investments in the United States is a use of funds. The final component of the current account is net transfer receipts, which include foreign aid, gifts, and other payments to individuals that are not exchanged for goods or services.

The capital account is where trade involving financial assets is recorded. The capital, in this account, refers to financial flows such as bank deposits, purchases and sales of stocks and bonds, and loans. A source of funds is the sale of an asset to a foreign resident or a loan from a foreign organization such as a commercial bank. A use of funds is a purchase of the assets that are owned by a foreign citizen or a loan to someone in that country. The total of source and use of funds must agree in order to balance the books between countries. A simple example, of an international sources and uses of funds statement, is shown below:

Sources of Funds   **Uses of Funds**
Sale of an asset   Purchase of an asset
Borrowing from a country   Lending to a country

When countries import more than they export, the difference must be made up in the capital account. In order to finance net imports, a nation has only two basic choices; that is to either sell some of its assets or to borrow from a country that has a positive position in net exports. Because of its propensity to consume more foreign goods than it sells, the United States has been forced to accumulate large amounts of foreign debt or to sell large amounts of its assets to foreigners. From 1986 through 1996, the United States has imported more than it exported every year. The resulting negative net export data from the Commerce Department is detailed in table 16-2. In addition, Table 16-3 provides a detailed example of an international sources and uses of funds statement.

Table 16-2

Net Exports from 1986 through 1996 ($ in Billions)

Year	Exports	Imports	Net Exports
1986	$319.2	$451.7	$ -132.5
1987	$364.0	$507.1	$ -143.1
1988	$444.2	$552.2	$ -108.0
1989	$508.0	$587.7	$ -79.7
1990	$557.1	$628.5	$ -71.4
1991	$601.5	$621.1	$ -19.6
1992	$640.5	$671.5	$ -31.0
1993	$660.1	$725.8	$ -65.7
1994	$722.0	$818.4	$ -96.4
1995	$807.4	$902.0	$ -94.6
1996	$855.2	$953.9	$ -98.7

Total 10 Year Accumulated Trade Deficit $-940.70

The Federal Budget Deficit

Many economists and politicians have pondered the question about the size of the gross national debt in the United States. One of the major questions that is asked about the gross national debt is its size. One way to answer this question is to compare the debt with something. The best vehicle available for comparing a nation's gross accumulated debt is that country's ability to produce goods and services, i.e., their gross domestic product. Figure 16-1 is a graph that compares the gross national debt to the gross domestic product of the United States for the years 1980 through 1996.

Table 16-3
U.S. Balance of Payments for 1996 ($ in Billions)

Balance of Payments	Sources	Uses	Balance
Current Account			
Merchandise Balance			
Exports	$ 615		
Imports		$ 802	
Balance of Trade			$-187
Services Balance	$ 240	$ 152	$ 88
GDP Net Exports	$ 855	$ 954	$ -99
Investment Income	$ 228	$ 237	$ -9
Unilateral Transfers		$ 42	$ -42
Total Current Account	$1,083	$1,233	$ -150
Capital Account			
Capital Inflows	$ 525		
Capital Outflows		$ 322	
Net Capital Inflows			$ 203
Statistical Error		$ 53	$ -53
Total Capital Account	$ 525	$ 375	$ 150
Total Sources and Uses			$ 0

Source: Survey of Current Business: April 1997.

Figure 16-1

Gross Domestic Product Compared to Gross National Debt - 1980 through 1996

Fiscal Year

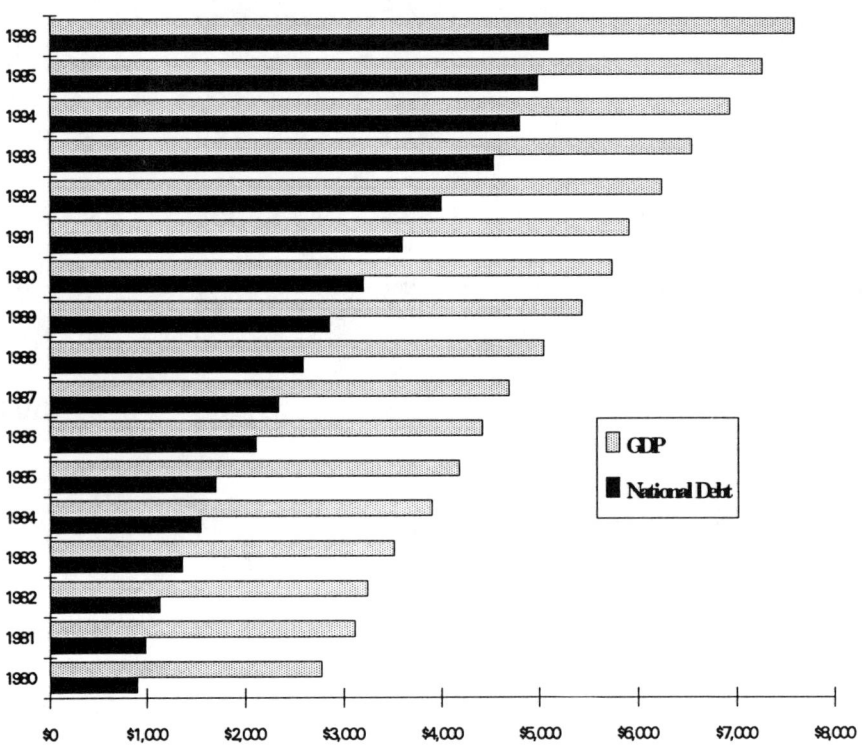

Dollars in Billions

Source: Survey of Current Business, February 1997

On the basis of the above graph in figure 16-1, we can see that the gross national debt has been steadily increasing as a percentage of gross domestic product since 1980. In 1980 gross national debt was 34 percent of gross domestic product. In 1995 the gross national debt was 69 percent of   GDP. Most commercial banks, when considering a loan to its customers, require a company to have no more than 50 percent of its assets in debt. If we consider gross domestic product as the total assets of the United States, this would equate to a debt to asset ratio of 69 percent. For 1996, the trend of debt to assets has moderated to 68 percent. This was the result of an increase in GDP of 4.5 percent and an increase in the gross national debt of only 3.1 percent. However, under the terms of the Maastricht Treaty, by 1999 European Union countries would have to reduce their gross national debt to GDP ratio to 60 percent to qualify for the new European common currency. Based on the current debt to asset ratio, the United States would not qualify for admission to the European common currency.

One of the major problems that a country with such a high debt to asset ratio could incur is the difficulty of borrowing. In the case of the United States, this country's banker is its own citizens and the rest of the world. If the industrial countries of the world elected to stop lending to the United States, we would have a problem. This would mean that the entire debt would have to be funded internally.

While the average citizen of the United States does not lose a lot of sleep over the gross national debt, many economists and even a few politicians, worry about it. By definition, the gross national debt is the dollar amount that the federal government owes its creditors at a given time. It is the cumulative legacy of the federal government's yearly budget deficits. Not all of the gross national debt is owed to the public. About 26 percent of the debt is held by the Federal Reserve banks and government agencies. Of the $4.9 trillion in gross national debt outstanding in 1995, $3.7 trillion was held by the public. This is called the net public debt.

The major portion of the net public debt is the internal debt. The internal debt is the portion of the debt owed to the citizens of the United States. The remainder is the nation's external debt, that portion of the debt that is owed to citizens of other nations. Payment of interest on the debt to a country's own citizens is a redistribution of income and therefore does not directly decrease total demand. However, as the portion of the debt held by foreigners increases, greater amounts of interest are paid out each year to foreign citizens. Payment of interest on debt held by foreigners sends money out of this country, which could contribute to a reduction in aggregate demand sometime in the future. As of December, 1995, 20.9 percent or $770 billion of the net public debt was owned by foreign and international citizens and governments. Many private citizens might ask the question, what does this deficit mean to me? One way to compare the net national debt is on a per worker basis. In 1995 the civilian labor force was over 123 million. If we divide the portion of the net national deficit that is owed to foreigners, by the civilian labor force, the result is that every working American, as of December 1995, owed $6.3 thousand to foreign nationals.

Will the federal government go bankrupt if it continues to run large deficits? There is very little risk of this happening because the federal government can increase taxes to pay the debt. However, there are two major problems that are a result of a large net national debt. The first burden of the debt is that a larger portion of the taxes paid by future generations of Americans will be used to pay interest on the debt. Interest on the net national debt currently amounts to about 20 percent of federal government expenditures. This means that currently 20 cents of each dollar in taxes is used to provide interest payments to holders of the debt and over 4 percent of our tax dollars go to paying interest to foreigners. These tax dollars could be put to a much better use, such as investments in infrastructure and education.

A second burden of the huge net national debt, is its effect on private investment. This was referred to earlier as the crowding-out effect. According to this theory, a growing net national debt will decrease private investment and reduce the growth rate of private capital stock. As the growth rate of worker productivity declines because of a decrease in the growth rate of capital, the growth rate per capita GDP (gross domestic product divided by the labor force), will decline. Therefore, a growing net national debt has the potential to retard the growth rate of a nation's future standard of living.[1]

The Burden of the Twin Deficits

The international current account deficit and the net federal deficit taken together are linked to the international financial markets. The current account deficit must be offset by capital inflows from foreign citizens and a large part of the net national debt is financed by foreigners. A simple sources and uses of fund's statement can be used to show the relationship of these twin deficits to the financial markets.

International Financial Markets -
Sources and Uses of Funds

Sources of Funds   **Uses of Funds**
Domestic Savings   Investments
Foreign Capital Inflow   Government Budget Deficit

A nation's economy can compensate for an increase in government budget deficits by reducing private investment, increasing the rate of savings, and increasing net capital inflows. Net capital inflows are created by net imports. Critics of the federal government's fiscal policy during the last 14 years, charge that the mismanagement of the budgeting process has left the nation burdened with debts owed to foreign lenders. This has caused export industries to lose market share in an increasingly competitive global economy and has reduced aggregate business investment as a result of the crowding-out effect.

EFFORTS TO REDUCE THE FEDERAL DEFICIT

By 1984, the federal budgetary process was in such bad shape that Herbert Stein, President Nixon's Chairman of the Council of Economic Advisors, wrote an article that was published in the December issue of the Economists. In that article Stein states that, "We have no long-run budget policy." In response to this and many other criticisms, Congress has passed three bills designed to reduce or eliminate the deficit.

The Gramm-Rudman-Hollings Act of 1985

This law established a declining set of deficit targets, beginning with a deficit target of $144 billion for fiscal year 1987 and to eliminate the deficit by fiscal 1991.

An exception was written into the law allowing the deficit ceiling to be waived in the event that real gross national product grew at an annual rate of 1 percent or less, for two consecutive quarters. The deficit targets were revised in 1987, which delayed balancing of the budget until 1993. The feature that was supposed to give this law some real ability to control expenditures was a provision for making mandatory spending cuts if Congress failed to provide a budget that would be within $10 billion of the Act's target. However, the targets developed by the Gramm-Rudman-Hollings Act were not met as the federal deficit was $221 billion in fiscal year 1990, compared to a target of $100 billion.

One of the major reasons that this act failed to meet its deficit reduction targets was that entitlements such as social security, Medicare, and aid to dependent families, were exempted from its cost reduction provisions. Alice Rivlin, who is currently President Clinton's budget director, wrote in the October 3, 1989, issue of the Wall Street Journal, that the Gramm-Rudman-Hollins Act was a "well intentioned experiment that failed."

The Budget Deficit Reduction Act of 1990

The growth of the deficit in fiscal year 1990 resulted in a new reform effort. This was the Budget Deficit Reduction Act of November, 1990. The act consisted of a negotiated package of spending cuts (primarily defense) and tax increases that were to total $500 billion for the five years from fiscal 1991 through fiscal 1995. In addition, this act included a new approach to automatic enforcement, a "pay-as-you-go" mechanism. Under this provision, spending was divided into three broad categories: defense, domestic, and international. In theory, if any new legislation pushed spending above a set ceiling for any category, all the programs in the category would be cut proportionately to bring the category back into balance.

On September 30, 1990, President Bush explained the new law to the public by stating that: "The bipartisan leaders and I have reached agreement on the federal budget. Over a period of five years, the deficit would be reduced by $500 million." However, the budget deficit continued to increase as spending increased faster than revenue, even with the new taxes that were enacted under the law. In fiscal year 1991, the federal deficit rose to $270 billion, in fiscal 1992 to $290 billion and was over $255 billion in fiscal 1993.

The Omnibus Budget Reconciliation Act of 1993

In August of 1993, Congress passed, by a one vote margin, a new deficit reduction law. The new law called for some spending cuts as a result of a proposed reduction in the federal civilian work force. The federal work force was reduced from an average of 2.989 million in fiscal year 1992 to 2.858 million in June of 1994, a decrease of over 130 thousand workers. However, the bulk of the savings from this staff reduction was used to fund the Clinton administration's 1994 crime bill. The revenue raising provisions of the bill called for marginal tax increases on the "wealthy" by raising the top rates, from 31 percent of adjusted gross income to 36 percent, for all married couples earning more than $140,000 per year. The 1990 bill increased the top rates from 28 percent to 31 percent. Also, the gasoline tax was raised by 4.3 cents per gallon following a raise of 5 cents per gallon in 1990.

The tax increase provisions of this bill were sold to the public as a way to make the rich pay their "fair share." However, the wealthy did not become rich because they are stupid. Rich people usually employ tax lawyers and accountants who advise them on how to pay a minimum of taxes legally. For example, the total income-tax receipts in 1991, the first year after the 1990 budget act was signed, actually fell. U.S. Treasury figures on income-tax receipts in 1991 show that the wealthy (defined here as people who earn $200,000 a year or more) paid $106.1 billion in income taxes in 1990, but in 1991, after the tax increase, paid $99.6 billion. The tax revenues received in 1991 from this group amounted to a reduction of $7.1 billion over the taxes received in 1990. This is because the wealthy found tax shelters in Municipal Bonds, stopped investing in business expansion and curtailed other activities that would increase their tax burden.

Therefore, the only addition to federal tax revenues that can be expected from the Budget Reduction of Act of 1993 are from the 4.3 percent increase in the tax on gasoline and additional taxes on social security payments from our so called wealthy senior citizens that earn over $34,000 per year.

CHAPTER 17

ECONOMICS AND PUBLIC CHOICE

"In order to get better government policy, we'd better look not to electing better people, but to changing the structure of the rules which constrain them." —James Buchanan

THE NATION-STATE TO THE FISCAL STATE

By the late nineteenth century, the nation-state that had been in existence since the sixteenth century, was being made over into an economic agency. This trend has been referred to by economists, including Joseph Schumpeter, as the evolution from the nation-state to the "fiscal state." The job of the leaders of the nation-state was seen as maintaining the climate for economic growth, keeping taxes low and encouraging savings. The great depression gave rise to the belief that the national government should control its country's economic environment.

Since World War II, most developed countries have come to believe that there are no economic limits to what government can tax or borrow and, therefore, no economic limit to what government can spend. Schumpeter pointed out that as long as governments have been around, the budget process has begun with an assessment of revenues. Expenditures would be allocated to causes based on available resources. Since the supply of "good causes" was inexhaustible, and the demand for spending was therefore infinite, the budget process consisted of deciding where to say no. As long as revenues were considered as a constraint, it was difficult for a government to act as either a social or an economic agent.[1]

Following World War II, most developed countries had adopted the financial theories of John Maynard Keynes. However, what was lacking from Keynes's theory was the role that would be played by government. Keynes assumed that a wise and efficient government, would faithfully apply sound fiscal policy. However, fiscal policy must be applied by people, in this case politicians and government bureaucrats. Economic theory can often become dangerous in the hands of politicians, who quite often assume that there are no limits to the revenues that government can obtain. In the hands of modern day politicians, government has become the master of the individual in society. By using taxes and expenditures, government can redistribute society's income. However, there is a serious question as to whether modern government's have succeeded in bringing about a meaningful redistribution of income. Vilfredo Pareto (1848-1923) the Swiss sociologist developed a law concerning income distribution. Pareto's Law stated that income distribution between major classes in society is determined by two factors: the culture of the society, and the level of productivity within the economy. According to Pareto, the more productive an economy was, the greater would be the equality of income. Taxes, Pareto argues, cannot change the inequality of income.[2]

THE PUBLIC CHOICE SCHOOL OF ECONOMICS

Keynesian economics assumes an efficient and benevolent government to carry out fiscal policy. However, governments in most developed countries, have become such heavy spenders that they can no longer use fiscal policy to counteract the effects of recession. In the United States, the federal government reached the limit of its ability to tax and borrow in the 1980's. This made fiscal policy practically useless during the recession of the early 1990's. Worst of all, the fiscal state has become a "pork-barrel state." If the budget process starts with the determination of expenditures rather than a realistic forecast of revenues, there is no fiscal discipline; government spending becomes the means for politicians to obtain votes. Politicians, therefore, run on platforms designed to convince local voters that they will extract a larger part of the federal budget for spending projects in their districts, then their opponents. In the fiscal state, the looting of the federal treasury is done by politicians to ensure their own election.

The pork-barrel state thus increasingly undermines the foundations of a free society. The elected representatives use the taxes of their constituents to enrich special-interest groups, who in turn, are heavy contributors to the elected official's campaign fund. Joseph Schumpeter warned in 1918 that the fiscal state would in the end undermine government's ability to govern. Eighteen years later, Keynes hailed the fiscal state as the great liberator of a depressed economy. Keynes argued, that government, no longer limited by restraints on expenditures, could govern effectively by manipulating government spending and taxation. However, in the 1990's, it is becoming quite clear that Schumpeter was right.

Economic Rent Seeking

One of the key elements of the Public Choice theory is economic rent seeking. Economists define economic rent, as any payment to a factor of production in excess of its opportunity cost. An example is the huge salaries that sport figures earn. Major league athletes usually earn much more than they could earn using the same time in, for example, teaching a course in economics.

Entrepreneurs are constantly attempting to earn such profits by lowering unit costs, introducing new products or creating brand images in the minds of consumers. When they are successful the income that they earn may be substantially higher than their competitors. However, economic profit that is earned as a result of private market activity is not the only category of economic rents. Many business managers and workers, through labor unions, often turn to government in search of economic rents rather than trying to gain a competitive advantage through the marketplace. An additional profit earned, because of a government program that raises prices or serves to reduce unit costs, is worth just as much as profit earned through the marketplace. Often profit earned from developing a competitive advantage in the marketplace is short term. This is because the competition may develop a new process or a new product that reduces unit cost or better satisfies customer needs. Government regulations, on the other hand, cannot only create opportunities to earn economic rents, but often shield those opportunities from competitors.

Political rent seeking is often referred to by economists as the act of obtaining and defending economic rent through government action. Government restrictions on market activity are often found in the areas of price controls and restrictions on competition. An example of price controls is the case of milk price supports. This occurs when the government places a floor on the market price of milk. If the price of milk falls below the floor price, the federal government purchases the excess milk in order to maintain the targeted price. Public choice economists see this policy as a classic case of political rent seeking. This is because a large portion of the benefits of price supports goes to farmers who are not in need of the supports. However, politicians who are in search of votes, would rather support a bill that has the backing from a large group of farmers instead of only the farmers that actually need assistance.

Government restrictions on competition are another way of generating rents. For example, tariffs and import quotas shield domestic firms from foreign competition. By eliminating foreign competition, firms are able to raise prices above the competitive market level. There are also examples of rent seeking within the domestic economy. For instance, licensing fees and professional examinations restrict the number of competitors who can enter such fields as public accountants, medicine and law.

The theory that government policies do not always promote efficiency and fairness is not a new one. Economists have long been aware of the law of unintended consequences. However, political choice theorists go beyond the tendency of government policies to have effects that are vastly different from their original intentions. Political choice economists argue that the element of rent seeking in the formulation of government policy suggests that there is a systematic tendency for government programs to cause rather than cure economic efficiencies.[3]

Fiscal Responsibility and Public Choice

As early as the 1970's, it had become apparent that the use of fiscal policy to counteract recession and inflation, did not always work. Fiscal policy to stimulate an economy and avoid a recession was used by President Johnson in the mid 1960's. However, fiscal policy was not effective in fighting the inflation of the 1970's. Also, as a result of the huge budget deficit's of the 1980's, fiscal policy lost its ability to combat a recession. A new school of economic theory was needed to explain why fiscal policy, the main tool of Keynesian economics, no longer worked. This new theory was developed by James M. Buchanan, who currently is a professor with George Mason University. In 1986, Buchanan won the Nobel Memorial Prize in Economics, for his work in what became known as "The Public Choice Theory." The public choice theory is a study of how people use the institutions of government to promote private ends. The public choice school attempts to explain some of the modern day economic and political problems, for example:

- Why does the United States suffer from continuing budget deficits?

- Why do special interest groups proliferate?

- Why do bureaucracies continue to expand despite presidential promises to trim them?

A basic principle of public choice theory is that people act in the same way in both public and private roles. In analyzing people's private choices, economists have long assumed that people act in rational pursuit of self-interest. As consumers, they maximize their utility; as entrepreneurs, they maximize profit. Therefore, public choice theorists assume that the actions of people, in public roles, are guided by self-interest as well.

The Problem of Budget Deficits

Buchanan, does not show politicians simply as economic villains. He searches for the reasons that encourage them to act hypocritically. Buchanan argues that it is the budgeting system that leads to government deficits. Buchanan uses the theories of Jeremy Bentham to explain the spending programs initiated by Congress. Politicians want to please their constituents. People, according to Bentham, would prefer pleasure to pain. Government spending programs bring visible pleasure to some groups of people, and taxes are painful. Therefore, politicians assume that constituents would prefer pleasure to pain or high spending and low taxes to balanced budgets. It does not take a financial wizard to conclude that this will translate into budget deficits.

Critics of the public choice school argue that if persistent budget deficits hurt the economy, people will begin to feel the pain and demand a balanced budget. Buchanan answers these critics by explaining that budget deficits do hurt, but the pain is not direct. Reductions in spending programs have an immediate effect. However, even though the result of reduced spending is a more healthy economy, the benefits of fiscal responsibility, are long-term. Budget deficits are created by lowering taxes and raising government spending. Both of these actions by government tend to please taxpayers and beneficiaries. Deficits may reduce the economy's ability to grow, but the effects are indirect. Deficits require people to imagine the future and to determine how they will be affected in the long run.

Buchanan argues that deficit spending ignores the future, and it harms future generations. He even raises a moral question; are deficits a form of taxation without representation? Congressmen today enhance their constituents' present welfare, as well as their own re-election probability, by jeopardizing the welfare of their grandchildren. The unborn cannot vote. Yet congress, by creating large deficits, is presenting each of them with a future financial liability.[4]

The Power of Special Interest Groups

Elected representatives often have interests of their own that do not match those of the voters that elected them. For a politician, re-election is the highest priority. However, getting elected costs money. Therefore, a representative must become proficient at raising campaign funds. Lobbyists for favor-seeking special-interest groups offer the richest sources of contributions for political candidates. Campaign contributions do not buy votes directly, but they buy time on representatives' crowded schedules. Often the side that receives the most time to present its viewpoint, is the side that wins the legislative battle.

In order to present their views to congress, special-interest groups hire people or firms to lobby for them. Lobbying, by definition, is any method used to communicate with elected officials for the purpose of educating or persuading them toward the views of a special-interest group. In order for an individual voter to communicate with their elected officials, they must send them letters or telegrams, take out newspaper ads or telephone their office directly. Few voters feel that they have enough at stake in any one issue to justify the effort of any of these means of communication. However, groups of people with common interest can share the costs of making their views known to their representatives. They can hire full-time lobbyists to present their views to state and federal legislatures. As a result, their influence may be much greater than would be possible if each member acted individually.[5]

The Expansion of Government Bureaucracies

The actual work of government, at all levels, is accomplished in the multitude of departments, agencies and bureaus that are collectively known as "The Bureaucracy." Government bureaus bear some resemblance to private firms. Both bureaus and firms use the hierarchical principle of management. However, despite the many similarities, bureaus are different from private companies. One of the major differences is the self-interest of the bureaucrats. Government managers are not judged on the basis of their contribution to profit or the building of market share for the firms' products. Bureaucrats are judged, and paid, on the basis of the size of their organization. Therefore, the major interest of the heads of government bureaus is the expansion of their organizations.

In a government bureau, the value of a job to the organization is determined by a staff of personnel specialists. As of June, 1994, the federal government had almost 2.9 million workers. The basic pay scale for government workers is broken down into 18 different pay categories with 10 different pay steps in each category.

This pay scale does not even include the executive service of the federal government, which has its own pay scale. This type of organization, by its very size and complexity alone, makes it impossible to accurately evaluate each job. Therefore, job grades in the federal government are, for the most part, determined by the size of the organization or the size of the staff, not on the complexity of the job.

Salary, perquisites such as office size, type of furniture, travel budgets, prestige and most promotions, all tend to increase as the bureau or staff that a manager is in charge of, increases. Thus, agency directors actively lobby congress and the administration for increases in their budgets and responsibilities. It is rare to see an agency argue that some function it now performs is not required. It is virtually unknown for an agency to return unspent funds to the treasury. Most agencies feel that if they do not spend all of the funds that are allocated to them, their next year's budget will be reduced. Therefore, there is no incentive to spend less than the budget allotment and every incentive to constantly lobby congress for additional funds. A consequence of the way agencies are managed is that they often grow larger than congress originally intended. Congress originally sets up an agency in response to lobbying pressure from an interested group of voters. However, after the agency has been set up, pressure for expansion comes from both interested voters and the agency itself.[6]

Economics and Public Choice

Many economists regard the public choice school with some skepticism. However, most economists admit that this theory offers at least one important lesson. The lesson is that the public should not assume that government takes economically prudent steps in the face of political opposition. Modern economic textbooks point out that market imperfections such as monopolies and the uneven distribution of income, may be cured by government action. Public choice theorists ask the question: will the government actually do its theoretical duty? Just as the market may have imperfections, government is not perfect. Adam Smith told us that people act in their own self-interest. Government employees are people too. Why then should we expect a government employee to be any different than the rest of us?

CHAPTER 18

ECONOMIC GROWTH, COMMUNISM, AND THE INTERNATIONAL MONETARY SYSTEM

"The first requirement for economic development in any country is an educated and, in consequence, a competent and socially and economically motivated population."
—John Kenneth Galbraith.

MEASURING ECONOMIC GROWTH

Previous chapters have concentrated on economic growth in the English speaking countries of the world. However, we now operate in a global economy where information is available to producers and consumers of all nations. In a global economy, the basic goals of consumers are often similar. These goals are, survival, growth, and prosperity. What makes countries different, from an economic point of view, is the probability of the attainment of each of these basic goals. In many of the world's developed countries, the goals of growth and

prosperity are obtainable and measurable. In almost all of
the undeveloped countries, the goal is often only survival,
and often that goal is not achieved.

Economists use two measures of growth, real
national income and per capita real national income. The
term real means that gross national income has been
adjusted for the effects of inflation using the country's
gross domestic product deflator. As more goods and
services are produced, the real income of a nation
increases, and people are usually able to consume more.
Per capita real national income is a term used by
economists to describe the ratio between a country's real
national income and its population. The ratio is
calculated as follows:

$$\text{Per capita real national income} = \frac{\text{Real national income}}{\text{Total population}}$$

On the basis of this formula, a country could
experience growth in its real gross domestic product, but
if the population is growing at an even faster rate, output
per person actually will fall. If economic growth is defined
as a rising real per capita national income, then a
nation's output of goods and services must increase faster
than its population.

Governments can facilitate economic growth in
many different ways. If a country is undeveloped, its
government must first establish a set of laws that provide
basic stability. In order to increase a country's total
output, it must increase its productive capability. To
increase the productivity of its assets a country must
increase its capital investment either through its internal
savings or foreign investment. Therefore, a stable

government is the first requirement for increasing a country's national income.

Governments can also facilitate the growth in real per capita national income through the use of macroeconomic policy. However, to increase a country's real per capita income, in the long-run, macroeconomic policy must be directed at increasing production, i.e., increasing aggregate supply. In order to increase the supply of goods and services, government investment must be directed toward improving the performance of the factors of production, i.e., labor, land, capital, and technology.

Labor

Economic growth depends on the size and quality of the labor force. Education and training are the key success factors in the quality of a nation's labor force. Therefore, government programs directed at improving education and training will result in increased productivity and, in turn, increased per capital output.

Capital

To produce goods efficiently, capital must be combined with labor. The ability of a country to invest in capital goods is tied to its ability to generate domestic savings. A lack of current savings can be offset by borrowing, but the availability of borrowing is limited by the prospects of a country's future potential to save. However, the lower the standard of living in a country, the harder it is for its people to forgo current consumption in order to save. Governments can facilitate capital investment with a tax system that rewards personal savings and by direct investment in their county's infrastructure, i.e., roads, bridges, and telecommunication systems.

Land

Capital and labor can be combined with land to produce goods and services. Abundant natural resources can contribute to economic growth, but natural resources alone do not generate growth. Government can help manage natural resources so that there is a maximum amount of value that is added to the resources through the production process. A country is usually better off if it can increase the value of its natural resources rather than selling the resource to other countries in its natural state. For example, government could prevent the sale of raw timber to foreigners and only permit the export of finished wood products.

Technology

Advances in technology allow the production of more output from a given amount of resources. This means that technological progress accelerates economic growth for any given rate of increase in the labor force and the stock of capital. However, technological change depends on the scientific community. The more educated a population, the greater its potential for technological advances. Education gives industrial countries a substantial advantage over developing countries in creating new products and in improving the manufacturing process. Government can assist in technological development by directly investing in research and development. The greater the investment made for research and development, by a country, the better its chances for technological advancement.

The above analysis of the factors of production provides a foundation for the next step in the examination of world growth and prosperity. Therefore, this model will be used to determine the probability of growth in real per capita national income in the undeveloped countries, the ex-communist countries, and the industrialized countries of the world.

PROSPECTS FOR GROWTH IN THE UNDEVELOPED COUNTRIES

As a group, developing countries have performed poorly compared to developed countries. Over the last half century, only two groups of countries have moved from the category of developing country to middle-income countries. These two groups are the Oil-Producing Countries and the Asian Tigers (Taiwan, South Korea, Singapore and Hong Kong). From 1950, the developing countries' growth rates were about equal to those of developed countries, but their per capita national income rate of growth was much lower. What makes it so difficult for developing countries to create a successful program for per capita growth is that social, political, and economic problems blend into one another and cannot be considered separately. The institutional structure that is taken for granted in the United States often doesn't exist in these countries.[1]

Economists have identified several general obstacles to real per capita national income growth in undeveloped countries. These problems include, political instability, excessive foreign debt, poor or inappropriate education, and overpopulation.

Political Instability

In order to perform properly an economy needs a
set of consistent rules and regulations. Any plan for
economic development requires financial investment,
either internally through savings or externally through
investment of borrowing. Foreign lenders will not invest
in a country that is subject to political instability.
Political instability also restricts internal investment.
There is usually only a small percentage of people who
have any money to save. However, these people often
channel their investments out of their own country as a
hedge against a revolution. Well-off people in developing
countries often provide major inflows of capital to
developed countries.

Excessive Foreign Debt

In the 1970's, developing countries borrowed from
foreign banks to finance development projects by private
domestic firms. However, as a result of political
corruption and economic mismanagement, the
investments were often unproductive. The governments
that had guaranteed these loans eventually were put in a
position of having to repay them without the financial
resources to do so. In many of these countries annual
interest payments exceeded their export earnings.
Meanwhile no payments were made on the principle.
Accordingly, the 1980's was a period of intense
negotiation designed to prevent developing countries from
defaulting on their loans. The United States government,
along with most of the developed countries and the
International Monetary Fund were active in these
negotiations. The result was that loans were restructured

to prevent default, but the undeveloped countries, for the most part, had exhausted their borrowing capability.

Poor or Inappropriate Education

In less developed countries, workers are often illiterate and they have little training. Low productivity is a result of poorly educated human capital as well as physical capital. Also, developing countries tend to empathize the wrong type of education. In developing countries only the well-off are usually educated. The best students qualify for scholarships in western countries. The training that they receive is often based on business techniques that are practiced in developed countries. Often their education is not relevant to the problems facing their own countries. This often causes a "Brain Drain," where the best and brightest students from the undeveloped countries move to developed countries to obtain jobs that are relevant to their education.

Overpopulation

There are two ways that a country can increase per capita real national income. These two methods are:

- Decrease the number of people in the country without decreasing total income.

- Increase national income without increasing the population.

Thomas Carlyle gave economics its nickname, "The Dismal Science." Caryle was commenting on the population growth theories of Thomas Malthus. Remember, from chapter number 4, Malthus predicted that society's prospects are dismal because population tends to outrun the means of subsistence. This view was cemented into economic thinking in the law of marginal productivity. According to this law, as more and more people are added to a fixed amount of land, the output per worker gets smaller.

Through technological progress, most western economies have avoided the fate predicted by Malthus because growth in output has exceeded growth in population. In contrast, many developing economies have not avoided the fate that Malthus predicted. This is because diminishing marginal productivity has exceeded technological change, and the economic growth that developing countries' experience isn't sufficient to offset the increased growth in population. The result is a constant or falling rate of growth in real per capital national income.[2]

On the basis of the history of per capita real national income growth in the world's richest countries, an iron law of economic development can be stated. No country can become rich without an extended period of good economic performance and an equally long period of very slow population growth. Therefore, when it comes to the prospect of getting rich, in most of the undeveloped countries, the dismal science provides a most dismal forecast.

THE FALL OF COMMUNISM

At the end of World War II, there were two military superpowers, the United States and the Soviet Union. However, there was only one economic superpower, the United States. In any economy, certain items can be produced at the expense of other products. When the Reagan administration increased its defense spending, in the middle 1980's, the Soviet Union had to increase their spending on defense in order to maintain military equity. Since the Soviet Union was not an economic superpower, their increased defense expenditures had to be funded through a decreased investment in civilian consumption. However, the reason for the fall of communism in the Soviet Union was even more fundamental than the trade-off between civilian and defense spending. The reason that Communism failed is due to the faults of the system itself.

The Soviet system, unlike capitalism, did not evolve gradually over time. The system came into being after the revolution of 1917. A semi-feudal society was taken over by a group of revolutionaries who were driven by the philosophy of Karl Marx. According to Marx, after the revolution, a temporary regime known as the "dictatorship of the proletariat," would take over the transition from capitalism to socialism. Once government was organized, a planned socialist economy would emerge that would set up the organization that was necessary for the production and distribution of goods and services. However, the revolution presented, Lenin, Trotsky and the other leaders of the new Soviet Union with problems far more complex than Marx's utopian design. One of the major problems of the new government was how to distribute food from the farms to the factory workers.[3]

In 1927, Joseph Stalin became the new leader of the Soviet Union. Stalin decided to solve the food distribution problem by taking over the farms. While the process of collectivizing both agriculture and industry solved the distribution problem, there was a tremendous social and economic cost. Many peasants slaughtered their livestock rather then hand them over to the new collective farms and others just refused to cooperate with the new system. In reprisal, Stalin acted with brutal force. Farmers that would not cooperate were executed or put in labor camps. In the cities, factory workers were given tasks by the central authorities. The right to strike was forbidden and trade unions were eliminated. Under Stalin, the Soviet Union was transferred from a utopian form of socialism, as advocated by Karl Marx, to a dictatorship.

Economists often define socialism as a system where the productive resources are owned by government. In a capitalist system, the market through the price system is used to produce and distribute goods and services. In the absence of a market, direct orders from a central planning agency must be used to distribute society's products. In a socialist economy, planners not consumers determine the demand for products. In a totally planned economy, every item that goes into the final plan must be in great detail. Schedules of production are needed down to the smallest items. Supplies of labor must also be planned. Thus, the master plan must be accompanied by a whole hierarchy of smaller plans in order to achieve the smallest of objectives. Even one little planning error, can have disastrous affects if it is part of the strategic link in the chain of production and distribution. In short, to effectively run a socialist system, the leaders of the system would have to know all of the possible available alternatives. The probability of success of such a system approximates the possibility that one group of people knows all the answers to all of the problems inherent in an economy. While it is possible to develop strategy for even a large economy, it is the execution of the plan that requires an ability greater than that which could be possessed by a small group of people.

With all of its improbabilities, central planning worked in the years following World War II. However, after the war the inherent problems of a socialist system began to appear. The problem of developing and implementing the basic framework of a modern industrial state became increasingly difficult. Under Stalin's successors Nikita Khrushchev and Leonid Brezhnev, the Soviet system began to show signs of failure. The system was becoming bogged down with a large bureaucracy. Consumer goods were produced in sufficient quantity, but they were of such poor quality that warehouses bulged with unusable shoes and shoddy clothes. Although the Soviet Union produced almost twice as much steel per capita as the United States, there was a chronic steel shortage because the material was used so wastefully. In summary, by the time that Mikail Gorbachev began to speak of "Glasnost" (openness) and "Perestroka" (the fundamental restructuring of the economic system), in 1985, the Russian system was apparently becoming an economic failure. Once the door had been opened by Gorbachev, the old system was dismantled by thousands of Soviet citizens who simply became unwilling to cooperate with it.[4]

In the early 1990's, political and economic changes in Eastern Europe have been fast paced and erratic. Their future choices are much larger than the selection of an economic system. The choices that must be made have both political and social elements. For example, the republics of the former Soviet Union are combinations of distinct nationalities with their own customs and allegiances. These differences have already led to political and social upheavals. Economic markets simply cannot exist in an environment of social unrest.

A second problem that the Eastern European countries face is a lack of consensus as to which direction to follow. Many countries lack the patience to wait until a system of markets evolves. However, a capitalist economy cannot be created by the vote of the people or the commands of a dictator. A well-functioning market requires the existence of a legal structure that can see that contracts are carried out, a well-defined structure of private property, and a work force that is trained in both technical and entrepreneurial skills. During the 1990's most of the Eastern European countries will be attempting to establish market driven economies. However, the economic and political problems that continue in these countries will, at best, make progress slow. The leaders of Eastern Europe that predicted an easy transition to a market economy will be proven wrong. Therefore, during the 1990's and into the twenty-first century, one of Western Europe's greatest problems will probably be immigration. After all, if the citizens of an Eastern European country become impatient with their country's attempts to establish a market driven economy, they can always decide to move west. In this case to Western Europe where a market economy is already established.

THE INTERNATIONAL MONETARY SYSTEM

The fall of communism in Eastern Europe will have far reaching affects on the economic development of Western Europe. In addition the evolution of the current international monetary system should have equally profound affects on tomorrow's world economy. The fuel that drives international economic growth is obviously money and the fuel injector that keeps the economic engine burning is the international exchange mechanism. Governments have three basic choices in determining a foreign exchange policy. They can develop a system of flexible exchange rates, partially flexible exchange rates or a fixed exchange rate. When governments do not enter into foreign exchange markets at all, but leave the determination of exchange rate up to the international money market, the country has a flexible exchange rate. When governments sometimes buy or sell currencies to influence the exchange rate, while at other times they let international currency market forces operate, they have partially flexible exchange rate. If government chooses a particular exchange rate and offers to buy and sell currencies at that price, it has a fixed exchange rate.[5]

An effective way to explain how the various foreign systems work is to present a brief history of the international exchange rate system. Beginning with the Paris Conference of 1867 and lasting until 1933, most of the world economies had a system of relatively fixed exchange rates under what was called a gold standard. Under a gold standard, the amount of money a country issued had to be directly tied to gold. Each country participating in a gold standard agreed to fix the price of its currency relative to gold. That meant a country would agree to pay a specified amount of gold upon demand to anyone who wanted to exchange that country's currency for gold. To do so, each country had to maintain a stockpile of gold. When a country fixed the price of its currency relative to gold, it fixed its currency's price in relation to other currencies. Under the gold standard, a country made up a difference between the quantity supplied and the quantity demanded of its currency by buying or selling gold to hold the price of its currency fixed in terms of gold. How much a country would need to buy and sell depended upon its balance of payments deficit or surplus. If a country ran a deficit in the balance of payments, it was required to buy its currency and to sell gold to stop the value of its currency from falling.

Since gold served as reserves to a country's currency, a balance of payments deficit would result in a flow of gold out of the country. This resulted in a reduction in a country's money supply often at times when an increase in the money supply was needed to fight a recession. It was in this way that the gold standard determined a country's monetary policy and forced it to adjust to any international balance of payments disequilibrium. Adjustments to a balance of payments deficit were often politically unpopular for they led to recessions and prevented the Federal Reserve System from counteracting the recession with monetary policy. For all practical purposes, President Roosevelt ended the gold standard in the United States, when he abandoned the gold standard in 1933.

As World War II was coming to an end, the United States and its allies met to establish a new international economic order. After a considerable amount of debate, they agreed upon a system named after the resort in New Hampshire where the meeting was held, i.e., the Bretton Woods system. The Bretton Woods system established the International Monetary Fund to oversee the international economic order. The IMF was empowered to arrange short-term loans between countries. The Bretton Woods system also established the World Bank, which was empowered to make longer-term loans to developed countries. Today the World Bank and the IMF continue their central roles in international financial affairs. The Bretton Woods system was based upon mutual agreements about what countries would do when experiencing balance of payments surpluses or deficits. It was essentially a fixed exchange rate system.[6]

The Bretton Woods system reflected the underlying political and economic realities that were present after World War II. The European economies were in a state of almost total destruction and the United States was the only one of the allies whose economy was almost untouched by the war.   In order to rebuild their economies, Europe would have to import large amounts of equipment and borrow large amounts from the United States to finance these purchases. The establishment of fixed exchange rates helped to provide the financial stability that was necessary to rebuild Europe. In addition, the Bretton Woods system provided a mechanism for long-term loans from the United States to Europe, that could help sustain the fixed exchange rates that were established. However, one of the major difficulties of the Bretton Woods system was the shortage of a currency in which countries could hold their liquid financial assets, i.e., a reserve currency. To offset that shortage, the IMF was empowered to create a basket of international currencies called "Special Drawing Rights." However, SDR's never became established as an international currency and the United States dollar soon began serving as a reserve currency. To get dollars into the hands of foreigners, the United States had to run a deficit in its international balance of payments current account. Remember that a current account deficit or net imports results in a reduction of the gross domestic product of a country.

By the early 1970's the number of dollars held by foreigners was far greater than the amount of gold the United States held in its vaults at the Fed. This meant that the United States could not redeem in gold all of the dollars that were held by foreigners. This situation came to a head when France in 1971 demanded a redemption in gold for the dollars held by the French central bank. As a result of this demand, the United States ended its policy of exchanging gold for dollars at the predetermined price of $35 per ounce and with that change, the Bretton Woods system effectively came to an end.[7]

The present international monetary exchange rate system is a partially flexible one. Most western country's exchange rates are allowed to fluctuate although, at various times, governments buy and sell their own currencies in order to affect short-term fluctuations. While most Western countries exchange rates are partially flexible, certain countries have agreed to fixed exchange rates of their currencies in relation to the rates of a group of certain other currencies. For example, the European Common Market countries allow their currencies' value to fluctuate only within a narrow range while other currencies are fixed relative to the dollar. Also, the European Common Market countries have all signed the Maastricht Treaty which is a document designed to establish the basic rules of trade between these countries. One of the goals of this treaty is to establish a European common currency by the year 1999. To obtain the goal of a uniform currency, the European Community governments are expected to set up the European Monetary Institute and a national European central bank. This they believe is a necessary step towards developing a truly common market for the 15 nations that make up the European Community.

CHAPTER 19

THE BATTLE OF THE TITANS

"In a Global Economy a worker has two things to offer; skills or the willingness to work for low wages." —Lester Thurow

THE NEW CAPITALISM

In 1996 the United States remains as the world's only military superpower. Concurrently, the United States is competing with Japan and Western Europe (centered on Germany), for economic supremacy. Because of their different histories and present circumstances, both Japan and Germany are going to be playing the capitalistic economic game with strategies very different from those found in the Anglo-Saxon world. Today's rules for the international economic game, were written after World War II and built on the realities that then existed. As a result, the system that governed the world economy in the last half of the twentieth century will not be the system governing the world economy in the first half of the twenty-first century.

Nowhere are the necessary changes going to be harder to make than in the United States, for in the past century it has been the most successful economy in the world. In the next century the United States will be just one of many equal players in a game where other countries will increasingly write the rules. Looking forward, the next half century will be a competitive-cooperative three-way economic game between Japan, Western Europe and the United States.

Militarily, the United States is going to be the dominant power in the first half of the twenty-first century. However, military power does not lead to economic power. Quite the reverse, if a country is to be a military superpower, it must be willing to cut its private consumption to levels that insure it is not cutting back on the investments needed to keep civilian productivity growing. An economic superpower must make large investments in civilian research and development, plant and equipment, public infrastructure, and human skills to remain an economic superpower. If a nation wishes to be both a military and an economic superpower, it must make both sorts of investment. While military power can sometimes outlast economic power for centuries, eventually military power depends upon having a successful economic base.[1]

Building upon the economic muscle of Germany, Western Europe is patiently engineering an economic giant. Also, halfway around the world, Japan's economic tiger has arisen from the ashes of World War II. From the world's perspective, replacing a military confrontation with an economic contest is a step forward compared with the military confrontations of the past century. This is because the winners and losers are both winners in the economic game ahead. The aggressive invasion of well-made Japanese or German products, from firms that intend to conquer American markets, is not at all equivalent to the threat of a military invasion from the Soviet Union.

The United States is still, the dominant economic power in the world. However, just as the fall of the Berlin Wall in November of 1989 marked the end of the old contest between capitalism and communism, so the integration of the European Common Market that took place on January 1, 1993, marked the beginning of a new economic contest that will continue well into the twenty-first century. Then the Unites States became the second largest economy in the world. This reality will become the symbol for the start of the competition that determines who will own the twenty first-century.[2]

Consumer Economics versus Producer Economics

The economic competition between communism and capitalism is over, but another competition between two different forms of capitalism is already under way. Using a distinction first made by George C. Lodge of the Harvard Business School, the individualistic, mainly British-American form of capitalism, is going to face off against the communitarian German and Japanese variants of capitalism. The essential difference between the two forms of capitalism is their stress on communitarian versus individual values as the route to economic success. What makes this comparison even more interesting is that two different forms of capitalism are currently in use within the Western European Community.[3]

According to Lodge, two very distinctive forms of capitalism have emerged within the world's developed countries. The first form of capitalism Lodge calls "Consumer Economics," and the other form of capitalism is referred to as "Producer Economics." Consumer economics stresses individual accomplishments while producer economics stresses communitarian values. The United States with its history of individualism is clearly in the camp of consumer economics. Japan with its partnership relationship between business and government stresses the theories of producer economics. The Japanese derive their economic theory from the American and British tradition; however, there is a much stronger Marxian influence. In Japan the state is the executive committee of the capitalist economy. The result of this combination of Marxist and capitalist theory, is an accepted cooperation between industry and government. Western Europe is a mixed bag between the two forms of capitalism. In Western Europe, producer economics is clearly identifiable in Germany, and the Netherlands. Also, France and Italy have aspects of this more socialistic approach to economic development. Britain, on the other hand, clearly follows the direction of consumer economics and the remaining European Community Countries such as Belgium, Greece, Ireland, Luxembourg, Portugal and Spain, are more closely aligned with Britain. Also, the members of the European Free Trade Association, Finland, Austria, Denmark, Sweden, and Switzerland exhibit identifiable tendencies toward producer economics.

America and Britain proclaim individualistic values: the brilliant entrepreneur, large wage differentials (especially for senior managers), individual responsibility for skills and training, easy to fire and easy to quit, profit maximization and hostile mergers and takeovers. In contrast, Germany and Japan stress communitarian values such as: business groups, social responsibility for skills, teamwork, firm loyalty and active industrial policies that promote long term growth.

Japanese business firms play a game that is better described as strategic conquest. British-American firms play a different game; their objective is to maximize profits.[4]

Consumer Economics

Consumer economics is based on the theory of individual values, performance and rewards. The major goal for a firm that practices consumer economics is profit maximization. For this type of company, the first objective is to maximize stockholder returns. Second, in the sequence of importance are the firm's customers and a distant third in importance are the employees. Wages are to be beaten down where possible and when not needed, employees should be laid off or fired. In individualistic firms, labor is not a member of the team. Labor is considered to be just another factor of production, along with money and physical assets. Labor is therefore, rented when it is needed, and gotten rid of when it is not needed. While these firms often preach the virtues of loyalty to their company, their actions do not encourage employee morale.

Mergers and acquisitions are an integral part of the structure of a firm practicing consumer economics. Bank loans and bond funding are used to purchase the assets of other companies. Often the company is purchased by a group of financial investors for the purpose of making a resale profit. These "Financial Vikings" are encouraged, by the potential for huge profits, to purchase the outstanding stock of a public company only to turn around and sell off the assets of that company for a profit. In the process, they often dismiss a company's entire labor force. This system of buying a company in the stock market and selling off its assets for a quick profit is totally unproductive. In fact, financial raiding is a misuse of investment funds that could have been put to much better use by adding to the economy's capital stock. The result of financial raiding is the enrichment of a few financial vikings and some stockholders at the expense of the economy's ability to grow in the long-term.

In a country that practices consumer economics, the relationship between government and business is often analogous to a police state. Government bureaucrats think that one of their major functions is to keep businesses honest. The government does not form a partnership with business. Instead of a partnership, government develops an adversary relationship with industry. The role of government is not to assist business, but to regulate business. In the United States, for example, banks cannot own industrial firms because the Glass-Steagall Act of 1933, prohibits it. Also, businesses cannot mutually plan their marketing strategies for that practice is outlawed by the antitrust laws.

Training in this economic environment is the responsibility of the individual. In the United States, local government provides mass education through high school; however, after the twelfth grade the individual is on their own as far as education and training is concerned. The United States has one of the best college systems in the world and a large amount of financial aid is available to encourage students to attend college. However, for those who do not go on to college, additional training is hard to find. Many companies have training programs, but they are often available for skilled, well-educated workers only. In a global economy where goods can be obtained in low-wage third world countries, the effective supply of unskilled workers has expanded enormously. Consequently, wages must fall for the unskilled who live in rich countries such as the United States. In the United States the skills of workers that do not attend college are simply not up to world class standards. Most non-college students in the United States could not pass the high school graduation examinations that they require in Japan and Western Europe. In addition, those students that do not finish high school in the United States are on a par with third world students.

Producer Economics

In communitarian capitalism (producer economics), individual and firm strategies also exist but these strategies are developed starting from quite different foundations. In Germany and Japan one joins a team and is then successful as part of that company team. In Germany and Japan, job switching is far less prevalent than it is in the United States. In a communitarian system, they view labor turnover as bad for business. This is because they feel that workers will not make sacrifices for the good of the company if they do not expect to stay with that company. In Japanese business firms the owners view employees as the number one stakeholder, the customers number two, and the shareholders a distant number three. Since the employee is the prime stakeholder, higher employee wages are a central goal of the firm in Japan. In countries such as Japan or Germany, the bottom two thirds of the work force is better skilled than in English-speaking countries. Their skills contribute to higher rates of productivity growth and validated higher wages.

The role played by profits in these two capitalist systems, is very different. In the profit maximizing firm, profits are the goal; the company's objective function. In the empire building firm, profits are the means to the end of a larger empire; i.e., a constraint to future growth. The goal of an empire building firm is market share not just profit maximization. A profit maximizing firm will devote its higher profits to individual consumption; an empire building firm will devote its higher profits to investment in expanding its empire.

Beyond personal and firm strategies, producer economics believes in both business groups and national strategies. Business groups such as the Mitsui Group in Japan or the Deutsche Bank Group in Germany are expected to have collective strategies. Companies should be financially interlocked and work together to strengthen each others activities. The Japanese break into vertical (Keiretsu) groups made up of suppliers, producers and retailers, and horizontal (Keiretsu) groups made up of firms in different industries. The Deutsche Bank directly owns 10 percent or more of the shares in 70 of the countries leading companies. Deutsche Bank executives sit on four hundred corporate boards. When an Arab group threatened to buy a controlling interest in Mercedes-Benz in the 1980's, Deutsche Bank intervened on behalf of the German economy to buy up the shares that were for sale. This type of intervention protects the managers of Mercedes-Benz from the raids of the so called Financial Vikings.[5]

Both Europe and Japan believe that government has a role to play in economic growth. They believe that Government has an important role in insuring that everyone has the skills necessary to participate in the workplace. Germany's socially financed apprenticeship system is the envy of the world. In Germany, they view social welfare policies as a necessary part of a market economy. In Japan industry representatives working with the Ministry of International Trade and Industry present "Visions" of where their economy should be going. Today these visions are used to guide civilian research and development funding. Key industries in Japan are targeted for future growth.

EVALUATING THE ECONOMIC CONTENDERS

After World War II, America served as the major stimulus for the world economy. Whenever the world sank into recession, the United States would use its fiscal and monetary policies to invigorate demand. Foreign exports to America would rise, pulling the exporting countries out of their economic slump. American macroeconomic stimulus, starting in the fall of 1982, pulled the industrial world out of its sharpest post-world War II recession. In 1983 and 1984 most of the growth in both Europe and Japan could be traced to exports to the American market. However, for the first time the United States found itself burdened with a large trade deficit. America's effortless exports became a thing of the past. In the 1990's, the total production of America's industries is no longer large enough to pull the entire world out of a recession.

In response to this new environment, governments are increasingly managing international trade. Non-tariff import barriers are rising everywhere. The trend is clear. America signs a free trade arrangement with Canada and Mexico. Europe talks about associate memberships in the European Community. In the twenty-first century the rules of the game will be written by that group of businesses or countries that control the largest markets. If the European Common Market becomes the world's largest economy, then they will informally write the rules for the new game, in Europe. The economy that controls the world's largest market will write the rules of the economic game in the twenty-first century.

The Case for Europe

If the Europeans are going to write the rules for international trade in the twenty-first century, it will be for a system of "Managed Trade" and "Quasi Trading Blocks." Free trade is great in theory, but in actual practice it interferes with what Adam Smith labeled as "Self-interest." If countries act in their own self-interest, only managed trade agreements are possible in the real world. In other words, countries will negotiate with other potential trading partners to develop contracts that define the rules of international trade. Both countries and trading blocks will negotiate the terms of the contracts based on their own interests not on the mutual interest of the entire world.

Two events make Europe the focal point of attention in the 1990's. First, in Western Europe on December 31, 1992, the European Community integrated, and instantly became the world's largest economic market. The countries that make up the European Community have almost 337 million citizens. In 1995, Sweden, Austria, and Finland all joined the European Community, bringing its number of countries to 15 and its members to more than 360 million people. Secondly, in Middle and Eastern Europe communism has dissolved and is being replaced by capitalism. The ex-communist economies have low wages, well-educated populations, and are located conveniently next to the world's largest market.

Some Middle and Eastern Europe countries will probably be offered associate memberships in the newly integrated European Community. Their special access could close Europe's markets for mid and low-income countries elsewhere in the world. While there will be problems along the way, the formation of the House of Europe is now unstoppable for the following reasons:

• The opportunities to create an integrated House of Europe are just too good to pass up.

• The need to compete against the Japanese in a global economy require a combined effort by the Europeans.

• Enough integration has now occurred to make it very difficult for anyone to withdraw.

Throughout history, those who control access to the world's largest market, wrote the rules of international trade. Britain wrote the rules of world trade in the nineteenth century. The United States did it in the twentieth century. As the world's largest market, Europe can write the rules of world trade in the twenty-first century. The combination of Western and Eastern Europe has 850 million well-educated people. Imagine what could occur if they paired the high-tech science capabilities of the former Soviet Union with the world-class production capabilities of the Germans, the financial capabilities of the British, and the design abilities of the French and Italians.

Although the wheels of European integration have been set in motion, the timing of the unification is still far from certain. For example, Germany with the largest industrial base of any European country, has many internal problems that must be addressed before unification can fully take place.

In the October, 1994, elections, German Chancellor Helmut Kohl won his fourth term in office. However, the coalition of Chancellor Kohl's Christian Democratic Union and the smaller Free Democratic Party together won only

49 percent of the vote. Mr. Kohl's greatly reduced majority will make it difficult for him to make any radical changes in the German government. Many Germans, including Chancellor Kohl, are troubled by the long-term prospects for economic growth, social restructuring, and the unification of East Germany. They believe that an overbearing bureaucracy and exorbitant labor, tax and welfare costs are stifling initiative and encouraging many businesses to leave the country. Financially, German unity has drained the country's strength and will continue to be a burden well into the twenty-first century.

Continued failure to come to grips with Germany's fundamental economic and social problems could have severe consequences both for Germany and for the rest of Europe. At the very least, a Germany that is financially weak and politically bogged down by internal problems won't be able to act as an engine to pull the rest of the European Community. Currently, inefficiency and red tape already clog the German production engine. For example, it can often take as much as three months just to change a telephone number in Germany. German's work fewer hours and take longer holidays than most other European workers. However, German labor unions continue to advocate a shorter work week.

Manufacturing production costs in Germany rank equally with over-regulation as a large constraint to long term economic growth. Wages and benefits of average German workers are almost $29 an hour, compared with $18 for American workers. As a result, many German companies are moving some of their production facilities out of the country. Germany's many internal problems such as an overbearing bureaucracy and exorbitant labor, tax and welfare costs, will tend to slow their economic growth. This, in turn, will serve to reduce the speed of the unification of all of Western Europe. In addition to the problems in Germany, all of the countries in the European Community have internal problems and many of these problems will have to be resolved before a truly unified Europe can emerge.[6]

However, there is a negative side to the integration of Europe. Middle and Eastern Europeans will not stay for long on their side of the border and earn one tenth of what those in Western Europe earn. Therefore, Eastern Europeans will have to be given access to the markets of Western Europe in order to accelerate their economic growth. If Eastern Europeans are not given access to these markets they will start moving West.

Another question that will require some strategy development is how will Europe deal with Japan? In Japan, the whole distinction between public and private has little meaning. To protect their international trade position against the Japanese, Europe will probably be forced to develop an exclusionary and projectionist trading block. As for the United States, this is one circumstance in which being the only military superpower will be beneficial. Europe cannot put up trade barriers against the United States and at the same time continue a military partnership.

As the Europeans continue their economic integration, they will become more involved in writing the rules for international trade in the twenty-first century. Some of the ex-communistic economies will succeed in moving to a market economy and will rapidly raise the living standards of their citizens. The number of ex-communistic countries that do succeed will depend upon the degree of outside help. Western Europe will have no choice but to help Eastern Europe to improve their economies. Preventing Western migration, reducing border tensions and lowering ethnic hatreds all demand economic success in Middle and Eastern Europe.

The Case for Japan

The ideas central to Japanese economic thought derive extensively from American and British tradition but with a stronger Marxian component than is thought reputable in the English speaking countries. The Marxian influence relieves Japanese economic and political thought of the notion of a social dichotomy, even conflict, between the private market economy and the state. In Japan the state is the executive committee of the capitalist class. The result is an accepted cooperation between industry and government that is unthinkable in the American and British tradition. Japan also, has a commitment to educate and train its people at all levels, not just its college educated people. The result of this commitment to education is the highly competent Japanese labor force with its ample engineering and management talent.

Central also to the Japanese success is the avoidance of relatively sterile, unproductive investment in military operations. The use of a generous flow of savings for civilian capital formation as opposed to military purposes and the availability of engineering, scientific and business talent for civilian industry goes far to explain the industrial success and eminence of Japan. We have seen that, in the classical view, a worker was added when his contribution at the margin exceeds his cost. The Japanese worker is added as an integral part of the enterprise, and for life. Not surprisingly, this induces a loyalty not likely in the Western tradition.

Consumer economics is based on the theory of the profit maximizing business firm. This is derived from the theory that rational individuals will attempt to maximize the benefit or utility of their purchases. According to this theory, increased consumption and more leisure are the sole economic elements of human satisfaction. The consumer economics model is not wrong. Individualism and the desire for consumption and leisure are all parts of human nature. However, they are not all of human nature. Business firms can be based on the historical, psychological, and sociological fact that individuals are also social builders who want to belong to empires that expand. Man is a consumer, but he is unique from all other mammals in that he is also a tool user. As a tool-using animal, work is not necessarily disagreeable. Belonging, esteem, power, building, winning, and conquering are all human goals. These goals are just as important to many workers as maximizing consumption and leisure. Work is where one achieves such goals as those listed above.[7]

Kenichi Ohmae, in his classic book "The Mind of a Strategist," explains the basic Japanese business strategy. The Japanese secret is that they have tapped a universal human desire to build, to belong to an empire, to conquer neighboring empires, and to become the world's leading economic power. Their goal is market-share maximization and value-added maximization not simple profit maximization. The Japanese business strategy, on bringing new products to market, is to enter the market on the low end. Their initial strategic emphasis is to improve their production technology and to test the market in Southeast Asia. The next step is to expand their products to the medium and high end of the market through economies of scale, improving the image of the products, and marketing the product worldwide. The final step in the Japanese business strategy is to "Win the World." They develop this final strategy through global brands, non-price competition and overseas production of products. The Japanese business strategy is not just to become a player in the world market. The Japanese business strategy is to dominate the world market.[8]

Those remembered in human history are not the great consumers. They are the conquerors, the builders, the producers. Being part of a collective effort, of a powerful group, may be more important to some individuals than a lot of personal consumption. As we saw in chapter 1, teamwork is an integral part of achieving economic efficiency. Together, individuals can build something bigger than they could ever dream of building by themselves. Men and women can conquer markets much as they used to conquer neighboring clans. Empires and nations attach citizens to them by offering external security (freedom from conquest) and internal security (law and order). Firms that effectively provide security to generate group solidarity obtain employees who are more directed in their focus, more willing to mobilize and prolong their effort to meet a firm's goals, more willing to sacrifice immediate self-interest, and more interested in achieving the goals of the firm, than those firms that do not provide these benefits. Japanese business firms recognize that they are in the empire building business.[9]

Two basic Japanese business goals are to lengthen time horizons and to accept a lower rate of return. To accomplish these goals, impatient consumption oriented stockholders must be kept under control. The Japanese have organized their business groups to do just that. Japanese business group members own 78 percent of the shares listed on the Tokyo Stock Exchange. With interlocking ownership, Japanese business firms hold impatient consumption oriented shareholders at bay. Members of the business group do not gain by being paid high dividends. They improve their profits because they receive preferential treatment as preferred suppliers and customers.

In developing national strategies, the Japanese goal is to focus on those industries with high income elasticity of demand. This is an economic term meaning that there is a high rate of response to changes in demand caused by a change in price. In addition, the Japanese strategy concentrates on industries that have high rates of growth in productivity, and high value added to products per employee. High value added means that high wages can be paid to employees. With falling prices due to reduced unit costs of production and high income elasticity of demand, markets will be expanding rapidly as consumer incomes grow, and there will be no need to reduce the labor force.

In the 1990's there are seven industries that the Japanese Minister of International Trade believes meets the high value added criteria. These industries are microelectronics, the new materials science industries, biotechnology, telecommunications, civilian aircraft manufacturing, robots plus machine tools, and computers plus software. The Japanese believe that their government has an important role to play in accelerating economic growth. This means raising investments in plant and equipment, skills, infrastructure, and research and development above the levels that would occur in unhindered markets. They believe that market participants have too much interest in the present. In Japan, the government essentially represents the interest of the future in the present.[10]

However, not all Japanese citizens are in love with their government. The Japanese worker faces a marginal federal tax rate of 20 percent that is about the same as the U.S. worker. In addition, the Japanese gross domestic product that totaled $3.927 trillion in 1993, was only 62 percent of the U.S. gross domestic product, while the Japanese per capita GDP was $31,450 or 27% higher than the U.S. per capita GDP. According to the yearly survey conducted by the World Bank, of the top ten countries ranked by per capita GDP in 1993, eight were in Europe, Japan was ranked third and the U.S. was ranked seventh. All ten of these countries could be characterized as having a high degree of domestic consumption with the exception of Japan. With one of the highest living standards in the world, Japanese consumers are already starting to demand an efficient domestic retail market that will provide them with the best products the world has to offer at the lowest possible cost.

Japan continues to have a large trade surplus with both Europe and the United States. The U.S. trade deficit with Japan was $67.318 billion in 1994. The United States has continued to negotiate trade agreements with Japan in an ongoing attempt to open Japanese domestic markets to American products and services. For example, in December of 1996, the United States and Japan reached an agreement, that would open Japan's $341 billion insurance markets, to foreign competition. The deal will give U.S. insurance companies a chance to compete for a bigger share of Japan's market that is now dominated by a Japanese cartel. The agreement ties into Japanese Prime Minister Ryutaro Hashimoto's "Big Bang" plan which is to deregulate Japan's entire financial sector by 2001.

Japan and the United States have a history of bitter disagreement on several trade fronts, most notably autos, alcoholic beverages, semiconductors and photography equipment and film products. The successful insurance agreement settles one of the biggest trade barriers between the two nations. Japanese policy holders under the agreement will have freedom of choice and new products will become available as a result of worldwide competition. If this becomes a standard for other agreements between the United States and Japan, for opening the Japanese domestic markets to international products and services, it could result in a severely reduced Japanese export surplus position with both the United States and Europe.

The Case for the United States

Economically, in the years after World War II, the United States had five overwhelming economic advantages over Europe and Japan.

- In 1950 the American market was more than nine times as large as the next largest market, the United Kingdom. Mass manufacturing was effectively an American monopoly, where unit cost levels were beyond the dreams of the largest foreign producers.

- Americans were superior in technology to the rest of the world. World War II had destroyed the scientific establishments in most of Europe and Japan.

- American workers were more skilled than those found abroad. Americans had invented mass compulsory public elementary and secondary education. With the passage of the GI bill, America was the first nation to give its veterans the opportunity for mass college education.

- America was the richest country in the world. Because Americans had more discretionary income, the first mass market for most consumer products began in the United States.

- American managers were the best educated and trained in the world.

However, in the 1980's, the rest of the world began to catch up with the income levels in the United States. As a consequence, the relative size of the American market got smaller. In addition, modern telecommunications, and transportation technologies have created a world where the size of one's internal market is less important than it used to be. Global market economies of scale and scope are open to everyone, even if they live in relatively small countries.

The Reagan Administration in the 1980's changed the emphasis of antitrust policy by returning to the "Rule of Reason" criteria for judging if an individual firm's action would substantially lessen competition. Also, the Justice Department now considers how a merger or acquisition would effect the total market for a firm's products not just the company's domestic market. This has led to the recognition that big business is not necessarily bad, but actually may be required to compete in international markets.

For 1996, this may wind up being called the "Year of the Merger" as Boeing's $13.3 billion offer for McDonnell Douglas Corp., which was announced in December, topped a year end flurry of deals. In addition to the Boeing/McDonnell Douglas agreement, Vons Companies Inc. agreed to a $1.6 billion offer from Safeway and Bristol Hotel Corp. agreed to pay $659 million for Holiday Inn Hotels, bringing the total value of mergers for the first half of December to over $15 billion. However, the Boeing/McDonnell Douglas deal is only the fourth largest of those made in 1996. The top three mergers in 1996 were Bell Atlantic's $21.3 billion offer for

Nynex, British Telecommunication's $21.3 billion offer for MCI Communications, and SBC Communication's $16.5 pact to acquire Pacific Telesis Group. Deregulation and the increased competition in the telecommunications industry, were major catalysts in these acquisitions. Including the December agreements, the total dollar amount of the mergers, acquisition and spinoffs for 1996 was $659 billion, an historical record for America.

The strong stock market is providing companies with increased value, at least on paper, that enables them to fund merger deals with stock swaps. However, many companies view this as a short term window of opportunity. The trend toward global markets is creating a "Musical Chairs" environment where companies believe that they have to merge so that they are not left without a chair. This is creating a perceived urgency to grow, to be able to compete in the global marketplace. So far, the Justice Department is showing little desire to challenge this wave of mergers. The result is that America, which already has more large corporations than any other country, is being allowed to increase the size of many of its companies in order to compete in the global economy of the twenty-first century.

American commercial banks are also getting into the growth mode in order to compete with the large foreign banks. The Federal Reserve has approved a large number of mergers among commercial banks in the 1990's. While some of these mergers and acquisitions were approved to improve the safety of the banking system, other mergers were allowed to give large banks the ability to compete on a global basis. One of the most notable of the large bank mergers was the combining of Manufacturers Hanover and Chemical Bank into Chemical Bank in the early 1990's. In addition, in 1996 the Fed allowed Chemical Bank to again merge with

Chase Bank to form a bank equal in size to Citibank, the nation's largest. California also got into the merger act as Crocker Bank and First Interstate Corp. were acquired by Wells Fargo and Security Pacific Bank was acquired by the state's largest bank, Bank of America. Even the American farmer, who was already the most productive in the world, is joining the trend toward large size and increased mechanization by using computer modeling techniques to improve their productivity.

The American government could add to the momentum already started by its large industrial and financial corporations, by adopting policies designed to aid businesses in financing international trade and by negotiating fair trade deals with competitive nations. America starts the twenty-first century with more large multinational companies than any other country in the world. If the American government could form a partnership with business, this would serve to enhance an already formidable group of very competitive multinational corporations.

While America has many competitive advantages, there are also reoccurring problems that have to be addressed. American research and development spending used to lead the world, but that is no longer true. Today American non-defense research and development spending is lower than it was twenty years ago, while the Germans and the Japanese have increased their investment in new economic capital. Also, the rest of the world noticed the payoff from America's system of mass education, copied it, and in many cases improved the system. Comparative international examinations given to elementary and secondary school students reveal that Americans at all age levels know less than citizens in other advanced countries. Those Americans who graduate from college catch up with their foreign counterparts,

since most of the rest of the industrial world has not made
the human and physical investments necessary to shift
from elite education to mass education, and America's
graduate schools are the best in the world. However, to be
a success, an economy requires more than just a college
educated labor force. To operate the manufacturing firms
of America, factory workers are also needed. The new
technologies that are coming into the office and factory
are going to require everyone to have levels of math
competence that are far above those needed in the past.[11]

For those that do not go on to college, a poor
education starting position is compounded by less on the
job investment in skills. Ordinary American workers
receive little training beyond what is required to perform
their assigned jobs. At the same time technology has
moved in directions that require a much better educated
and more skilled work force. Today's factories require
workers to use linear programming, and statistical
quality control. To use statistical quality control, every
production worker must master it. To master statistical
quality control requires learning some simple operations
research, but to learn what must be taught, workers must
know algebra. Our politicians often tell their constituents
that they will spend more tax dollars to retrain displaced
factory workers. We should ask these politicians one
simple question about this proposed training. Training in
"What?" During the 1990's, the United States has
experienced large job losses in its manufacturing
concerns. Often these job losses result in structural
unemployment. This is a type of unemployment where the
job skills do not match the available jobs. For example, if
a worker in a large steel mill loses his job, can he be
retrained to work in a computerized mini-steel mill? The
answer to this question, for all practical purposes, is no.
This is because the worker in the large steel mill must be

re-educated before they are retrained. Therefore, retraining in this circumstances, means going back to school to learn the mathematical skills that were not acquired in the first place.

In the 1990's education attainment and increases or decreases in earnings will be highly correlated. American society is now divided into two different earnings groups; a skilled group with rising real wages and an unskilled group with declining real wages (the less educated, the bigger the income reduction; the more educated, the bigger the income gains). What is needed in the United States is a program that is directly related to the problem of structural unemployment not just more political rhetoric.

America starts the twenty-first century with a position second to none. America has the world's largest gross domestic product, the most manufacturing companies and the largest homogeneous market. However, America no longer enjoys the economic dominance that it had in the past. America has many problems both social and economical that it must solve. The first hurdle that America must climb is simply to recognize that problems do exist. The American economy will succeed or fail in the century that lies ahead to the extent that it recognizes its shortcomings and learns to play the new economic games that the Europeans and the Japanese are defining.

CHAPTER 20

NEW STRATEGIES FOR
AMERICA

"The future becomes the present, the present the past, and the past turns into everlasting regret if you don't plan for it." —Tennessee Williams

CONSUMPTION AND INVESTMENT

America's problem is not winning the new economic game, but forcing itself to notice that the game has changed. America needs to recognize that they will have to play a new economic game by a new set of rules and with new economic strategies. A country that wants to win in the economic arena starts by closely studying the competition. Studying the competition is necessary when developing business strategy and just as necessary when evaluating competing countries. First, find those counties in the world that are the best at each aspect of economic performance. Next, measure your performance against their performance to determine your relative strengths and weaknesses. Finally, develop a set of goals and objectives designed to take advantage of your strengths and to improve your weaknesses.

America must recognize that it has a problem relative to its major trading partners. The problem is that American consumers save less than many of their foreign counterparts and American businesses invest at a lower rate than businesses in many other countries. Companies that are located in countries that practice producer economics, usually allocate greater amounts of their total expenditures to new capital investment, than American companies do. America needs to develop strategies specifically designed to improve their economic investment relative to their trading partners. Outlined below is a proposal that, if adopted, could improve this country's ability to compete on an international level.

- The first step is for Americans to stop running large government deficits. Thirty-nine of the states in America have a balanced budget amendment in their constitutions. Perhaps it is time to impose this basic discipline on the federal government as well. During the 1995 secession, the Senate fell two votes short of passing a balanced budget amendment.

- Step two is to adopt a tax system with powerful incentives to save, and powerful disincentives for consumption. During the 1996 Republican primary, several proposals for a flat tax were presented to the public. The basic premise of these plans was to simplify the current federal income tax system and to reduce taxes on investment income.

- Step three is to establish strong incentives for private investment such as an elimination of the double taxation on corporate profits and to increase the incentives for consumer savings for retirement through such programs as Individual Retirement Accounts and 401K programs.

- Finally, the federal government must reduce their propensity to consume and increase their allocation of spending for capital investment. In the long run, the only way for a country to improve both the quality and quantity of its output is to increase its productivity. Productivity is improved through increasing the efficiency of the factors of production. Therefore, the federal budget should be modified to direct more of its spending towards projects that improve the efficiency of labor, capital and natural resources. This can be accomplished through training and educational programs, by increased investment in research and development projects, and as a result of improved land management and mineral production and conservation programs.

In principle, a government could run a surplus in its budgets large enough to finance private investment. However, this principle does not hold up to the evaluation of what government bureaucrats actually do. American governments are not going to run surpluses large enough to obviate the need for private savings because the current system does not encourage this type of action. If American government deficits were produced by increased public investment its citizens could relax about the borrowing necessary to finance them. However, America's budget deficit was not caused by higher public investment. It was caused by higher public consumption. As a result, private savings were being borrowed to finance public consumption. Therefore, the economic analysis of businesses investing the unspent savings of consumers no longer is of value. This is because government is taking a major portion of private savings and consuming it. The result of government using consumer savings for consumption purposes is that fewer funds are left for the private sector. Therefore, business investment had to go down unless additional funds could be borrowed abroad. We have previously referred to this shift in investment spending from businesses to government as the crowding out effect.

If the federal government continues to accumulate large budget deficits, then the amount of money that American citizens owe to foreign investors, will also continue to increase. If government deficits are financed by external borrowing, taxes have to be collected from Americans to make government interest payments to foreign bondholders. The eventual result of increased taxes to pay off foreign debt is that American incomes will fall. Therefore, this trend of increased debts to foreigners requires Americans to ask themselves some serious questions. Can Americans stop this trend of borrowing today and reducing the future incomes of their people? Can a Congress whose historical direction was to extract as much of the federal budget for the purpose of spending money for projects in their home states, somehow develop the discipline necessary to balance the federal budget? In short, can Congress really be expected to act fiscally responsible without the discipline of a balanced budget requirement or at the very least a presidential line item veto? If we rely on history to solve these questions the answer is no. A growing number of Americans are coming to the conclusion that America must first, by law, restrict the size of the federal budget (restrict expenditures to revenue projections) and then let Congress choose how the resources should be allocated. In a vote in 1994, Congress fell four votes short of passing a balanced budget amendment.

In a large business organization, planning starts with developing strategy, i.e., the long-run direction of the firm. Part of developing a framework for strategy is to determine the scope of your markets and products. In other words, the first step in developing business strategy is to determine the possible revenue stream based on realistic goals. To be effectively run, the federal government must be looked upon as a very large business.

The executive branch of the federal government must take the lead in developing a strategic plan for the future allocation of projected revenues. If fiscal policy is to have any future value in controlling business cycles, then a strategic plan must be developed that would balance the federal budget during times of economic growth and increase spending during periods of recession. One of the first steps in developing a fiscal strategy is to divide the current government expenditures into consumption and investment. The next step is to develop strategies based on a planned ratio of investment to consumption. Finally, the federal government should develop a budget structure that analyzes both operating and capital expenditures. All major American businesses require their financial managers to prepare both a capital and an operating budget. This basic financial discipline would be extremely valuable if it were adopted by each of the agencies of the federal government.

If Americans can get everything that they want without saving, what incentives do they have to save? When consumers do save, the government steps in to effectively penalize this effort, by taxing the interest earned on individual savings' accounts. The federal tax system should be changed in a manner that would penalize consumption, not savings. For example, an income tax credit could be established on the first $15,000 of individual savings. To offset the reduction in federal revenue, individual tax rates could be raised slightly. If the government changed its tax system in the above way, these tax-free savings' accounts would be a powerful instrument for raising private savings. If this tax change were introduced, small savings' accounts would effectively be exempted from taxation, and this would turn America's progressive income tax system into a progressive tax on consumption.

Also, to encourage corporate investment, the double taxation of dividends on corporate stock should be eliminated. Currently, corporations pay out dividends to shareholders with after tax dollars. In addition, the individual shareholders must declare these dividends on schedule B of their individual federal income tax returns as dividend income. Therefore, the government taxes this money twice. If the government's strategy is to increase corporate investment in new plant and equipment, then the double taxation of corporate profits is not an effective course of action.

DEVELOPING NATIONAL STRATEGIES

To compete in a world economy, products and services must be speedily designed and precisely tailored to the needs of the customer. To do this, corporations must work with their suppliers and customers, but in the American system of arms-length business relationships, cooperation usually fails. American firms play in a world economy where they face off against Japanese and German business groups. Business groups make it hard for American firms to penetrate foreign markets. With business groups, the American market becomes harder for foreigners to penetrate. Also, American business groups will make it much harder for financial Vikings to raid a company and to sell off the companies' assets. In the words of Adam Smith, the individual search for profits would always promote the nation's economic growth. However, in practice a problem developed. Too often, Adam Smith's "Invisible Hand" became the hand of a pickpocket. Practical experience has taught us that profit maximizing did not necessarily lead to output maximizing.[1]

At the turn of the last Century, America redirected the profit making ambitions of the "Robber Barons" with the Sherman Antitrust Act of 1890 and the Clayton Antitrust Act of 1914. The new laws were designed to insure that the name of the game was to make money by building a better or cheaper product. However, antitrust laws were developed to protect consumers from the industrialist that were prevalent at the turn of the twentieth century. General Motors, for example, is permitted to engage in a joint venture in California, with Toyota that will effectively attack Ford and Chrysler; whereas it would not be permitted to engage in a joint venture with Ford and Chrysler to repel the Japanese auto invasion.

What needs to be done is that the entire regulatory framework of governing finance and industry must be altered so that the biggest profits and highest incomes are paid to those who expand productivity and output rather than to those who manipulate financial assets. To put real capitalists back into American capitalism, today's short-term financial traders must be remade into tomorrow's long-term capitalist builders. The key to this proposed new direction for American firms is changing the financial regulations that prevent American banks and other financial institutions from becoming merchant banks, i.e., the Glass-Steagall Act of 1933.[2]

To be successful, American firms have to be able to build dominant market shares when they have technological leadership. If this is prohibited by foreign industrial policies, others will effectively compete in the United States market when they have technical superiority, but American firms will not be able to compete effectively in foreign markets when Americans have technological superiority.

America's corporations require at least a defensive trade policy to have any chance of winning the economic game. The United States should announce that it will duplicate any policies put in place in the rest of the world. Foreign industrial policies in wealthy countries will be matched dollar per dollar. Any subsidy going to Airbus Industries in Europe will be matched by an equivalent subsidy to Boeing and McDonnald Douglas in America. Japan and Germany do not have less government or more motivated individuals. They are countries noted for their careful organization of teams. These teams involve workers and managers, suppliers and customers, and also, government and business.[3]

America's tough problem is realizing that there are problems that must be solved. Without that realization, nothing can be done. Americans are no longer in a position to force the rest of the world to play the economic game by its rules, but Americans can play the game by their competitor's rules. If the international community wants to play hardball, we'll play hardball, after all the game of hardball was invented in America.

EDUCATION, TRAINING AND ACCOUNTABILITY

The United States is unique among industrial countries in that it does not have an organized post-secondary education for the non-college bound. The Germans have an apprentice system that is the envy of the rest of the world. With lifetime employment, Japanese firms know that they must either train or have an untrained labor force. However, the American secondary education system is not yet the equivalent of our international competitors.

The business entrepreneur produces a product for sale in the market by manipulating the factors of production. In the nineteenth century the supply of skilled labor was scarce in America relative to the demand. Therefore, the industrialist was forced to use labor saving devices to make up for this shortage. In the late nineteenth and the early twentieth centuries, the industrialists began to provide labor with more machines and tools to perform their jobs more efficiently. The next step in this process of improving manufacturing efficiency was to develop ways to better manage the method of work itself. This was accomplished through the theories of scientific management.

In the twenty-first century technology will become less important and the ability of each employee to add value to a product or service will become much more important.

Currently, there is no economic theory of the productivity of knowledge investment. However, we do know that making knowledge productive is a management function. This responsibility is not a function that should be performed by government; and it also cannot be directed by the invisible hand of the price mechanism. Knowledge development requires a systematic and organized partnership between business, government, parents and the students themselves. In the twenty-first century, we will become what Peter Drucker calls "The Knowledge Society." In the knowledge society, school becomes the institution of the adult as well as the traditional student. Above all, in the knowledge society, the school will become accountable for the future performance of its students.[4]

Technology will not be the most important factor of production in the twenty-first century. Most important will be the knowledge level of both management and workers. This will require society to re-evaluate the role and function of schooling; its focus, purpose, and values. Universal literacy is the foundation that is needed for America, or for that matter, any society, to perform in the world of tomorrow. To equip individual students with the tools to perform, to contribute, and to be employable is the most important responsibility and perhaps the biggest challenge of the American education system in the twenty-first century. To meet this challenge, America must develop an education system that is equal to our competitors' systems on all levels, not just for college graduates.

In the school of tomorrow the students will increasingly become their own instructors, and the personal computer will be their technological partner in learning. However, even with the advances in technology, improvements in the level of total literacy pose great challenges. The fundamental skills of reading, writing, and arithmetic will still be needed, but literacy will require numerical achievement; it requires a basic understanding of science and technology. However, the twenty-first century will require education beyond the basics; it will require learning how to be effective as members of an organization. Japanese and German students are already universally taught how to be a member of a team, of a work force. American students that do not go to college, need to have some support system that teaches them how to perform on the job; in short, how to work as part of a team.

Universal literacy implies a clear commitment to the priority of schooling. It demands that the school, especially the elementary school children, subordinate everything else to the acquisition of foundation skills. Unless the school system successfully imparts these skills to the young learner, it has failed in its most important responsibility. That responsibility is to give beginners self-confidence, to give them competence, and to make them capable of performing and achieving in the twenty-first century. However, this requires a reversal of the prevailing trend in American education. In the 1950's and 1960's America reversed its educational priorities. Instead of putting the task of learning first, the American school system became a social institution. However, schools are not designed to be social institutions; they are designed to be learning institutions. Like every other organization, the schools are good only at their special task. Subordinating learning to social goals may have become a major factor in the decline of the basic American educational system. What America has to do to compete in the knowledge society is to reassert the original purpose of its school system. The major purpose of a school system is not social reform or social amelioration; the purpose of school is individual learning.[5]

This assertion could possibly be attacked by our liberal politicians as an elitist position. However, the most elitist school, the Japanese school, has created the most egalitarian society. Even those who do not shine in the intensely competitive educational race in Japan still acquire what by any traditional standard is extremely high literacy and an extremely high ability to achieve and perform in modern society. Yet in the Japanese school, literacy is put first, and everything else is subordinated to it. Still there are those academicians and politicians that might not agree with the scenario that America needs to get back to the basics and to increase the productivity of its educational system. Perhaps, a few statistics on the subject of educational expenditures and achievement might persuade these critics.

Total expenditures on public elementary and secondary schools have increased more than 200 percent since 1960. For example, the following contains an analysis of expenditures, on elementary and secondary education in the United States, from 1960 through 1992. The dollar amounts have been adjusted for inflation using 1989 as the base year. When the dollars spent are compared to the results achieved, as measured by the average SAT scores, there does not appear to be any correlation between the amount of dollars spent on education and the level of academic achievement.

Table 20-1
Amount Spent on Education

Year	Billions of Constant 1989 Dollars
1960	$ 67.5
1965	$ 83.2
1970	$136.8
1975	$159.0
1980	$157.0
1985	$164.5
1990	$205.3
1992	$216.8

Source: U.S. Department of Education

However, since 1960, the scholastic aptitude test scores among all students have dropped 73 points.

Table 20-2
Scholastic Aptitude Test (SAT) Scores

Year	Verbal	Mathematical	Combined
1960	477	498	975
1970	460	488	948
1980	424	466	890
1985	431	475	906
1990	424	476	900
1993	424	478	902

Source: The College Board

In addition, even with the increase in educational expenses, there is no systematic correlation between spending by state on education and student achievement, i.e.,

---

Table 20-3
Top States in SAT Scores: 1992 - 1993

State	Achievement Rank	Expenditure Rank
Iowa	1	27
North Dakota	2	44
South Dakota	3	42
Utah	4	51
Minnesota	5	25

Source: U.S. Department of Education

Table 20-4
Top States in Expenditures: 1992 - 1993

State	Expenditure Rank	Achievement Rank
New Jersey	1	39
Alaska	2	31
Connecticut	3	33
New York	4	40
District of Columbia	5	49

Source: American Legislative Exchange Council and Empower America.

There are many other statistics that could be presented to prove the same point; however, the facts are clear; throwing more money at education does not necessarily improve its quality. What is needed, in fact will be required by tomorrow's businesses, is improved productivity in education. A message from David Kearns the Chairman of Xerox Corporation, can be used to summarize the importance of improving the quality of education in America. "Education must increase its productivity; we must get more education for the dollar. Not just to squeeze more out of the system, but to demonstrate that a good education is worth paying for. Business leaders know that these two ideas are related; unfortunately, educators do not. The public will support productive education willingly; it is reluctant to support unproductive education."[6]

Over the last decade, the United States has witnessed a change in the type of knowledge that is required to perform on a job. The job market of the 1950's and the 1960's, where a student could drop out of high school in the tenth grade and earn a respectable living in a factory is a thing of the past. Where twenty years ago it was common for a man to work for thirty years at the same job, today, a professional can expect to have at least seven different jobs during his career. This has led to a new demand in education; to provide education for the adult worker. This means that tomorrow's society has to create an educational system that offers the individual at any age the opportunity to continue their formal education. In addition, society has to be willing to accept people into whatever work they are qualified for, regardless of their age.

No society today is organized for this. In fact, most developed countries are organized to keep people in the station that they begin their working careers. The system is most rigid in Japan, but nearly as rigid in Europe as well. The United States has gone the farthest in creating educational opportunities for adults. The growth area in American education these last twenty years has been the continuing education of adults at any age, and the willingness to offer even more advanced knowledge to already highly educated people. This gives the United States a tremendous advantage over other developed countries. However, even in the United States, there is still a reluctance to accept people in knowledge work unless they have acquired the basic qualifications fairly early in life. Any professional, over the age of forty, in the United States will attest to the fact that it is almost impossible to change industries once they reach this age.

America also has an outstanding system of education that is located between high school and the college or university. This is the American community college system. The number of community colleges in the United States is much smaller than the number of colleges and high schools. Community colleges are also controlled by the state in which they are located. This equates to only 50 different controlling authorities as opposed to fifteen thousand secondary education authorities. The current community college system in America presents an opportunity for the states and the business community to organize a partnership for the purpose of bringing America's non-college graduate students up to world class standards. However, America is currently under utilizing this resource. The community college system offers a perfect opportunity to develop a partnership between educators and business leaders. The current community college system provides an atmosphere where both academic and apprenticeship training can go on within the same institution. It can offer training in functional skills such as diesel mechanics and academic skills as economics within the same location.

Education in the future will accommodate both an intellectual association and a society of organizations. The educated person will therefore have to live and work simultaneously in two cultures, that of the intellectual and that of the business manager.

Intellectuals see the organization as a tool that enables them to practice their specialized knowledge. Managers see knowledge as a means to the end of an organization's performance. The intellectual's world, unless counterbalanced by the manager, becomes one in which everybody does their "own thing," but nobody ever achieves anything. The manager's world, in contrast, can often lead to the stultifying bureaucracy of the "Organizational Man." However, if the two balance each other, there can be creativity and order, fulfillment and the accomplishment of the overall goals of economics. These goals are a high level of employment, a low rate of inflation and a steady growth in the standard of living of a nation's people.[7]

CHAPTER 21

ECONOMICS AND POLITICS
IN THE 1990's

"The Taxpayer - that's someone who works for the Government but doesn't have to take a Civil Service Examination." —Ronald Reagan

THE CONGRESSIONAL CAMPAIGN OF 1994

In the summer of 1994, the majority of the Republican members of the House of Representatives gathered on the steps of the Capital to start the fall election campaign. By this time it was clear that a majority of the middle class voters were fed up with the entire political process. Many voters had begun to question the goals and promises made to them by their representatives. More and more, the conservative middle class voters were questioning whether the small amount of "Pork" that was brought back into their states was worth the price they had to pay in additional taxes to fund the national debt. There was a growing feeling among voters that Congress is not held accountable for its actions and does not follow the rules that it imposes on the rest of the American people. To take advantage of this sentiment, 367 of the Republican canditates for seats in the House of Representatives, led by House Minority Leader Newt Gingrich of Georgia, responded with a new set of written promises, a "Contract with America."

THE CONTRACT WITH AMERICA

The purpose of the Republican contract was to draw a distinction between a campaign promise and a signed contract. The House document was designed to address the key concerns of the American People. The Contract stated that, within the first one hundred days of the 104th Congress, they would bring to the House Floor the following bills:

1.   **The Fiscal Responsibility Act:** A balanced budget/tax limitation amendment and a legislative line-item veto to restore fiscal responsibility to an out-of-control Congress, requiring them to live under the same budget constraints as families and businesses.

2.   **The Taking Back Our Streets Act:** An anti-crime package including stronger truth in sentencing, "good faith" exclusionary rule exemptions, effective death penalty provisions, and cuts in social spending from the 1994 crime bill to fund prison construction and additional law enforcement to keep people secure in their neighborhoods and kids safe in their schools.

3.   **The Personal Responsibility Act:** Discourage illegitimacy and teen pregnancy by prohibiting welfare to minor mothers and denying increased AFDC (Aid to Families with Dependent Children) for additional children while on welfare, cut spending for welfare

programs, and enact a tough two-years-and-out provision with work requirements to promote individual responsibility.

4.   **The Family Reinforcement Act:** Child support enforcement, tax incentives for adoption, strengthening rights of parents in their children's education, stronger child pornography laws, and an elderly dependent care tax credit to reinforce the central role of families in American society.

5.   **The American Dream Restoration Act:** A $500-per-child tax credit, begin repeal of the marriage tax penalty, and creation of American Dream Savings Accounts to provide middle-class tax relief.

6.   **The National Security Restoration Act:** No U.S. troops under UN command and restoration of essential parts of our national security funding to strengthen our national defense and maintain our credibility around the world.

7.   **The Senior Citizens Fairness Act.** Raise the Social Security earnings limit, which currently forces seniors out of the work force, repeal the 1993 tax hikes on Social Security benefits, and provide tax incentives for private long-term care insurance to let older Americans keep more of what they have earned over the years.

8.   **The Job Creation and Wage Enhancement Act:** Small business incentives, capital gains cut and indexation, neutral cost recovery, risk assessment/cost-benefit analysis, strengthening of the Regulatory Flexibility Act and unfunded mandate reform to create jobs and raise worker wages.

9.   **The Common Sense Legal Reform Act.** "Loser pays" laws, reasonable limits on punitive damages, and reform of product liability laws to stem the endless tide of litigation.

10.   **The Citizen Legislature Act.** A first-ever vote on term limits to replace career politicians with citizen legislators.

The Contract with America was an attempt by the Republicans to personalize the congressional elections by asking voters:

- How much of your taxes does Congress waste?

- Why doesn't Washington listen to your concerns?

- Can social programs be increased in the long-run through borrowing and running huge deficits?

The contract promised specific actions on what the voters perceived to be the country's greatest problems. The contract ended by stating: "Respecting the judgment of our fellow citizens as we seek their mandate for reform, we hereby pledge our names to the Contract With America."

THE MIDDLE CLASS REVOLT

On November 8, 1994, the "Contract with America," was put to the test of the American voters. The results of the election were beyond even the most optimistic of the Republican pollsters. When the 104th Congress convened, in 1995, conservative Republicans were in charge of both houses of Congress. The Republicans won a majority in the Senate, by seizing 9 new seats bringing their total to 53 versus 47 for the Democrats. In the House, Republicans gained an almost unprecedented 52 seats. The races for Governor throughout the country reported an equally devastating blow for Democrats as 11 state houses were lost to the Republicans. In addition, every incumbent Republican Representative and Senator won reelection.

Many of President Clinton's allies were defeated in the election. Among the defeated incumbents were: Senators Harris Wofford (Pennsylvania), Jim Sassier (Tennessee), House Speaker Tom Foley (Washington), House Judiciary Committee Chairman, Jack Brooks (Texas), and the ex-chairman of the House Ways and Means Committee, Dan Rostenkowski (Illinois). In their place, conservative Republicans were put in key positions of power in both the House and Senate. For example, Bob Dole (Kansas) took over as the Senate Majority Leader, Newt Gingrich (Georgia) became the Speaker of the House, and Dick Armey (Texas) the House Majority Leader.

ACCOMPLISHMENTS OF THE 104th CONGRESS

Following is the record of the legislation that was passed by 104th Congress and signed by President Clinton:

- Telecommunications: Congress rewrote the nation's telecommunications laws, to promote competition and remove some of the regulations on telephone, cable and broadcast companies.

• Welfare: Congress ended the federal guarantee of cash assistance to all low-income mothers and children, gave states broad authority to run welfare programs, and also gave the states block grants to offset the additional costs.

• Health: This law made it easier for workers to keep health insurance coverage if they lose or leave their jobs. Also, they enacted a pilot program for Medical Savings Accounts.

• Farm Bill: This bill replaced the decades old commodity subsidy programs with fixed, but declining subsidy payments that aren't linked to market prices or farmers' planting decisions.

• Minimum Wage: This bill raised the minimum wage by 50 cents, to $4.75 an hour, to take effect on October 1, 1996, and then to $5.15 on September 1, 1997. Also the bill included $10 billion in small business tax breaks over a five year period. This legislation was initiated by the Democrats and approved by a majority of both houses.

• Line-Item Veto: This gave the President power to rescind individual items in spending bills unless Congress passes a "disapproval bill," which is subject to a veto.

• Immigration: Cracked down on illegal immigration by authorizing a large increase in the U.S./Mexico boarder patrol officers.

• Shareholder Lawsuits: Limited lawsuits initiated by disgruntled investors against companies who had a large drop in the market value of their stock holdings in those firms.

• Terrorism: The legislation expanded the federal power to prosecute and punish certain crimes related to terrorism.

However, the 104th Congress had several initiatives that either failed to pass or were vetoed by the President, as follows:

• Budget Reconciliation: The Republican sponsored bill to balance the federal budget was vetoed by President Clinton. This resulted in a shutting down of the federal government during two separate occasions. The bill included $245 billion in tax cuts over seven years, and spending restrictions on the growth in Medicare and some other entitlement programs.

• Balanced-Budget Amendment: A constitutional amendment requiring the federal budget to be balanced was defeated in the Senate by two votes.

• Term Limits: A constitutional amendment to limit the terms of members of Congress, was defeated by the House of Representatives.

• Regulatory Overhaul: This legislation would have required the federal government to document costs and benefits of proposed regulations.

• Product Liability: This bill would have capped punitive damages in product liability suits. The bill was vetoed by the president.

The spending agreement for fiscal year 1997 reached between the President and the Republican-led Congress marked a major retreat from the promises, in the Contract with America, on the issue of a balanced budget. After two years in power, Republicans can boast of cutting spending on general government programs, below the levels approved by the Democratic-led Congress, in the fiscal year 1995 budget. However, what began as a crusade is ending in a reversal of direction that is raising doubts about Congress' ability to reach its goal of a balanced budget in seven years.

THE ELECTIONS OF 1996

Borrowing from the theme of Ronald Reagan's "Morning in America" campaign, in 1984, President Clinton presented a positive message to the voters, in the elections of 1996. The president cast himself as a moderate centrist, a defender of core government services and a provider of modest new "tools" to help families with the twin constraints of time and money management. Even as Republican challenger Robert Dole began to attack the President's alleged ethical lapses, Mr. Clinton simply kept smiling, stayed on a positive course, and offered nothing in rebuttal.

The strategy worked and William Clinton became only the third Democrat, beside Woodrow Wilson and Franklin D. Roosevelt to be re-elected to the presidency in the twentieth century. As Karl Rove, a top Republican strategist for Governor George Bush of Texas, noted in the Wall Street Journal; "Its awfully hard to knock off an incumbent Democratic who's willing to run as a Republican." The President had engineered a great comeback after the Republicans gained control of both the House and Senate in the 1994 elections. The key to the

President's re-election was the perception that the Republicans had gotten on the wrong side of popular issues such as Medicare, education, and the environment. In addition, the economy was expanding and consumer confidence was building. However, the voters decided to hedge their bets on the newly positioned, more moderate President Clinton, by electing Republicans to a continued majority in both Houses of Congress.

While the campaign was a success, it provided virtually no road map for the re-elected President to follow over the next four years. There remains a question in the minds of many political analysts as to whether America will have a liberal, conservative or middle-of-the-road President. Big government proposals have little chance of passage in a Republican Congress. Therefore, the President must work with Congress on specific programs that are targeted for improvement. The following are some of the key areas that will probably be on the President's agenda, during his second term in office.

Balance The Federal Budget

The federal budget deficit was reduced to $107 billion for the fiscal year ended September 30, 1996. This is the lowest federal deficit recorded since 1981 when it was $79 billion. However, the job of balancing the budget needs to be finished. The President is aware of the awards offered by the bond markets and the Federal Reserve in lower interest rates. Still nothing has fueled the perception that Washington is out of control more than persistent deficits. Economic expansion and increased tax revenues along with modest reductions in expenditures have served to reduce the current deficit. While this is a good start, it will not balance the budget.

The budget can only be balanced by making tough decisions on the reduction of the growth in expenditures, including entitlements.

Improve Education

Education finance reform was one of the President's key campaign issues. The centerpiece of the education reform proposals is a tax break for tuition and a program to make two years of community college almost as universal as the twelfth grade. A deal may be worked out on education tax breaks as it serves both liberal (increased government involvement) and conservative (improved business productivity through a better educated labor force) interest.

Health Care and Medicare

There will be no attempts for a government takeover of the health care system. The main health care proposal that is on the agenda, is to set up a government fund that will help people who lose their jobs, continue insurance coverage for up to six months. The President will bill the measure as an appropriate next step following the Kennedy-Kassebaum legislation that made it easier for people who change jobs to keep their medical policies.

Many Republicans are resentful of the perceived election-year demagoguery on Medicare, where they were accused of cutting this program by several hundred billion dollars. The President wants to establish a bipartisan commission to recommend a solution to Medicare's long-term problems. However, he will have to reduce the long-term growth rate of Medicare expenses to ensure its stability. If he's prepared to make a deal, including about $150 billion in savings over the next five years, the GOP Congress will probably go along.

Welfare Reform

After signing a welfare-overhaul bill in 1996 with provisions he disliked, President Clinton will attempt to modify this bill. His budget submission to Congress included increased funds for welfare programs; for example, the President wants to rollback some of the cuts in aid to legal aliens and to offer a tax credit to employers who hire long-term welfare recipients. However, Republicans will resist spending any more money on welfare reform, probably approving only modest changes. In addition, any program of tax incentives to hire welfare recipients will have to include some educational incentives. Offering tax incentives for employers to hire workers who are not qualified to perform on the job, is really a false solution to the welfare problem.

Trade

The President will attempt to expand the North American Free Trade Agreement (NAFTA) by including Chile. Also, he will attempt to negotiate a free trade agreement with the remainder of the South American countries. The first step in these negotiations is to get the authority from Congress to negotiate trade agreements that they can only approve or disapprove. Countries are reluctant to enter into talks with the United States which lead to agreements that Congress can amend. Administration officials claim that it is imperative to get "Fast-Tract" authority from Congress. However, not only must Congress be convinced, a compromise must be worked out between labor and environmental groups. The compromise must advocate that fast-tract authority includes stipulations that each country adhere to international labor and environmental standards.

Also, the trade deficit between the United States and China continues to grow topping $29 billion in 1994. The administration needs to negotiate some kind of managed trade agreement with China that includes adherence to international labor standards. The trade deficit with Japan also continues to grow reaching $67 billion in 1994. Negotiations with Japan will continue in order to open Japan's domestic markets to foreign products.

Taxes

The Republican proposed 15 percent across-the-board tax cut will not be approved. The President will put forth a package of middle-class targeted tax cuts. The Republicans in Congress will counter with a broader capital-gains tax cut. The outcome of the negotiations will most likely be that the President will get middle-class reductions, including a $500 per child tax credit and some tax credits for education. However, in return he will have to settle for greater cuts in capital-gains taxes.

The Election of 1996

In summary, the verdict of the electorate in 1996, was a divided government balanced between liberal and conservative philosophy. Corporate America, as witnessed by the week long increase in stock prices after the election, was pleased with the outcome. If Republicans and Democrats can somehow refrain from partisan blood-shedding, the election might result in a centrist agenda for the next four years. This is probably the best that the voter could expect in an America of diminished expectations for government and a reduced faith in politicians.

THE PAST, PRESENT AND THE FUTURE

On April 27, 1994, Richard Nixon, the thirty-seventh President of the United States, was laid to rest. Speaking for his country President Clinton said, "On behalf of former Presidents Gerald Ford, Jimmy Carter, Ronald Reagan and George Bush, and on behalf of a grateful nation, we bid farewell to Richard Milhous Nixon." It was an extraordinary day of reconciliation. Strong men expressed humility. Partisan men laid aside their differences. Henry A. Kissinger, who was President Nixon's Secretary of State, in his speech noticeably fought to hold back his tears as he led the audience of 2,800 invited friends, family and foreign dignitaries in saying good-by to his friend. Kissinger spoke fondly of Nixon as he said; "He stood on pinnacles that dissolved into precipice. He achieved greatly and he suffered deeply, but he never gave up."

Henry Kissinger's fond farewell to Richard Nixon can be used as a lesson for all Americans to remember. We have as a country a certain dignity or a certain class that no other nation has ever achieved. When the Soviet Union first sent a man into space, we responded by making not one but two trips to the moon. When a nation that was one of our close friends and ally was invaded by a dictator, we responded in the Gulf War, with the greatest military might the world has ever witnessed. When our entire automobile industry was threatened by an economic invasion of well-made Japanese products, we responded with a whole new line of well-made American automotive products.

The June 19, 1995, issue of The Wall Street Journal, Stephen K. Yoder presented an article entitled, "Back In The Running: U.S. companies are once again competing for a big piece of the consumer electronics market." According to the article, during 1994, Americans for the first time spent more on personal computers and software than on color televisions. The result of this trend in spending habits is that the consumer electronics market has changed in a way that puts U.S. companies in the running again. This is because households are increasingly purchasing computers, printers, phone equipment and other electronic gadgets that use computer chips as their electronic brains. U.S. companies are once again becoming key players in this industry because consumer electronics is moving from analog technology toward digital technology. U.S. companies are strong in digital electronics because of their lead in computers and their experience selling advanced electronic devices to industry and the military.

Macroeconomic policy still has the same three basic goals: full employment, long-run price stability, and economic growth. So in the 1990's we are left with two basic but less than perfect theories about how to achieve these goals. A conservative government that does nothing to improve the standard of living of its people is not acceptable. On the other hand, a liberal government that spends unwisely and one that creates burdensome regulations is no improvement. What is needed is a new theory, perhaps one that incorporates the best of the two existing ones.

There is an old saying in business that, "A rising tide carries all boats." Businesses need to invest in improving the productivity of the factors of production. Government programs that assist this process are good for the economy and should be continued and even strengthened. In a January 21, 1997, article in The Wall Street Journal, author Bernard Wysocki Jr. describes a new approach to long-term prosperity. The theory, was developed by Paul M. Romer, an economist at Stamford University. His ideas go by the name of "New Growth Theory." According to Dr. Romer, ideas and technology discoveries are the driving engines of economic growth, especially ideas that are codified in a chemical formula, or embodied in a peace of computer software or, in some way, improve the efficiency of the factors of production.

And finally, who will win the twenty-first century? On the basis of the evidence developed throughout this book, it is this author's opinion that the United States will retain its position as the economic leader of the world because it is already the leader and there is no clear cut evidence that any other country can overtake America. The second largest economy in the world is Japan. However, Japan's gross domestic product is only about 65 percent of America's and their domestic market, is inefficient compared to those found in the United States and Western Europe. As for the European Union, the current trend is toward more nationalism. This trend makes the transition toward a unified Europe even more difficult. Therefore, in its quest toward remaining the world's largest economic power, it is difficult to see how the United States could lose the twenty-first century; unless America defeats itself.

With only a few years remaining in the twentieth century, the debate continues over the role of government in business. Should the federal government emphasize the regulation of business and risk the possibility of "shooting itself in the economic foot"? Or should government form a partnership with business and develop strategic visions for the future? Here, at least, is one vote for "Team America."

GLOSSARY OF
ECONOMIC TERMS

A

Aggregate demand. The market value of all planned expenditures.

Agricultural Adjustment Administration. A federal agency created by the Roosevelt administration to control farm prices by setting minimum prices, controlling production and providing for the storage of quantities that was over the established limits.

American value system. A term used to describe the attitudes of American workers, towards their jobs, during the industrial revolution.

Antitrust policy. A set of laws that seek to control the competitive behavior of firms.

B

Balance budget amendment. A proposed amendment to the U.S. Constitution that would require Congress to balance the federal budget by the year 2002.

Bank Holiday of 1933. An action, taken by President Roosevelt, that closed the nation's entire banking system, for one week in 1933, in order to stop the run on bank deposits.

Bourgeoisie. A term, used by Carl Marx, to describe the industrial capitalist.

Brain drain. A situation where the brightest students of an undeveloped country move to a developed one.

Bretton Woods System. An agreement that governed international exchange rates from after World War II until 1971.

British Mercantilism. An economic system that existed from the sixteenth century through the end of the eighteenth century, where British Colonies were to provide the "Mother Country" with raw materials in return for British finished goods.

Omnibus Budget Reconciliation Act of 1993. A law designed to reduce the federal deficit by $400 billion in 5 years. This was to be accomplished through tax increases on gasoline, adjustments of the tax tables on individuals making over $125,000 per year, and some small expenditure reductions.

Budget Reconciliation Act of November 1990. A law designed to reduce the federal budget deficit. This law consisted mostly of defense cuts and tax increases that were designed to reduce the budget deficit by $400 billion from 1991 through 1995.

Bureaucracy. The system of managers and workers that are employed by the government.

Business cycle. A pattern of the economies repeated expansion and contraction of business activity.

Business groups. Associations where groups of businesses, that compete in the same industry or that are suppliers to an industry, get together to promote economic activity.

C

Capital. The means of production that is created by people including tools, equipment and structures.

Capital account. An account that consists of purchases and sales of assets and international borrowing and lending.

Capital Inflow. Are inflows of money into a country to pay for a deficit in the current account.

Capital Outflow. Are outflows of money from a country that result from a trade surplus.

Capital gains tax. A tax that is levied on personal income based on the profit from an investment.

Cartel. A group of producers that jointly attempt to maximize their profits by limiting production and controlling prices.

Central economic planning. An economy in which the political leaders decide the direction that the country will take.

Ceteris Paribus. A Latin term meaning, "Other things being equal." A method of analyzing economic data, that was first developed by Alfred Marshall, where the elements of the particular analysis are considered under the assumption that all other elements, that could affect the analysis, remain constant.

Christianity: A religion based on the teachings of Jesus.

Circular flow. The flow of goods and services between households and firms balanced by the flow of payments made in exchange for goods and services.

Clayton Antitrust Act. A law, passed by congress in 1914, that outlawed mergers that would substantially lessen competition.

Communism. A form of government, based on the "Communist Manifesto," by Karl Marx and Frederick Engel. This publication predicted a violent revolution, by the working class, against the industrial capitalists.

Comparative advantage. The ability to produce goods or services, at a relatively lower opportunity cost, than someone else.

Conspicuous consumption. A term coined by Thorstein Veblen to describe the actions of rich capitalists in showing off their wealth.

Conspicuous leisure. A term coined by Thorstein Veblen to describe the actions of rich capitalists and their offspring who did not work.

Constant dollars. Dollars that are adjusted by a price index.

Consumer durable goods. Consumer goods that are expected to last more than one year.

Consumer economics. A theory, that is based on individual values, performance and rewards. The major goal for a firm that practices consumer economics is profit maximization.

Consumer price index. An index, based on the price of a market basket of goods and services, that are purchased by a typical urban household.

Consumption expenditures. The total amount that is spent on the purchase of goods and services, by consumers, in one year.

Contract With America. A set of written promises, that were made by the Republican members of the House of Representatives, in September of 1994. The purpose of the contract is to draw a distinction between a campaign promise and a signed contract.

Crowding-out effect. The tendency of expansionary fiscal policy to raise interest rates and thereby cause a decrease in real planned investment.

Current account. The international balance of payments account that includes imports and exports of goods and services plus unilateral transfers.

D

Deficit. The yearly difference between the federal government's gross revenues and expenses.

Demand. The desire and ability to obtain goods and services.

Demand deposit. Money, deposited in commercial banks and thrifts, that can be used to write checks that are acceptable to pay debts.

Depreciation (of a currency). A decline in the value of a country's currency, relative to that of its trading partners.

Diminishing marginal utility. The theory that, as individuals continue to increase their consumption of a good the level of satisfaction, from the consumption of additional units of that product, will steadily be reduced.

Discount rate. The interest rate that is charged, by the Fed, on loans to banks.

Dismal Science. A term that was given to the field of economics by Thomas Caryle. The term was based on the writings of Thomas Malthus.

Disposable income. Personal income minus personal taxes.

Double taxation of profits. The federal taxation of both corporate profits and the after-tax dividends that are paid to the owners of the corporation.

E

Economic forecasting. The application of economic variables to forecast future business events.

Economic history. The subject that deals with the ways in which man has used his limited resources to satisfy his wants and with the institutions he has developed to organize economic activity.

Economic Investment. An investment that adds to the capital stock of an economy. Capital stock includes, fixed investment such as new plant and equipment and machinery and changes in the stock of finished inventory.

Economies of scale. A situation where long-run average costs decreases as output increases.

Economics. The social science that seeks to understated the choices people make in using scarce resources to meet their demands.

Elasticity. A ratio that measures the response of one variable to a change in another one. The ratio is stated as a percentage change.

Entrepreneur. A term coined by Joseph Schumpeter to describe the businessman who develops new products and manufacturing processes to improve the quantity and quality of products.

European Common Market. An economic and political union among the major trading countries of Europe, that allows free trade between its members.

Excess reserves. Total reserves in the banking system minus required reserves.

Exchange rate. The rate at which one country's currency can be traded for currency of another country.

Executive Branch. The part of the U.S. federal government that is controlled by the President and the federal agencies.

Exports. Consist of goods and services that are sold from one country to another country.

External debt. The amount of debt that a nation owes to foreigners.

F
Factor market. The markets in which firms obtain the necessary factors of production.

Factors of production. The resources, or inputs that are necessary to produce goods or services. The factors include, labor, technology, capital investment and natural resources.

Federal Deposit Insurance Corporation. A federal agency, that was created by the Roosevelt administration in the 1930's, to insure consumer demand deposits at commercial banks and thrifts.

Federal Emergency Relief Agency. A federal agency, that was created by the Roosevelt administration in the 1930s', to assist the unemployed. The agency made grants to the states to support a program of work relief during the great depression.

Federal Open Market Committee. The Fed's authority to purchase and sell government securities rests with this committee.

Federal Reserve Bank of NY. The decisions regarding changes in the Fed's holdings of securities are carried out through the open market trading desk at the Federal Reserve Bank of NY.

Federal Reserve Board. This is the policy making body of the Federal Reserve System. The board has seven members who have the power to approve changes in the interest rate on loans made to member banks and to set minimum levels of reserves that banks and thrifts are required to hold.

Federal Reserve System. An independent agency of the federal government, that was established in 1913. The Federal Reserve Bank is the central bank of the United States.

Financial Vikings. A group of companies or individual investors who buy the stock of a company and sell the individual assets of that company, for more than the cost of the stock purchase.

Financial flows. The continuing process of trading stocks and bonds and making loans.

Financial intermediaries. A set of institutions whose function is to channel the flow of funds from net savers to net investors.

Fiscal policy. The policy that is concerned with the federal government's purchases, taxes, and transfer payments.

Fiscal State. The belief that the federal government should play an active role in the economic development of a country.

Fixed exchange rate. This occurs when a government selects an exchange rate and offers to buy and sell currencies at that rate.

Flexible exchange rate. This occurs when the foreign exchange market determines the rate of exchange between two country's currencies.

Fundamental Analysis. An analysis of the basic income and expense, balance sheet, and cash flow positions of a company.

G
GDP as expenditures. The market value of all final goods and services produced in a country in one year. The GDP accounts include household consumption, business investment, government purchases, and net exports.

Glasnost: A policy, developed by Mikail Gorbachev, to open up the political system of the Soviet Union.

Glass-Steagall Act. Legislation, passed by the Roosevelt administration, to separate the business of the securities and the banking industries.

Gold standard. A system, established by the Paris conference of 1876, which made gold the medium of exchange of all participating countries. Under the system, a country must maintain a stockpile of gold large enough to cover the market demand for their currency.

Government expenditures. Purchases of goods and services that are made by the federal government.

Gramm-Rudman-Hollings Law. A law passed by Congress, in December 1985. This law established a declining set of deficit targets which if implemented would have balanced the federal budget by the year 1991.

Greenbacks. Paper money that was issued by the U.S. government to fund the Civil War.

Gross domestic product. The total market value of all goods and services produced in a country in one year.

Gross domestic product deflator. A weighted average of the prices of all final goods and services produced in a country.

Gross national debt: The total of all accumulated federal government deficits. This is the total amount that the federal government owes to its creditors.

Gross private investment: Expenditures, that are made by businesses on fixed assets and new inventory, and residential and non-residential structures.

H
Horizontal merger. A combination of two or more firms that are in the same industry.

I

Immigration. This occurs when the citizens of one country set up residency in another country.

Imports. Are goods and services produced in another country and sold in the home country.

Indirect business taxes. Taxes that are levied by government on the final sales of businesses. For example, sales taxes and excise taxes.

Industrial Capitalist. The name often used to refer to the owners of businesses during the nineteenth and the early twentieth centuries.

Industrial Revolution. A period from 1750 through 1900 where technology and machines rapidly modernized industrial production.

Inflation. A sustained increase in the average level of prices of all goods and services.

Infrastructure investment. These are additions to the underlying structure of the economy, such as transportation facilities, highways and utilities.

Installment plan buying. This occurs when consumers borrow from financial organizations, for the purpose of buying durable goods.

Interest. The income paid to consumers for the use of their savings.

Internal debt. The portion of the net public debt that the federal government owes to its own citizens.

International balance of payments. The record's of all the transactions that occur between the citizens of one country and those of foreign countries.

International Monetary Fund. An international financial institution that is concerned with monetary issues.

Investment Trusts. These are non-operating companies that purchase stock for their own account and sell shares of their company's stock to the public.

Invisible Hand. A term developed by Adam Smith to describe the workings of the price system in a market economy.

Iron Law of Wages. A theory, developed by David Ricardo, which held that wages are the price that is necessary to enable the laborers to subsist and to perpetuate their race. The theory established that those who worked were meant to be poor and were not to be rescued by a compassionate government.

K

Keiretsu Groups. Japanese business groups that are financially interlocked and work together to strengthen each other's activities.

L

Labor. The contribution to productivity made by people.

Labor theory of value. Developed by Adam Smith, the theory argued that the worth of any possession is measured ultimately by the amount of labor for which it can be exchanged.

Laissez Faire. A term that was coined by the eighteenth century French Physiocrats. The term is most often used to argue that the government should keep its hands out of business affairs whenever possible.

Law of Accumulation. The economic theory proposed by Adam Smith which stated that the money to build manufacturing facilities mostly came from the profit of the enterprise or the accumulated savings of the capitalist.

Law of demand. The principle that an inverse relationship exists between the price of a good and the quantity of that good that buyers demand.

Law of supply. The principle that more of a good will be supplied the higher its price, other things being equal.

Learning by doing. A theory which states that workers get better at their jobs as they gain experience in performing the required tasks.

Line item veto. A change, in the federal government procedure, that would allow the president to veto a single expense item in a new bill without rejecting the entire bill.

M

Machine tools. Are machines that are used to automate a factory. Such tools include milling machines, grinding machines and turret lathes and die casting machines.

Macroeconomics. The part of economics that studies large scale aggregates including, employment, inflation and economic growth.

Managed trade. International trade based on a written contract between the two trading countries.

Marginal costs. The additional cost required to increase production by one unit.

Marginal propensity to consume. The proportion of each additional dollar of real disposable income that households use to buy goods and services, and the amount of disposable income that is saved.

Marginal utility. The amount of added satisfaction that a consumer gets by adding one additional unit of a good or service.

Market economy. A capitalist system that relies on the price mechanism to distribute its products.

Market equilibrium. A condition in which buyer and seller plans exactly mesh in the marketplace.

Market share. An individual firm's sales of a specific product compared to the entire sales of all companies in the market.

Market Structure. The conditions under which a firm operates in the market. The key traits of a market include the number and size of firms, the nature of the products, the ease of entry and exit from the market and the information available to the competing companies.

Mass compulsory public education. A system where a country requires all of its citizens to attend school up to a certain age.

Mass consumption. A situation that occurs when enough people are located in a specific geographical area to establish a built in market for a product.

Mass production. A situation where a manufacturer produces large quantities of standardized products.

Merchandise balance. The international balance of payments account that shows the total amount of exports and imports of goods.

Merchant Capitalism. An economic system where government decides who engages in economic activity. This system dominated Europe and America from the sixteenth to the eighteenth centuries.

Merger. The Combination of two or more companies where the resulting firms maintain the identity of the acquiring firm.

Microeconomics. The part of economics that studies small economic units including, individual households, business firms and government agencies.

Mismatching of assets and liabilities. An occurrence where a financial institution funds its long term assets, mainly loans, with short term liabilities.

Monetarism. A theory of long term macroeconomic equilibrium that emphasizes the steady growth of the money supply at a rate that is consistent with the economy's ability to produce goods and services.

Monetary policy. The policy conducted by Fed that influences the economy through changes in the money supply and credit availability.

Monetary target. A financial variable for which the Fed sets a short-term target, which it then uses as a guide in the day-to-day conduct of open market operations.

Money. An asset that serves as a means of payment, a store of purchasing power and a unit of account.

Monopolistic competition. A market structure where there are many small firms and easy entry and exit. Firms in this market invest additional amounts of money into expanding the features of their products to add value for their customers.

Monopoly. A situation where there is only one seller of a good or service.

Moving assembly line. A manufacturing process where parts travel along a conveyor belt to the workers in a factory. This technique was first introduced in the automotive industry by Ransom Olds.

Multiplier effect. The theory that there is a tendency, for a given initial shift in any component of real aggregated demand, to cause a larger shift in the total real aggregate demand. This occurs because money can be spent more than once.

N

National Banking Act. A law enacted by Congress in 1863 for the purpose of providing a uniform currency to eliminate the oversupply of state bank notes.

National Income. The total income earned by a country's residents. This income includes wages and salaries, rental income, interest payments and business profits.

National State. This arose as a response to transnational attempts to unify Europe by force during the seventieth century. The national state consists of a political structure that allows for a government to create laws for the entire nation.

National income accounting. The system that provides a way of measuring the total output of an economy over a designated period of time.

National strategies. A national policy that is developed by a federal government for the purpose of defending their citizens from the unfair trading practices of other countries.

Natural Resources. Mineral deposits that are found in their natural state in the ground; for example, iron ore, gold and oil.

Natural selection. The theories of Social Darwinism which claimed that companies prospered because they had the best products, the best delivery systems and the best managers. The theory claimed that only the most fit would survive. All other companies would go out of business.

Net exports. The difference between total exports and total imports.

Net public debt. The amount of the gross public debt that is not owned by the Federal Reserve or by government agencies.

Net taxes. The amount of taxes paid to government authorities minus transfer payments that are made by the government.

Neutrality of money. The theory that, in the long run, changes in monetary policy can only effect the general price level.

Normative Economics. The parts of economics that is concerned with judgments about which conditions or policies are good or bad.

O
Old-age pensions. Payments to people who are retired from the full time work force. Social Security is the federal government's largest system of old-age pensions.

Oligopoly. A situation where a few large companies dominate an entire industry. The theory of oligopoly was first developed by Edward Chamberlin and Joan Robinson.

Open market operations. Purchases or sales of government securities that are made by the Federal Reserve either to or from the public.

Opportunity cost. The cost of the best alternative that could have been chosen.

Overproduction of consumer goods. This occurs when manufacturers produce more goods than they can sell to consumers. This results in a buildup in inventories and often leads to a recession.

P
Partially flexible exchange rate. An international monetary exchange system where rates are allowed to fluctuate. However, governments can intervene in the market to alter the value of their currencies.

Pent-up demand. A situation where consumer demand to purchase a product is restricted by government action. The demand increases after the restrictions are eliminated.

Per capita national income. The result obtained when national income is divided by the total population. This is an indication of the standard of living in a country.

Perestroka. A strategy developed by Mikail Gorbachev that meant to restructure the economic system of the Soviet Union.

Personal income. The total income received by households that includes, earned income, payroll deductions and transfer payments.

Physiocrats. A group of eighteenth century French philosophers who developed the idea of an economic system, as an interconnected and interdependent structure of concepts; a controlling natural law of economic behavior, the prominence of agriculture and a laissez faire approach towards government interference in business.

Political rent seeking. Any policy designed to obtain or defend economic rent as a result of government action.

Pork-barrel State. A government where elected representatives use the taxes of their constituents to enrich special interest groups, who in turn, are heavy contributors to the officials campaign fund.

Positive economics. The part of economics that is concerned with analyzing data and coming to conclusions based on efficiency.

Producer economics. A form of communitarian capitalism that is practiced by Germany and Japan. In these countries one joins a team and is then successful as part of that company team.

Producer Price Index. Is a ratio of a composite of prices based on a sample of goods and services bought by business firms. Economists use the PPI as an early indication of the future direction of inflation.

Productivity. The ratio of output produced to the amount of input that was contributed by the factors of production.

Productivity Revolution. A period from 1900 through 1960, where knowledge began to be applied to the work itself.

Profit maximization. The financial concept that emphasizes maximizing the wealth of a firm's shareholders.

Proletarian. A term used by Carl Marx to describe the workers in a capitalist society.

Public Choice Theory of Economics. A theory developed by James Buchanan to explain why fiscal policy no longer worked in the United States.

Purchasing power of the dollar. A measure of the quantity of goods and services that can be purchased for one dollar.

Q
Quantity Theory of Money. The Classical economic theory that argues that price levels vary, in response to changes, in the quantity of money.

R
Real gross domestic product. Gross domestic product adjusted for inflation using the gross domestic product deflator.

Recession. A cyclical contraction of gross domestic product that lasts for two consecutive quarters.

Reserve requirement. The minimum amount of reserves that the Fed requires depository institutions to hold. These funds must be set aside at the Fed or in the vaults of the individual banks.

Return on investment. A measurement of the amount of profit that is received from an investment compared to the total investment.

Rugged Individualism. A theory that was championed by American Socialist William Graham Sumner during the latter part of the nineteenth century. The theory held that all social systems develop and change by a natural process that results in a maximization of individual wealth.

S
Say's Law of Markets. Developed by eighteenth century economist John Baptiste Say, the theory states that the production of goods creates a level of demand sufficient to purchase all of the products that are marketed.

Scientific management. A theory and method developed by Frederick Taylor that represented the utilization of research as an approach to the solution of management problems. The theory stressed the standardization of products and manufacturing process, time and motion studies, incentive plans, and selection and training of workers.

Sherman Antitrust Act. A law, passed by congress in 1890, that outlawed all contracts and conspiracies in restraint of trade.

Shooting ourselves in the foot. Acting in a way that makes it much more difficult to achieve stated goals and objectives.

Single tax. A recommendation made by Henry George, to tax away the unearned gain in land values that did not derive from the effort of the land owners.

Skilled workers. Workers with special training that is marketable to business corporations.

Social Darwinism. A theory based on the works of English economist William Spencer. Spencer wrote that all social systems develop and change by a natural process that results in a maximization of individual wealth.

Social Security Act of 1935. Legislation that was passed by the Roosevelt administration to relieve the hardships of the depression. The act directed aid to those unable to work, provided a system of retirement benefits and established unemployment insurance.

Socialism. An economic system that is associated with government ownership of productive resources. The system includes a central planning authority for the purpose of producing and distributing goods and services.

Special interest group. An organization that seeks to persuade government to increase spending in a way that will benefit the members of the group.

Stagflation. An economic term used to describe an economy where real GDP is stagnant and inflation is growing.

Stock purchases on margin. Using funds that are borrowed from a financial institution to purchase corporate stock.

Strategic planning. A management tool that is used to systematically determine the future direction of a firm.

Structural unemployment. A condition where the available jobs do not match the training of the potential applicants for those jobs.

Supply. The amount of goods and services that will be delivered to the marketplace at various prices.

Supply shock. An event that raises prices for most firms and increases the workers cost of living. An example is the large increase in the cost of foreign oil created by OPEC in the 1970's.

Synergy. A term used in business to describe a situation where resources can be shared among different businesses within the organization.

T
Technology. The use of machines and other production systems, for the purpose of increasing output per man hour.

Term limits. A proposal that would limit the amount of times a person could run for political office.

The Great Society. The name used to describe the social welfare programs that were developed by the Johnson administration in the 1960's.

The New Deal. The name used to describe the social welfare programs that were developed by the Roosevelt administration, during the depression of the 1930's.

The World Bank. An international financial institution that works with undeveloped nations to secure international loans.

Trade deficit. A situation where a nation buys more goods and services from foreigners than it sells to them.

Twin deficits. The current account deficit plus the federal budget deficit is often referred to as the twin deficits.

U

Underemployment equilibrium. A term, used by John Maynard Keynes, to describe a situation where an economy could fall to a level of production below its normal trend. Keynes argued that an economy in this state could stay there until the federal government took steps to increase aggregate demand.

Unilateral transfers. A situation where one country or its citizens give something to foreigner.

Utilitarianism: An early defense of the capitalist system that identified happiness or utility with that property in any object that tends to produce more benefit's than pain.

V

Velocity of money. A measure of the average number of times each dollar of the money stock is used each year for income producing purposes.

Vertical merger. The purchase, by an acquiring firm, of other firms that are suppliers to the company or markets the organization's products.

W

Wage and price controls. The establishing of legal limits on prices and wages by the federal government.

NOTES:

Chapter 1
The Economic Way of Thinking

1. Marshall, Alfred, <u>Principles of Economics, 9th Edition</u>, London, England, Macmillan, 1920, p. 1.
2. Dolan, Edward S. & Lindsey, David E., <u>Economics, Seventh Edition</u>, The Dryden Press, Orlando, FL, 1994, p. 9.
3. Dolan and Lindsey, p. 10.
4. Hyman, David N., <u>Economics, Third Edition</u>, Boston, MA, Irwin, 1994, p.10.
5. Dolan and Lindsey, p. 14

Chapter 2
The Roots of Political Economics

1. Aristotle, <u>Politics, Book I, In Early Economic Thought, Edited by A.E. Monroe</u>, Cambridge, MA, Harvard University Press, 1924, p. 10.
2. Aristotle, Politics, Book I, p. 19.
3. Saint Thomas Aquinas, <u>Summa Theological, in Early Economic Thought</u>, pp. 54-55.
4. Oresme, <u>Traictie de la Premiere Invention des Monnoies, in Early Economic Thought</u>, p. 95.
5. Bodin, Jean, <u>Les Six Livres de la Republic, In Early Economic Thought</u>, p 127.

6.   Galbraith, John Kenneth, <u>Economics in</u>
       <u>Perspective</u>, Boston, MA, Houghton Mifflin
       Company, 1987, p. 38
7.   Hume, David, <u>On Money, " In his Writings on</u>
       <u>Economics,"</u> Edited by Eugene Rotwein, Madison,
       WA, University of Wisconsin Press, 1955.
8.   Galbraith, p. 56

Chapter 3
American: The Colonial Years

1.   Krooss, Herman, <u>American Economic Development</u>,
       Englewood   Cliffs, N.J., Prentice-Hall, Inc., 1966,
       p. 150
2.   Lester, Richard A., <u>Monetary Experiments</u>,
       Princeton, N.J., Princeton University Press, 1939.
3.   Brownlee, Elliot, W., <u>Dynamics of Ascent</u>, Belmont,
       CA, Wadsworth Publishing Company, 1988, p. 104.

Chapter 4
The Foundations of Classical Economics

1.   Smith, Adam, <u>An Inquiry into the Nature and</u>
       <u>Causes of The Wealth of Nations</u>, R.H. Campbell,
       A.S. Skinner and W. B. Todd, Editors., Oxford, En,
       Clarendon Press, 1977 [1776], Introduction.
2.   Smith, Book I, Chapter 2.
3.   Smith, Book I, Chapter 5.
4.   Smith, Introduction.
5.   Smith, Book 4, Chapter 1.
6.   Gailbraith, John Kenneth, <u>Economics in</u>
       <u>Perspective</u>, Boston, MA, Houghton Mifflin
       Company, 1987, p. 75.
7.   Heilbroner, Robert L., <u>The Wordly Philosophers</u>,
       New York, Simon & Schuster, Inc., 1986, p. 65.

8.   Heilbroner, p. 66.

9.   Malthus, Thomas A., <u>An Essay on the Principle of Population, 6th Addition</u>, London, England, Ward Lock, 1890, p. 15.

10.   Sraffa, Piero, <u>The Works and Correspondents of David Ricardo</u>, Cambridge, England, Cambridge University Press, 1951, p. 11.

11.   Ricardo, p. 77.

12.   Gailbraith, pp. 100-101.

Chapter 5
The Foundations of Democracy

1.   Hughes, Jonathan, R., <u>American Economic History, Third Edition,</u> Chicago, IL, HarperCollins Publications, 1990, p. 86.

2.   Hughes, p. 90.

3.   Hughes, p. 91.

Chapter 6
Finance and Banking (1800-1900)

1.   Puth, Robert, C. <u>American Economic History</u>, Orlando, FL, The Dryden Press, 1993.

2.   Esterlin, L. Davis, <u>American Economic Growth: An Economists History of the United States</u>, New York, N.Y., Harper and Row, 1971.

3.   Calomiris, C., <u>Is Deposit Insurance Necessary? A Historical Perspective</u>, Journal of Economic History, June 1990.

4.   Lee, S. and Passell, P., <u>A New Economic View of American History</u>, New York, N.Y., Norton, 1979, pp. 112-113.

5.   Puth, p. 240.

6.   Bureau of the Census, <u>Historical Statistics</u>, 1:1020.

7.   Fogel and Engerman, The Reinterpretation of
       American Economic History, New York, N.Y.
       Harper and Row, 1971.

Chapter 7
The Evolution of Classical Economics

1.   Galbraith, John Kenneth, Economics in
       Perspective, Boston, MA, Houghton Mifflin Co.,
       1987, p. 108.
2.   Bentham, Jeremy, Introduction to the Principles of
       Morals and Legislation, New York, NY, Haffner,
       1948, p. 1.
3.   Buchholz, Todd G., New Ideas From Dead
       Economists, New York, NY, Penguin Books, 1989,
       p. 99.
4.   Buchholz, p. 102.
5.   Marx, Karl and Engels, Friedrich, The Communist
       Manifesto, Edited by Francis B. Randall, New
       York, N.Y., Simon & Schuster, 1964. p 11.
6.   Marx, p. 16.
7.   Marx, p. 16.
8.   Marx, p. 57.
9.   Marx, p. 61.
10.   Galbraith, p. 133
11.   Fusfeld, Daniel R., The Age of the Economists,
       Fifth Edition, Glenview, IL, Scott Foresman and
       Co., 1986, p. 72
12.   Fusfeld, p. 72.
13.   Galbraith, p. 122
14.   Fusfeld, p. 74.

Chapter 8
The Industrial Revolution (1800-1900)

1.   Brownlee, W. Elliot, <u>Dynamics of Ascent - A</u>
      <u>History of the</u> <u>American Economy,</u> Wadsworth
      Publishing Company, Belmont, CA, 1988, p. 129.
2.   Brownlee, p. 135.
3.   Krooss, Herman, E., <u>American Economic</u>
      <u>Development</u>, Englewood Cliffs, N.J. Prentice-Hall,
      Inc., 1966. p. 349.
4.   Krooss, Herman, E., p. 351.
5.   Brownlee, p. 186.
6.   Krooss, Herman E. <u>American Economic</u>
      <u>Development, Second Edition</u>, Englewood Cliffs,
      NJ, Prentice-Hall, Inc., 1966, p. 343.
7.   Krooss, p. 343.
8.   Krooss, p. 155.
9.   Krooss, p. 160.
10.   Krooss, p. 161.
11.   Krooss, p. 162.
12.   Krooss, p. 163.
13.   Krooss, p. 164.
14.   Boyes, William and Melvin, Michael, <u>Economics</u>,
      Boston, MA, Houghton Mifflin Co., 1991, p. 715.
15.   Boyes, p. 716.
16.   Puth, Robert C., <u>American Economic History, Third</u>
      <u>Addition</u>, Fort Worth Texas, The Dryden Press,
      1993, p. 348.
17.   Krooss, p. 241

Chapter 9
Neoclassical Economics

1. Buchholz, Todd G., New Ideas From Dead Economists, New York, NY, The Penguin Group, 1987, p. 152.
2. Marshall, Alfred, Principles of Economics, 9th Edition, London, England, 1961, p. 316.
3. Buchholz, p. 160.
4. Marshall, p. 3.
5. Keynes, John Maynard, "Alfred Marshal," in Essays in Biography, London, England, Macmillan, 1972, p. 164.
6. Galbraith, John Kenneth, Economics in Perspective, Boston, MA, Houghton Mifflin Company, 1987, p. 167.
7. Galbraith, P. 171.
8. Galbraith, P. 176.
9. Heilbroner, Robert L. The Worldly Philosophers, New York, NY, Simon & Schuster, 1986, p. 295.
10. Heilbroner, P. 296.
11. Galbraith, P. 183.
12. Krooss, p. 362.

Chapter 10
Scientific Management, Mass Production and World War I

1. Drucker, Peter F., Post Capitalist Society, New York, NY, HarperCollins, 1993, p. 19.
2. Drucker, p. 34.
3. Drucker, p. 35
4. Drucker, p. 32.

5. Krooss, Herman, E. <u>American Economic Development</u>, Englewood Cliffs, NJ, Prentice-Hall, 1966, p. 380.
6. Krooss, p. 382.
7. Ford Henry, <u>My Life and Work</u>, Garden City, N.Y., Doubleday & Co., 1992, pp. 91-92.
8. Krooss, p. 384.
9. Krooss, p. 171.
10. Nelson, R.L., <u>Merger Movements in American Industry, 1895- 1956</u>, Princeton, NJ, Princeton University Press, 1959.
11. Puth, Robert C., <u>American Economic History, Third Edition</u>, Fort Worth, TX, The Dryden Press, 1993, p. 492.
12. U.S. Department of Commerce, Bureau of the Census, <u>Historical Statistics of the United States</u>, Washington, DC, Government Printing Office, 1975, Volume 1 - p. 511.
13. Historical Statistics, Volume 2 - p. 1140.

Chapter 11
The Roaring Twenties-Prosperity and Depression

1. Krooss, Herman E., <u>American Economic Development</u>, Englewood Cliffs, NJ, Prentice-Hall, Inc., 1966, p. 176.
2. Krooss, p. 244.
3. Brownlee, W. Elliot, <u>Dynamics of Ascent, Second Edition</u>, Belmont, CA, Wadsworth Publishing Company, 1988, p. 380.
4. Hughes, Jonathan, <u>American Economic History, Third Edition</u>, Evanston, IL, 1990, p. 450.
5. Brownlee, p. 412.
6. Brownlee, p. 415.

7.   Puth, Robert C., <u>American Economic History, Third Edition</u>, Orlando, FL, The Dryden Press, 1993, p. 541.

Chapter 12
The Great Depression and the New Deal (1929-1939)

1.   Puth, Robert C., <u>American Economic History, Third Edition</u>, Fort Worth, TX, The Dryden Press, 1993, p. 569.
2.   Chandler, L., <u>America's Greatest Depression, 1929-1941</u>, New York,   N.Y., 1970, p. 196.
3.   Galbraith, John Kenneth, <u>Economics in Perspective</u>, Boston, MA, Houghton Mifflin Company, 1987, p. 215.
4.   Puth, p. 577.

Chapter 13
Keynesian Economics

1.   Galbraith, John, Kenneth, <u>Economics in Perspective</u>, Boston, MA, Houghton Mifflin Company, 1987, p. 222.
2.   Galbraith, p. 225.
3.   Buchholz, Todd, G., <u>New Ideas From Dead Economists</u>, New York, N.Y., Penguin Books, 1989, p. 205.
4.   Buchholz, p. 206.
5.   Buchholz, p. 207.
6.   Buchholz, p. 212.
7.   Galbraith, p. 249.
8.   Galbraith, p. 255.

Chapter 14
Economic Measurement and Forecasting

1. Colander, David, C., Economics, Burr Ridge, IL, Richard D. Irwin, Inc., 1994, p. 166.
2. Colander, p. 171.
3. Valentine, Lloyd M., Business Cycles and Forecasting, Cincinnati, OH, South-Western Publishing Co., 1991, p. 126.
4. Galbraith, John Kenneth, Economics in Perspective, Boston, MA, Houghton Mifflin Company, 1987, p. 261.
5. Fiedler, Edgar, Across The Board, New York, N.Y., The Conference Board, 1977.

Chapter 15
Inflation and Monetarism

1. Galbraith, John Kenneth, Economics in Perspective, Boston, MA, Houghton Mifflin Company, 1987. p. 267.
2. Galbraith, p. 270.
3. Galbraith, p. 275.
4. Buchholz, Tod, G. New Ideas From Dead Economists, New York, N.Y., Penguin Books, 1989, p. 231.
5. Buchholz, p. 234.

Chapter 16
The Federal Deficit

1. Hyman, David, Economics, Third Edition, Irwin Business Publications, Burr Ridge, IL, 1994, p. 809.

Chapter 17
Economics and Public Choice

1. Drucker, Peter, <u>Post Capitalist Society</u>, Harper Business, New York, N.Y., 1993, p. 126.
2. Drucker, p. 131.
3. Dolan, Edwin G. & Lindsey, David E., <u>Economics, Seventh Edition,</u> The Dryden Press, Orlando, FL, 1994, p. 460.
4. Buchholz, Todd G., <u>New Ideas From Dead Economists</u>, Penguin Books, New York, N.Y. 1989, p. 252.
5. Dolan & Lindsey, p. 710
6. Dolan & Lindsey, p. 715.

Chapter 18
Economic Growth, Communism, and the International Monetary System

1. Colander, David, C., <u>Macroeconomics,</u> Irwin Business Publications, Burr Ridge, IL, 1994. p. 471.
2. Colander, p. 478.
3. Heilbroner, Robert, <u>Making of Economic Society, 9th Edition,</u> Englewood Cliffs, N.J., Prentice Hall, 1993, p. 229.
4. Heilbroner, p. 229.
5. Colander, p. 456.
6. Colander, p. 457.
7. Colander, p. 458

Chapter 19
The Battle of the Titans

1.   Thurow, Lester, <u>Head To Head</u>, New York, N.Y., William Morrow and Company, Inc., 1992, p. 20.
2.   Thurow, p. 25.
3.   Lodge, George, C., <u>Perestroika in America</u>, Boston, MA, Harvard Business School Press, 1992, pp. 15-16.
4.   Thurow, p. 32.
5.   Thurow, p. 34.
6.   Gumbel, Peter, <u>Kohl Wins Narrowly In German Elections</u>, The Wall Street Journal, October 17, 1994, p. A11
7.   Thurow, p. 117.
8.   Ohmae, Kenichi, <u>The Mind of the Strategist</u>, New York, NY, Penguin Books, 1988, p. 113.
9.   Thurow, p. 118.
10.   Thurow, p. 145.
11.   Thurow, p. 159

Chapter 20
New Strategies for American

1.   Thurow, Lester, <u>Head To Head</u>, New York, NY, William Morrow and Company, Inc., 1992, p. 285.
2.   Thurow, p. 288.
3.   Thurow, p. 296.
4.   Drucker, Peter F., <u>Post Capitalist Society</u>, New York, NY, Harper Business, 1993, p. 194.
5.   Drucker, p. 200.
6.   Bennett, William J., <u>The Index of Leading Cultural Indicators</u>, New York, NY, Simon & Schuster, 1994, p. 94.
7.   Drucker, p. 215.

INDEX